Spanish Chronicles of the Indies: Sixteenth Century

Twayne's World Authors Series

Spanish Literature

Janet Pérez, Editor
Texas Tech University

TWAS 847

Spanish Chronicles of the Indies: Sixteenth Century

James C. Murray

Georgia State University

Twayne Publishers ■ New York

Maxwell Macmillan Canada ■ Toronto

Maxwell Macmillan International ■ New York Oxford Singapore Sydney

Spanish Chronicles of the Indies: Sixteenth Century
James C. Murray

Twayne Publishers   Maxwell Macmillan Canada, Inc.
Macmillan Publishing Company   1200 Eglinton Avenue East
866 Third Avenue   Suite 200
New York, New York 10022   Don Mills, Ontario M3C 3N1

Library of Congress Cataloging-in-Publication Data
Murray, James C.
    Spanish chronicles of the Indies: sixteenth century / James
C. Murray.
    p. cm. – (Twayne's world authors series; TWAS 847. Spanish
literature)
    Includes bibliographical references and index.
    ISBN 0-8057-4306-5
    1. Spanish prose literature – Classical period, 1500-
1700 – History and criticism. 2. Latin America – History – To
1600 – Historigraphy. I. Title. II. Series.
PQ6136.M87 1994
868'.309355 – dc20   93-29499
                                                        CIP

The paper used in this publication meets the minimum
requirements of American National Standard for Information
Sciences – Permanence of Paper for Printed Library Materials,
ANSI Z39.48-1984.

10 9 8 7 6 5 4 3 2 1

Printed in the United States of America.

To the memory of my parents,
Michael and Helen

Contents

Preface

The Spanish chronicles of the Indies of the sixteenth century constitute both literature and history and belong to both Spain and Spanish America. As Spanish literature they fall within the Golden Age.
Spain's Golden Age literature is well known to Hispanists and some
masterpieces – Cervantes's *Don Quixote,* Calderón's *La vida es
sueño* (*Life Is a Dream*), and Tirso de Molina's *El burlador de
Sevilla* (*The Trickster of Seville*) – are read by an international
general reading public. The chronicles are known largely to
specialists in colonial Spanish American literature and to historians
of Spanish America who treat them as historical documents, but, by
and large, the chronicles remain unknown to the general reader.
General critical studies of the chronicles of the Indies in Spanish are
older and often inaccessible. There is thus a need in English for a
general introduction or reference work on the chronicles. Since the
early 1980s interest in the chronicles of the Indies has grown in
phenomenal proportions, sparked by the five-hundredth observance
of Columbus's first voyage to the Americas. To make the chronicles
more accessible and better known, new editions of the texts, critical
studies in book and article form, scholarly conferences, and popular
workshops have been held. Studies of specific historical figures, like
Columbus and Cortés, have appeared. This book on the chronicles
of the Indies of the sixteenth century attempts to present a general
overview and introduction for students of Spanish and Spanish
American literature, for English readers, for nonspecialists in Hispanic studies, and for those with an interest in history.

The number of writers and titles of the chronicles is daunting.
Not all merit equal consideration. I have limited the chronicles
studied in this book to those written in the sixteenth century, which
is the great period of discoveries, explorations, conquest, evangelization, and colonization, and to authors born in Spain. In the same
century there exist a good number of *criollo, mestizo,* and Indian
writers of chronicles, but separate books could be devoted to each
one of those categories of writers. I have selected those works com-

monly accepted as the important chronicles for primary reference. Some, of lesser importance, are treated briefly or merely mentioned when relevant.

The chronicles do not constitute a genre but a discourse type that embraces several subtypes. The development of the chronicle parallels and is marked by the historical events the chronicles record; the same discourse types may be found under the different groups, but they may change and evolve according to the nature of the enterprise they chronicle. This volume traces this development and examines how the individual chronicle exemplifies the characteristics of a particular group, how it is different, and how it is unique. Occasionally, a chronicler, for example, Las Casas, will be discussed in two chapters because his chronicles fit two different groups.

The introductory chapter surveys the state of the secondary literature and describes the historical, social, and cultural framework in which the chronicles emerged and developed. The main historical movements in Spanish America in the sixteenth century – discovery, conquest, exploration, evangelization, and colonization – govern the division of the chronicles in this book. Within each division, the several types of discourse range from letters and journals to histories, chronicles, and *relaciones* (accounts). Given the panoramic scope and introductory nature of the present volume, no in-depth studies of individual writers or works are attempted.

The chronology highlights key historical events related to the world of the chronicles and the major chronicles, with their Spanish titles followed by English titles. English titles of chronicles discussed are given on first occurrence in the text and English translations of chronicles, when available, are listed in a section of the bibliography. Primary works in the bibliography include only the major chronicles analyzed in the text and their English translations when available. Since the notes contain specific references, the secondary sources in the bibliography are limited to (1) general works on the chronicles and (2) general studies of individual chronicles, with emphasis on books in English, primarily those of more recent publication.

This book could not have been written without the support of my former chairman, Dr. David O'Connell, of the Department of Modern and Classical Languages, who encouraged my project throughout the research and writing stages and who granted me a leave from teaching in the last quarter of writing. I am indebted to the staff of the Interlibrary Loan Department of the Pullen Library at Georgia State University for facilitating access to primary and secondary sources, and to the office staff of the Department of Modern and Classical Languages, especially Rickie Wesbrooks, for secretarial support.

Chronology

1526   Gonzalo Fernández de Oviedo, *Sumario de la natural historia de las Indias* (*Natural History of the West Indies*).

1527   Bartolomé de las Casas begins the *Apologética Historia* (Apologetical History) and the *Historia General de las Indias* (*History of the Indies*).

1529   Treaty of Zaragoza setting limits for Spain and Portugal in the Pacific.

1533   Francisco de Xerez (Jerez), *Verdadera relación de la Conquista del Perú* (*Reports on the Discovery of Peru*).

1534   Conquest of Peru finished by Pizarro and described by Jerez, *Verdadera relación de la conquista del Perú* (*True Account of the Conquest of Peru*).

1535   Gonzalo Fernández de Oviedo, *Historia general y natural de las Indias*, primera parte (General and Natural History of the Indies, first part).

1537   Paul III declares equality of Indians and their capacity to become Christians.

1538   First university in New World founded in Santo Domingo.

1540   Fray Bernardino de Sahagún, *Historia general de las cosas de la Nueva España* (*General History of Things in New Spain*).

1541   Fray Toribio de Benavente (Motolinía), *Historia de los Indios de la Nueva España* (History of the Indians of New Spain).

1542   The New Laws promulgated.

1545-1552   Pedro de Valdivia, *Cartas* (Letters).

1552   Las Casas, *Brevísima relación de la destrucción de las Indias* (*The Devastation of the Indies: A Brief Account*). López de Gómara, *Historia General de las Indias* (General History of the Indies).

1553   Pedro Cieza de León, *Crónica del Perú*, primera parte (Chronicle of Peru, first part).

1554   Ulrich Schmidel, *Warhaftige Historien einer wunderbaren Schiffart (The Conquest of the River Plate [1535-1555])*.

1555   Agustín Zárate, *Historia del descubrimiento y conquista del Perú (The Discovery and Conquest of Perú)*. Alvar Núñez Cabeza de Vaca, *Comentarios (Commentaries)*.

1556   Philip II becomes king of Spain.

1560   Cervantes de Salazar, *Crónica de la Nueva España* (Chronicle of New Spain).

1564   Diego de Landa, *Relación de las cosas de Yucatán (Account of the Affairs in Yucatán: The Maya)*.

1565-1566 Pedro Menéndez de Avilés, *Cartas* (Letters).

ca. 1566 Fray Diego de Landa, *Relación de las cosas de Yucatán (Diego de Landa's Account of the Affairs of Yucatán: The Maya)*.

1568   Díaz del Castillo, *Historia verdadera de la conquista de la Nueva España (The Conquest of New Spain)*.

1569   Fray Bernardino de Sahagún, *Historia General de las Cosas de la Nueva España (General History of the Things of New Spain)*.

ca. 1570 Alonso de Zurita, *Breve y sumaria relación de los señores y maneras y diferencias que había en ellos en la Nueva España (Life and Labor in Ancient Mexico: The Brief and Summary Relation of the Lords of New Spain)*.

1571   Juan López de Velasco begins *Geografía y descripción universal de las Indias* (Geography and Universal Description of the Indies). Fernando Colón's *The Life of the Admiral Christopher Columbus by His Son Ferdinand* published in Italian in Venice.

1573   Fray Gerónimo de Mendieta begins his *Historia eclesiástica indiana* (Ecclesiastical History of the Indies), which he finished in 1597.

Chapter One

The Literature on the Chronicles and Colonial Society: An Introduction

The chronicles are primarily historical works, but they are also included in the literary canon. They provide a grounding in the historical events of a particular time and society, the sixteenth-century Hispanic world. The discovery that took place in 1492 is now being echoed by a rediscovery of the texts recording that discovery and the subsequent conquest. New scholarly approaches that emphasize the variety of discourses and their rootedness in the sociohistoric context facilitate the rediscovery for readers. This chapter will orient the reader of the chronicles to both the secondary literature spawned by the chronicles and the sociohistoric context reflected therein.

The State of the Secondary Literature

Given the hybrid historiographical-literary nature of the discourse that we call chronicles, these works have attracted both historians and scholars of literature. The chronicles are "hybrid" in belonging both to the literatures of Spain and of Spanish America. Peninsular histories of literature often include remarks on the chronicles, and anthologies of literary and historical texts present selections from the major sixteenth-century chroniclers. Even when editions and studies of the chronicles are published in Spain, they are considered more and more as part of the literature of the New World. Editions are currently appearing in Spain mainly in response to the five-hundredth anniversary of the Discovery. Scholars of Spanish-American literature today are the primary researchers on the chronicles. The chronicles from the period 1492-1599 are fairly numerous and have spawned a sizeable body of secondary literature. A computer-as-

sisted search conducted for titles of recent studies treating the
chronicles as listed in the Modern Language Association's bibliography and in Historical Abstracts reveals that historians published
more studies on the chronicles – 195 items over a 15-year period
(1973-88) – than did scholars of literature – 102 items over a 24-
year period (1964-88). In historiographical studies, U.S. and Spanish
journals dominated the field in publishing articles on the chronicles;
Mexican and French journals tied for third place. In the last 10 years,
however, literary studies have proliferated, with articles appearing in
the major U.S. Hispanist journals. Two journals in particular should
be singled out for the attention given to the chronicles: *Revista
Iberoamericana* and *Dispositio*. The latter, published by the
Department of Romance Languages at the University of Michigan, has
published several articles on the chronicles, especially in volume 21.
Within academic circles, the number of doctoral dissertations dealing
with the chronicles has increased over the 10-year period (1979-88).
From an informal survey of the list of dissertations in the Hispanic
and Luso-Brazilian languages and literatures published annually in
Hispania, 25 dissertations out of a total of 1,499 dealt with the
chronicles and related topics; Inca Garcilaso de la Vega was the most
studied, followed by Guamán Poma de Ayala.

Bibliographic Sources and Reference Works

Despite the tremendous amount of secondary literature on the
chronicles, there is no bibliography specifically dedicated to them.
Abundant material appears in Benito Sánchez Alonso's three-volume
classic bibliography of Spanish and Spanish American history,
Fuentes de la historia española e hispanoamericana, but the work
needs to be updated (the last edition includes entries only up to
1950). Volume 1, chapter 6, contains an introduction to Spanish
American historiography and the history of Spanish America 1492-
1517; volume 2, chapter 7, includes entries for the period of the
House of Austria (1517-1700). Sánchez Alonso includes texts he calls
poetic works on the Indies that he esteems more as sources of history than for their literary value. The introduction to Spanish American historiography has brief sections on chroniclers of the Indies,
religious historiography, poetic historiography, collections of texts,
publications resulting from the four-hundredth anniversary celebra-

tion of the Discovery in 1892, documentary and bibliographic sources, and an overview of trends in modern Spanish American historiography. Although Sánchez Alonso's work deals with the political history of Spain and its former overseas provinces from a Spanish perspective, the entries, which are not annotated, are drawn from material published in Spain, Spanish America, the United States, and several other countries. Offering more recent coverage and accessibility to English-speaking readers are the annual bibliographies published by MLA and, in particular, the British publication *The Year's Work in Modern Language Studies*, published by the Modern Humanities Research Association, with annotated entries that give good coverage to the chronicles. Especially noteworthy is the *Handbook of Latin American Studies* from the University of Florida Press in Gainesville, indispensable for the study of Latin American history and literature. From its inception in 1935 until 1963 the *Handbook* annually included items on the chronicles in its section on colonial literature; since 1964 the literature section has appeared biennially. Bibliographic collections that are particularly helpful for following quantity and trends of studies on the chronicles are the *Handbook of Latin American Studies* and *The Year's Work in Modern Language Studies*. Both compilations strive to follow trends and present annotated entries. The Modern Language Association's International Bibliography is also a valuable source. The fairly new Spanish publication from Torre de Babel, *Prólogo*, and its inserts titled *Biblioteca Quinto Centenario*, provide a very good way to keep abreast of the numerous publications being generated by the five-hundredth anniversary in many fields of interest.

Traditionally, specialists and the general public interested in the chronicles have had to rely on collections formed in earlier centuries. The earliest collections date from the eighteenth century: the scholar Andrés González de Barcia was the first to make accessible the original sources in his *Historiadores primitivos de las Indias Occidentales*. In the nineteenth century Martín Fernández de Navarrete published the three-volume *Colección de viajes y descubrimientos*. The *Biblioteca de Autores Españoles* (founded in 1846 by Manuel Rivadeneyra, with volumes still being issued) was probably the most used series until editions were published in this century, in particular since the 1960s. Spurred by the five-hundredth anniversary celebration, several publishing houses, particularly in Spain, have been issuing new editions and reeditions of chronicles.

Dictionary and encyclopedic reference works in Spanish and in English devoted to peninsular and Latin American letters testify to the chronicles' Hispanic nature and appeal. *Diccionario de literatura española*, published in Spain by Revista de Occidente, includes short entries on the major chroniclers. In English, *The Oxford Companion to Spanish Literature*, edited by Philip Ward, likewise devotes space to these writers. Scribner's excellent three-volume series *Latin American Writers*, a result of the 500th anniversary celebration of the Discovery, is a critical anthology presenting representative Spanish American and Brazilian authors to English-speaking specialists and nonspecialists. The collection has lengthy articles in volume one on Las Casas, Fernández de Oviedo, Díaz del Castillo, Ercilla, Inca Garcilaso de la Vega, and Acosta. Irving A. Leonard's *Portraits and Essays: Historical and Literary Sketches of Early Spanish America*, edited by William C. Bryant (1986), gathers essays presenting biographical and textual information on several of the major chroniclers ("Toward the Setting Sun: Christopher Columbus," "Tidings of a Vast New Continent: Amerigo Vespucci," "Discoverer of the Mississippi: Hernando de Soto," "Conquistador and Chronicler: Bernal Díaz del Castillo"). Some of these Leonard had previously published elsewhere, although some are published for the first time in this volume. Carmen Bravo-Villasante's anthology *La maravilla de América: los cronistas de Indias* (1985) presents verbal portraits of several chroniclers and passages from their writings selected in accord with the organizing theme of the wonder America produced in the discoverers, conquerors, and the public in Spain.

The reader who wants to sample the literary and cultural wealth of the chronicles can turn to general as well as more specialized anthologies in Spanish. *Voces de Hispanoamérica: antología literaria* (1988), edited by Raquel Chang-Rodríguez and Malva E. Filer, is a recent literary anthology of Spanish American literature for college students containing selections from three chroniclers: Columbus, Las Casas, and Díaz del Castillo. The introduction discusses issues relevant to the period of the chronicles: oral tradition and writing, European influences, the "Invention of America," the first indigenous writers, and the representation of American reality.

Emir Rodríguez-Monegal's *Noticias secretas y públicas de América* (1984) is the most comprehensive recent edition devoted exclusively to the chronicles. Rodríguez-Monegal's premise is that the linguistic, legal, and religious unity of Latin America (believed for centuries to have been forged during the period of the discovery and conquest) never existed and that a plurality of languages and cultures in dialogue characterizes Latin America. Thirty-five selections in luxury format constitute the anthology that exemplifies that dialogue. Each author is introduced with a page or more of information on his life and works. A special characteristic of this anthology, illustrating cultural plurality and dialogue, is the inclusion of authors and texts from non-Spanish cultures: Portuguese (Pero Vaz de Caminha, Fernao Cardim), Indian (Chilán Balán, Guamán Poma de Ayala), French (Jean de Léry), and German (Hans Studen, Ulrich Schmidel).

The notion that the literature of the chronicles is journalistic reporting of events in the New World guides the organization of Manuel Ballesteros Gaibrois' combined introductory study and anthology of the chronicles, *La novedad indiana: Noticias, informaciones y testimonios del Nuevo Mundo* (1987). For Ballesteros, the discovery of the New World is an on-going process that over the centuries reveals to the reporters – men of arms, missionaries, and government functionaries – unknown aspects and new impressions. The anthology is arranged by centuries and within centuries by a variety of subjects: the physical world (geography, climate, landscape) and plant, animal, mineral, and human life. A geographically limited anthology, suitable as a school text, is Francisco Carrillo's *Cartas y cronistas del descubrimiento y la conquista* (1987), whose selected texts report the discovery and conquest of Peru. Introductory sections discuss the development from Spanish chronicle to American chronicle, the role of the Castilian language in Peruvian literature, and the historical background. Some of the authors included are Francisco Pizarro, Fray Gaspar de Carvajal, Hernando Pizarro, Cristóbal de Mena, Francisco Xerez, Pedro Pizarro, Pedro Cieza de León.

Idea y querella de la Nueva España, edited by Ramón de Xirau (1973), contains a specialized collection of texts focusing on the topic of humanism in chronicles limited to Mexico; authors included are Las Casas, Fray Toribio de Benavente (Motolinía), Fray Julián Garcés, Fray Juan de Zumárraga, Vasco de Quiroga, Fray Bernardino de Sahagún, Francisco Cervantes de Salazar. The collection does not follow a strictly chronological order but places texts in dialogue with one another – for example, it presents Fray Toribio de Benavente after Las Casas because the former's works are a response and challenge to Las Casas's ideas. The dialogue among the authors concerns crucial problems of the conquest: the right to wage war on the Indians, their evangelization, and their equality with the Spaniards.

Literary Histories

Literary histories that include the chronicles run the gamut from the more general and older to the more specialized and relatively recent. Literary histories have lately come under criticism in the general reconsideration of critical approaches. Rolena Adorno has criticized the traditional model of literary history, which considers the text and not discourse as the analytical category and presents the works according to a lineal order creating the illusion of uninterrupted progression while eliminating any consideration of points of view in dialogue and conflict.[1] Walter Mignolo advocates broadening the scope of the study of colonial discourse to permit consideration of texts produced orally, not written in Spanish or even in the Roman alphabet and not limited to Spanish America.[2] A traditional work, Enrique Anderson-Imbert's history of Spanish American literature, limits discussion to texts that fit the author's esthetic definition of literature and omits works written in Latin and in the Indian languages.[3] Anderson-Imbert admits the chronicles that, he claims, were written without artistic intentions, because he values their "literary portions" (16). According to his view of history as "an indivisible succession of events" (17), writers are presented in chronological order, which is divided into three historical-political periods, of which the first, "The Colony," discusses the chronicles.[4] In contrast with Anderson-Imbert's *History*, Giuseppe Bellini includes precolumbian and postconquest indigenous literature in his *Historia de la literatura hispanoamericana* (1985).[5] In a variation on the trend to trace later Spanish American literature back to the chronicles and colonial literature, Bellini finds close spiritual and expressive links between the indigenous and later Spanish American literatures reaching down to Asturias, Neruda, Roa Bastos, and Octavio Paz. There is a pro-Spanish bent in Bellini's suggestion that indigenous

culture was saved by being synthesized into the Spanish American
mentality and reached a worldwide audience through the Spanish
language. The discovery and conquest projected Spanish American
reality onto the world stage.

   Historia de la literatura hispanoamericana. I: Época colonial,
edited by I. Madrigal (1982), presents individual chapters by a variety
of scholars in essay form. This history offers the best coverage as far
as length and current approaches (for example, discourse analysis)
are concerned. The volume's first major division contains two informative chapters on colonial Spanish American background, the one
by Manuel Lucena Salmoral on social, political, and economic aspects and the other by Jean Franco on the cultural framework
(which gives considerable attention to the indigenous cultures). The
second major division, "Cartas, Crónicas y Relaciones," has contributions by Walter Mignolo on the historiography of the chronicles,
André Saint-Lu on Fray Bartolomé de Las Casas, Manuel Alvar on
Bernal Díaz del Castillo, Bernard Lavalle on Inca Garcilaso de la
Vega, Eduardo Camacho Guizado on Juan Rodríguez Freile, and
Rodolfo A. Borello on Alonso Carrió de la Vandera.

   Some recent literary histories in English include sections on the
chronicles. An important recent contribution to literary history is
David W. Foster's *Handbook of Latin American Literature* (1987).
Conceived to meet the need for reference works in English for
scholars and the general reader, it has information on the national
literatures of Latin America and incorporates recent cultural and literary issues. The essays present an ideological approach to Latin
American literature. It is within the context of separate national literary traditions that individual chroniclers are discussed; a chronicler
whose work draws on several countries is discussed under each of
the countries. One recent history in English of a national literature
that touches on the chronicles is James Higgins's *History of Peruvian Literature* (1987). Besides a chapter on Quechua literature are
a few pages devoted to historical writings on the conquest of Peru
and, in particular, to the chronicler Pedro Cieza de León.

Historical Accounts

By and large, the chronicles have received more attention in literary
histories than in histories of historiography. Benito Sánchez Alonso's

classic, two-volume *Historia de la historiografía española: ensayo de un examen de conjunto* (1941, 1944) places the chronicles within the overall development of Spanish history. Sánchez's primary focus is Spain's political history, but he seeks to give a rounded view with sections on foreign, religious, and urban history; biography; and travel books. The volumes are divided into periods within which histories or texts are grouped according to genre. The presentation is more useful to the nonspecialist. The first group of chroniclers, which includes among others Columbus, Vespucci and Cortés, is presented in a chapter titled "Christian History" and under the sections "History of the Indies" and "Autobiographical Reports." These reports, says Sánchez, were produced without any literary purpose and are not, strictly speaking, historiographical. In contrast to the first group, Sánchez presents the first real historians of the Indies, numbering among them Pedro Mártir de Anglería, Gonzalo de Oviedo, Fray Toribio de Benavente, Francisco López de Jerez, and Fernando Colón.

A later and more specialized history of the chronicles is Francisco Esteve Barba's *Historiografía indiana* (1964). Among the topics covered by the introduction are the initial purposes of the history of the Indies; types of historians; use of old forms; general, natural, and moral history; accuracy and fantasy; history and epic; and the development of the history of the Indies. This volume is helpful for the amount of chronicle literature included, its panoramic view, and the valuable notes.

New Critical Approaches to the Chronicles

Since the 1980s a new focus has developed in colonial Spanish American literature that has particularly affected studies of the chronicles.[6] Mignolo pointed out the manifestation of a new paradigm in colonial literary studies, one that recognized the cultural and linguistic complexity of colonial discourse. Mignolo traced four directions in colonial studies appearing from 1980 onward and contributing to the reevaluation of the traditional image of colonial literature: the study of non-Castilian literatures (neo-Latin and Nahuatl) in colonial Mexico; the attribution of esthetic and "literary" qualities to colonial texts and the location of the origin of Spanish American literature in the sixteenth century; interest in what the discourses have in common and in the reconstruction of the rhetorical norms that governed the production and reception of discourses in the sixteenth and seventeenth centuries; and an expansion of studies to include discourses of the colonial period (155-57). Such studies have led to an examination of the meaning of literature and the term *Spanish American*. The emerging model now includes texts not written in Castilian, nonliterary texts, transcription of oral tales, and texts in nonalphabetic writing. Adorno, continuing the direction of Mignolo's perceptions of a new paradigm in colonial studies, emphasizes the importance of discourse and the process of transculturation within which the question of the "other" has an important role.[7]

To resolve genre and hermeneutic problems posed by the chronicles studies, one must examine the historiographical metatext, historiographical treatises containing precise rhetorical norms that governed the writing of history in the sixteenth and seventeenth centuries. A comparison of historical texts and treatises helped Mignolo clarify the issue of whether the chronicles belong to history or literature. To the surprise of the modern reader, some texts called chronicles were not intended by their authors or understood by their early readers to be part of the historiographical discursive formation. Columbus's letter to Luis de Santángel about the first voyage and Cortés's letters, for example, were admitted to historiography because subsequent culture considered them important documents of its history. Some so-called chronicles, annals and *relaciones*, assumed the characteristics of historiographical discourse, and those terms became synonyms for history toward the end of the sixteenth century and in the seventeenth.[8]

Roberto González Echevarría recently probed the possibilities of expression available to writers desiring to narrate and describe the reality and events of the New World. The variety of forms in the group called chronicles can be explained by the rhetorical possibilities of the period and their blending and changing according to the social and cultural circumstances.[9] Chroniclers explicitly or implicitly compared their texts with the model of humanist historiography, a model reflected in treatises by writers such as Juan Luis Vives, Páez de Castro, Fox Morcillo, Pedro de Navarra, and others.[10] According to González Echevarría, the principal characteristics of Spanish humanist historiography at the time the chronicles were produced include a medieval providentialist scheme (which sees all events as part of a divine plan), eloquence and lofty tone, presence of moral and theological dilemmas of the period (although more importance is given to courtly and knightly morality of both Indians and Spaniards), and elegant, rhetorical prose (19-20). Chroniclers such as Pedro Mártir, López de Gómara, and Fernández de Oviedo strove to conform to the precepts of humanist historiography. Despite the predominance of the humanist historiographical model, González Echevarría sees in the chronicles a mixture of humanistic historiographical and notarial forms as represented by the *relación* (a legal document presenting the particular case of a person, including incidents of daily life, and without an attempt to reflect a transcendental truth). Writers such as Pané, Columbus, Cortés and Bernal Díaz wrote *relaciones*. The *relación* was important for literature as the model for the picaresque novel.[11]

Alfonso Reyes termed the chronicle and the missionary theater "nascent genres" of Spanish American literature.[12] González Echevarría places the chronicles in Spanish American literary tradition as the source of the narrative; he pointed out that modern writers like Neruda and García Márquez also considered chronicles as the origin of Spanish American letters (9). How did works of a historical nature enter the canon of Spanish American literature? To approach this and similar problems posed by the chronicles, scholars consider the works from the contexts of their production and reception. Margarita Zamora proposed a "bipartite critical strategy," studying colonial works in the sociocultural context in which they were written in order to understand their cultural function, discursive type, and classification, and later viewing them in the context of the eighteenth and nineteenth centuries when they were first classified as part of Spanish American colonial literature. According to Zamora, historical works were incorporated into Spanish American literature in the nineteenth century because of a change in the historiographical concept of truth and the literary-political need to posit a beginning for Spanish American literature, then in the process of identifying itself vis-à-vis Spanish and European literatures.[13]

In the colonial period, historical truth was understood in relation to ideology. The predominant ideology included a belief in Christian providentialism – that events occurred as part of a divine plan. Under the influence of eighteenth-century rationalism and particularly of nineteenth-century positivism, historiography underwent a change that recognized the true as "what is verifiable" (338). With this change, works that did not fit the positivist concept were relegated to literature. The chronicles were also declared to be literary in Spanish America in the nineteenth century for political reasons. As part of their movement for independence from Spain, Latin Americans required a beginning for their emerging literature. According to González Echevarría, early critics in their search for a *medium aevum* for Spanish American letters decided upon the colonial period and included various types of discourse in the literary canon.[14]

The presence of esthetic and literary qualities in historiographical texts requires an explanation and an interpretation of their meaning. Historiographical studies until most recently have rejected anything in texts that smacked of the imaginative, while literary studies concentrating solely on the text ignored metatextual research in historical archives and documents. Enrique Pupo-Walker rejects the approaches of both today's literary criticism and historical criticism. He accepts the historiographical vocation of the chronicles, while finding that they also have a literary vocation because of their imaginative spaces that belong to the area of literature.[15] Narrative schemes – myth, legend and broad parodic fragments – in the historiography of the Indies continue in later periods of Spanish American literature down to the present, for example, in nineteenth-century *costumbrismo*, in Ricardo Palma, and in twentieth century authors such as Alejo Carpentier (9). If the "imaginative spaces" are taken into consideration, a truer reading of the texts as history will result.

Stephanie Merrim explains the presence of literary elements in the chronicles in terms of the Renaissance concept of history when writers translated history into stories to shape historical facts, in the process relying on the techniques of literature. The ancient concept of history viewed history as a subgenre of fiction.[16] Merrim hopes her position regarding the story and literary model underlying history will serve as a beginning for a research method. From her investigation of the literary framework in Columbus's letter on the discovery of the New World, Díaz del Castillo's *Historia verdadera*, Cabeza de Vaca's *Naufragios*, and Inca Garcilaso's *Comentarios reales*, Merrim concludes that these writers chose certain literary or esthetic forms to best express a moral or spiritual value.

Discourse of the Chronicles

Scholars today have noted (in addition to the literary elements present in the chronicles) a density of discourses fusing in a work to
produce a hybrid discourse. Zamora cites the *Memorias* of Fray Ser-
vando Teresa de Mier as an example of the hybrid nature of some
colonial works. She finds several genres melding in Mier's *Memorias:*
the *relación*, the philological commentary, the sermon, the
picaresque novel, forensic oratory, and autobiography (344). From
studying noncanonical works, Adorno came to the realization that
scholars must disentangle the different discourses – historical,
mythical, theological and legal – functioning in a text and examine
the way in which the different discourses influence one another.[17]
Hybridization of genres results, she argues, from the "positions" of
the subject. To illustrate the various possibilities of the subject's
positions, Adorno uses a passage from the 1611 work by Alonso Fernández, *Historia eclesiástica de nuestros tiempos*, where the subject, Fray Bartolomé de las Casas, speaks as a saint, a tourist, a
theologian, and an eyewitness. For Adorno, the passage from Fernández suggests a paradigm possibly at work within colonial discourse, that is, a simultaneity of several positions of the subject
demanded by the different facets (political-administrative, religious-
theological, etc.) of the project of colonialism (14).[18] González
Echevarría describes something similar to hybridization and the positions of the subject in the case of Bernal Díaz del Castillo. In a
chronicle like that of Bernal's history, an author needed different
styles: for the material of the conquest, he needed a lofty rhetorical
style; for his position as an eyewitness and his purpose of obtaining
concessions from the Spanish government to meet his economic
needs, Bernal required the style of a letter or the formulas of notarial
rhetoric (11).

Beatriz Pastor's *Discursos narrativos de la conquista: mitificación y emergencia* (1988) is representative of the trend to consider not the literary text but discourse in analyzing the chronicles.
The narrative discourse of the conquest incorporates texts by participants in the discovery and conquest of America whose writing
was motivated by their desire to become part of history. Two processes are at work in the texts Pastor examines: the transformation of
the conquistador and his perception and vision of the New World,

and the emergence of an incipient new literature. Within the narrative discourse of the conquest she sees three fundamental discourses: the myth-making discourse based on a concept of the world and ways of representation not connected to the reality the authors try to report, and two demythifying discourses. One, the "narrative discourse of failure," questions the myths and models created, and the other, the "discourse of rebellion," demythifies the New World and the conquest.[19] René Jara and Nicholas Spadaccini describe the inscription of the New World in terms of allegory. Columbus's allegorization of the New World was in turn allegorized throughout the sixteenth century in narratives of the conquest by Cortés, Fernández de Oviedo, and Núñez Cabeza de Vaca. The rise of a counter-discourse created a negative allegory exemplified by Las Casas and others who inserted the indigenous "other" in their discourses. Inca Garcilaso placed indigenous and Spanish cultural values on an equal footing.[20]

Among new trends in colonial studies is heightened interest in the concept of the "other." The other, according to Tzvetan Todorov, can be interior or exterior to a society.[21] Todorov's study concentrates on the Indian as the exterior and remote other, defined as someone "whose language and customs I do not understand, so foreign that in extreme instances I am reluctant to admit they belong to the same species as my own" (3). Todorov approaches the treatment of the other through the story of the discovery and the conquest, searching for ethical meaning applicable today. Todorov's book takes into account the presence of the other, but the reader essentially views the Indian through Spanish eyes, with the exception of the presentation of Montezuma and the Indians who engage in dialogue with Durán and Sahagún.

The Indigenous Perspective

Collections of texts seldom let the Indians speak for themselves. Philip A. Means's *Biblioteca Andina* (1928), an older but still useful collection, limited to the Andean region, belongs to a series planned by Means to describe ancient and modern works on the history and governmental organization of the Andean region. In the only volume published, Means presents sixteenth- and seventeenth-century Spanish writers – there is one indigenous writer included, Juan de Santa Cruz Pachacuti Yamqui Salcamayhua – who treated pre-His-

panic Andean history and culture. A supplement treats writers who
dealt with the native languages before 1700. One modern collection,
Textos de cronistas de Indias y poemas precolombinos, edited by
Roberto Godoy and Angel Olmo (1979), contains writings chiefly by
Spanish chroniclers of Aztec and Maya culture – Fray Bernardino de
Sahagún, Fray Diego Durán, Juan de Torquemada, Fray Diego de
Landa – and Inca culture – Martín de Morúa, Juan de Betanzos,
Pedro Sarmiento de Gamboa, Inca Garcilaso de la Vega, and Fran-
cisco López de Gómara. A few surviving indigenous texts – *Popol
Vuh, Chilam Balam* – describe customs, rites, poetry and other as-
pects of Indian life.

The problem confronting Spanish authors who wrote about the
Indian and indigenous subjects was, as Adorno writes in her
"Literary Production and Suppression," how to introduce the Indian
into literature, especially in the same context where magic, sorcery,
divinations, cures, and superstition (considered morally and spiritually dangerous) would be discussed.[22] Writers felt the need to justify
their treatment of Indians. Writers often wished to exploit the sensa-
tional while avoiding the suppression of their texts (2). Epic poets
used references to chivalric romance, which contained magic and
other practices similar to those of the Indians, to lessen the aspect of
the forbidden when they introduced Indian topics (18).

More attention is being given to Indian voices in the context of
the conquest in an attempt to reclaim Spanish America's cultural
heritage. Studies today focus on the Indians' use of writing to gain
some degree of empowerment in a society ruled by Spaniards.
Raquel Chang-Rodríguez's *Violencia y subversión en la prosa colonial hispanoamericana, siglos XVI y XVII* (1982) deals with violence
and subversion in several authors: Inca Titu Cusi Yupanqui, Inca
Garcilaso de la Vega, Juan Rodríquez Freile, Núñez Pineda y Bas-
cuñán, and Sigüenza y Góngora. The process of conquest and colonization did violence to the indigenous world. Indigenous discourse
is subversive because it narrates the Indians' lives, and while expos-
ing the errors of colonialism, makes demands to be heard. The New
World experience could not be adequately communicated using the
Metropolis' norms so, in a sense, authors had to do violence to the
writing process. The problem of expression was not unique to
indigenous authors; their contemporaries in Spain experienced a
similar dilemma. Chang-Rodríguez advocates broadening the picture

of Spanish American colonial letters by reclaiming these historical and literary documents. Their decoding requires the assistance of interdisciplinary studies, history, anthropology and literary criticism. Rolena Adorno's *Guamán Poma: Writing and Resistance in Colonial Peru* (1986) treats Peruvian writer Guamán Poma in an attempt to decolonize historical literary scholarship.[23] Indigenous writers were doubly marginalized, in their political and social world and later in literary scholarship. Adorno reconstructs the ways an Indian writer conveyed his experience in the language of the conqueror. Poma offers a case study of cross-cultural communication in the century after the Spanish invasion.

Women and the Chronicles

Women constitute an important other in the chronicles and in their literary study. The collection of essays by Beth Miller, *Women in Hispanic Literature: Icons and Fallen Idols* (1983) was a major effort to overcome scholarly marginalization of Hispanic women; because of its broad scope, however, only one chapter focuses on a woman of the conquest, Rachel Phillips's study of Doña Marina or Malinche.[24] C. R. Boxer's *Women in Iberian Expansion Overseas, 1415-1815* (1975) offers more information on the place of women in a wider context, Spanish and Portuguese colonies in Africa, the Atlantic Islands, the New World, Portuguese Asia, and the Philippines, and from the perspective of historical documents. Julie Greer Johnson's *Women in Colonial Spanish American Literature: Literary Images* (1983) focuses on literary images of women in history, poetry, satire, and theater from 1492 to 1800. In addition to the views of men, Johnson gives women's views of themselves. Chapter 1, "Women in Early Historical Writings" provides the best coverage of women in the chronicles. The first view of women in America is found in these historical works. Bernal Díaz's *Historia verdadera* contains "the most extensive and varied testimony about women during the conquest years."[25]

The myth of Amazon women and the conquistadors' observation of warring women contributed to forming an image of the American woman as morally and physically strong. That image influenced the figure of the *mujer varonil* in Spanish Golden Age drama. Under the title of "The Woman as Conqueror," James Lockhart and Enrique

Otte have published an English version of a letter by the Spanish woman Isabel de Guevara, who wrote in 1556 to another woman, the regent doña Juana, about the heroic deeds of women like herself who arrived with the first conquistadors in the La Plata region.[26] Nati González Freire claims that Isabel de Guevara is the first woman writer in the New World.[27] Isabel's letter details the great hardships she and other women endured as they struggled with the conquistadors to found the city of Buenos Aires. She laments the lack of recognition and recompense from colonial authorities and presents certain demands.

Sociohistorical Context: Spain

Even more than works of fiction, the chronicles are organically connected to the society in which they arose. Basic notions of the chronicles' historical context derived from a variety of disciplines – history, anthropology, economics, sociology, and philosophy – are essential to understanding the chronicles. Owing to limitations of space, a panoramic view can only touch on highlights of the background. Most histories of Spanish and Spanish American literature include (in varying degrees of completeness) information on the relevant background. Hernán Vidal, *Socio-historia de la literatura colonial hispanoamericana: tres lecturas orgánicas* (1985) argues for the publication of global studies that show the organic relationship between colonial culture and literature, and faults studies that do not make that connection.[28] One successful attempt to connect literature and society is Jean Franco's study, "La cultura hispanoamericana en la época colonial," which relates indigenous and Spanish American literary texts to political, economic and social influences.[29] The first two volumes of *The Cambridge History of Latin America* (1984) synthesize knowledge drawn from many disciplines dealing with Colonial Latin America. Viewpoint in this compilation is not limited to the European perspective but equal importance is accorded the indigenous.[30]

Spain's enterprise of discovery, exploration, and conquest was prepared over time and on several fronts. Within Spain, a unified base emerged from which exploration and conquest could be launched. The explorers and conquistadors came from a nation that had achieved unification and thus was poised to provide a unified base of political and economic support for the undertakings of the last decade of the fifteenth century and during the sixteenth. Three important elements made unification possible: the termination of the Reconquest, the union of the crowns of Castile and Aragon in 1479, and the drive for religious homogeneity. The marriage of Isabella of Castile and Ferdinand of Aragon in 1469 preceded the union of the two crowns in 1479. Earlier tolerance vanished; in the 1470s, Isabella instituted the Inquisition to investigate converts whose faith was suspect; in 1492 the forced conversion or expulsion of the Jews was ordered and, in 1502, the same lot befell the Muslims remaining in the country. During the eight centuries of the Reconquest, Spanish Christians fought intermittently to regain control of their territory from Muslim domination. The Reconquest, above all, had a major impact on the enterprise of conquest. The Reconquest was both a religious crusade and a drive for land and wealth. Serving the king as a soldier resulted in wealth and also in important intangibles, honor and social prestige. With no more peninsular territory to be retaken, the persistent demand for land created a pressure for outward expansion. Migration to the recently discovered lands across the Atlantic became a way to relieve the pressure for territorial expansion.

Spanish overseas growth occurred within the context of European expansion of the later Middle Ages and the Renaissance. Models for Castilian overseas ventures came partly from Portuguese and Genoese practice. The Portuguese were the first on the Iberian peninsula to undertake voyages of exploration. The Castilians' rivalry with the Portuguese most likely influenced their desire to expand overseas. Models developed by the Portuguese began with the capture of Ceuta in North Africa in 1415 and exploration of the west coast of Africa; they also set up trading posts on Madeira, the Azores, and the Cape Verde Islands. In 1488, a Portuguese, Bartholomeu Dias, rounded the Cape of Good Hope and opened a route to India and the spice lands of the East. Genoese financiers and merchants had their largest community in Seville. The Castilians, along with merchants of Barcelona, Seville, and Lisbon, engaged in foreign trade. Overseas exploration and expansion was facilitated by technological advances in sailing instruments – the astrolabe, the quadrant and the magnetic compass – and in the construction of new vessels, especially the development of the caravel, the type of ship Columbus and his crew sailed.

During the process of commercial exploration, America was "discovered." Today this discovery is viewed more as an invasion and, at best, an encounter of two widely different civilizations. Edmundo O'Gorman put forth the thesis that America had not been discovered but invented. The thesis is based on his understanding of discovery that "implies that the nature of the thing found was previously known to the finder, i.e., that he knows that objects such as the one he has found can and do exist, although the existence of that particular one was wholly unknown."[31] We cannot speak correctly of Columbus's discovering America because he did not know of its existence prior to his first voyage, and once he came upon it he mistakenly thought it was Asia. The discovery of America is an idea originating in Columbus's day but largely developed over subsequent centuries. O'Gorman traces the development of the idea from the sixteenth to the nineteenth century in such writers as Oviedo, Gómara, Ferdinand Columbus, Las Casas, Herrera, Beaumont, Robertson, Navarrete, Washington Irving, and Humboldt.

Sociohistorical Context: The Americas

The New World to which the Spaniards came was populated by a variety of indigenous peoples.[32] Of the many Indian groups in the New World, the best known are the Aztecs of Central Mexico, the Incas of western South America, and the Mayas of the Yucatan peninsula. The native population in the New World in 1492 may have been 35-45 million. The Aztecs and Incas were militaristic societies. The Aztecs under the rule of Moctezuma II, who was both supreme ruler and high priest, were at the peak of their power and civilization. Aztec society consisted of several levels: hereditary nobility (the *pipiltin*), land-owning commoners (the *macebuales*), ordinary commoners (the *mayeques*), and slaves. As in the rest of Mesoamerica, the Aztec economy was basically agricultural, involving the cultivation of maize, beans and chilies. Although the Mexicans worshiped a number of gods – Quetzalcóatl, a benevolent god, Tezcatlipoca, a war god, Tlaloc, the rain god – the cult of Huitzilopochtli was in the ascendancy when Cortés and his soldiers arrived. Huitzilopochtli continually demanded human sacrifice; the daily sacrifice of human hearts guaranteed the rising of the sun and the continuation of the world's existence.[33] The Aztecs fought wars and expanded their territories for the purpose of obtaining human victims. Through territo-rial expansion, the Aztecs subjugated surrounding peoples. Exploita-tion as forced laborers and the levying of tribute left the victims disgruntled and disposed to join the Spaniards to overthrow the Aztec oppressor.

The Incas constituted the largest indigenous empire that the Spaniards encountered in the Western Hemisphere. Like the Aztecs, the Incas had enlarged their territory through conquering other groups in the region; unlike the Aztecs, the Incas treated their subju-gated peoples somewhat better. Incan lands were efficiently orga-nized and administered by a centralized government from the capi-tal, Cuzco. The organization included an excellent system of roads in the Andes; state-operated warehouses of food, clothing and weapons; and a communication network of runners to carry mes-sages throughout the empire. Public works were constructed by laborers serving their turn in the *mita*, obligatory work for the state done on a rotational basis. The Incan social structure consisted of several levels: the family, kin groups known as *ayllus*, a class of hereditary nobles, and the Incan royal family headed by the Supreme Inca. The *yanaconas* were a group of laborers not attached to an *ayllu*. Religion, an important factor in Incan life, involved the wor-ship of ancestors and *huacas* or sacred objects, persons and places as well as the cult of the royal mummies. Incan rulers believed they were descended from Inti, one of the manifestations of the sky god. Human sacrifice among the Incas was rare compared with Aztec practice.

At the time of the Spaniards' encounter with the Aztecs and the Incas, the two Indian empires had several characteristics in common. Both were highly centralized nations whose subjugated peoples were desirous of relief from oppression. The societies contained a well-structured hierarchy, aspects of which the Spaniards would use later to establish their own New World empire. Religion for both peoples was a key organizing element that marked the principal events of one's life and gave meaning to day-to-day existence.

The Spaniards broke suddenly into this organized and relatively peaceful world, and the conquest began.[34] Following the pattern developed by the Genoese and the Portuguese, the intention of Columbus's first voyage was trade and the establishment of trading stations called *factorías*. To their initial purpose of trade and the establishment of trading posts, the Spaniards added the objective of settlement and colonization. The conquest followed a pattern: from the Caribbean the conquistadors moved on to the mainland (Mexico) and finally south to the South American continent. The pattern was not preordained; it developed from pressures on the islands and lands discovered, particularly with the dwindling of gold resources and the decimation of the indigenous population needed to work in the mines and on the *encomiendas* (holdings of natives and lands). The conquistadors moved beyond Hispaniola, because little gold was left on the island and the Indian labor force was dwindling, mainly because of harsh working conditions and illnesses. The conquistadors constituted the first immigrants to Spanish America. The majority were commoners from Andalusia, Extremadura, and Castile. Some of the motivation of the soldiers during the Reconquest reappears among the conquistadors in the New World, in particular, the desire for land, wealth, and improved social rank. The image of the conquistador was formed in the years of frontier raids during the Reconquest, where survival demanded a sense of individualism balanced by membership in a group of soldiers. The conquistador formed part of a band led by a *caudillo*.[35]

Even while the conquest was progressing, the colonies' governmental, legal, and economic structures were being set up and were fully developed by 1570. With the exception of municipal government, the impetus for organization came down from the top in Spain. Founded in 1524 to oversee colonial affairs, the Council of the Indies issued laws, recommended policies to the monarch, and exercised fiscal and judicial powers.[36] The next administrative level was on American territory in the form of the two major viceroyalties. New Spain, with its capital in Mexico City, was established in 1535 to include the northern region of Panama, the Caribbean islands, Mexico, part of today's United States, and a part of Venezuela. Peru was next established in the 1540s to take in the rest of Panama and South America except for a part of Venezuela. The viceroy was responsible for the levying and collection of taxes, the construction of public works, maintenance of internal order, defense against external aggressors, support of the church, and protection of the Indians. A cultural derivative of the viceroyalty were the spectacular festivities held to welcome a new viceroy. To administer justice in the vast viceroyalties, *audiencias*, or courts, were set up under a president-governor.[37] At the town level, colonists established *cabildos* (town councils) to administer local affairs. The *Casa de contratación* in Seville was the economic arm of the Spanish government for regulating trade with the New World.

Documents by Indians capture in retrospect the ominous atmosphere prevalent in Mexico and Peru on the eve of the Spanish arrival. Prophecies, like that in the Mayan *Chilam Balam*, and signs among the Aztecs and Incas indicated the imminent end of time. The *Chilam Balam* foretold the coming of a new ruler and a new epoch. Among the signs in Mexico were a column of fire each night for a year in Tenochtitlán, the destruction by fire of the temple of Huitzilopochtli, and the appearance of a strange bird with a mirror in its head; in Peru, frequent earthquakes and damage by lightning to the Inca's palace seemed ominous.[38] Thinking that the prophecies of their sacred texts were being fulfilled, the natives at first received the Spaniards as gods in the belief that their own gods had been defeated. The Indians were amazed at the appearance of the Spaniards and, as Wachtel has pointed out, Indian descriptions of the conquerors from Mexico to Peru stress the same characteristics of white skin, beards, horses, writing, and firearms.[39] In Central Mexico before the arrival of the Spaniards there was a population of 25 million inhabitants; 30 years after the invasion 90 percent of that population had disappeared. In the Incan empire there were about 10 million, also reduced by about 90 percent, except in the cold highlands, or *altiplano*.[40] The main reason for the decline of the native populations was disease brought by the Europeans, such as smallpox, measles, and the flu; other factors included loss through warfare, hard labor in the mines and on the *encomiendas*, and attempts by the Indians themselves to escape their suffering through suicides, abortion, and birth control (see Wachtel, 213).

Issues of Indigenous Rights

The "discovery" of the lands hitherto unknown to the Europeans resulted in two issues: who would have title to the lands and how the inhabitants should be treated. Ferdinand and Isabella obtained title to the new lands from the Spanish pope Alexander VI in 1493. Along with the papal donation came the obligation to bring the inhabitants to the Christian faith. The conquest posed the question

whether the Spaniards had a right to wage war on the native inhabitants. Several positions emerged in the ensuing debate.[41] Some
Spaniards claimed that the papal donation authorized them to wage
war if the native population rejected evangelization. The Dominican
Francisco de Vitoria, considered the founder of international law,
advocated the doctrine of a just war against the Indians if they
opposed the spread of Christianity. The matter was also argued
between the Dominican protector of the Indians, Fray Bartolomé de
las Casas, and the humanist Juan Ginés de Sepúlveda. Las Casas
opposed forced conversion and mistreatment.[42] Sepúlveda sought
support for his position in the papal donation of 1493 and in Aristotle's doctrine, which propounded the idea that some people are
slaves by nature. Since the Indians were culturally inferior, a just war
could be waged to civilize them. In 1537, Pope Paul III stated the
church's official position on the Indians in the bull *Sublimis Deus*,
which proclaimed that the Indians were human, that they could be
converted to Christianity, that they could own property, and that
they must not be enslaved. Despite ecclesiastical condemnation,
exploitation of the native populations continued.

Two economic institutions, the *repartimiento* (distribution of
Indians) and the *encomienda*, had far-reaching effects on the
indigenous population. In the Antilles the *repartimiento* was the
allocation of a group of Indians with their *cacique* (chief) to a Spanish settler who used them to work in the mines or in the fields. With
some changes, the *repartimiento* was transplanted to the mainland
as the *encomienda*. Spanish landlords of *encomiendas* (*encomenderos*) were to provide for the spiritual and material needs of the
Indians entrusted to them. The *encomendero* with his Indians could
also defend the surrounding region, thus serving as an army for
Spain. Indians worked in their own towns under the direction of
their *cacique*, or chief, but all were answerable to the *encomendero*.
The crown did not want the *encomiendas* to become hereditary
fiefdoms as in medieval Spain. The New Laws of 1542, issued in an
effort to improve the Indians' lot, mandated the return of an
encomienda to the crown on the death of the current *encomendero*.
Compulsory labor by the Indians was abolished in 1549. Afterwards,
the Indians were to pay tribute.[43]

The system of tribute levied by the Spaniards was oppressive; at
first the level was arbitrarily set and later when tax laws or limits

were promulgated they were not always respected. In the face of economic oppression by the Spaniards, Indians in Peru struggled to exert some control over their destiny. They controlled the production of silver in the early days of the colony because the Spaniards had to rely on the Indians' knowledge of the silver producing process until 1574 when the European system of amalgamation was introduced into Peru (see Wachtel, 221-22). Some of the Indians' social and political structures survived the conquest, but were weakened when adapted to the Spaniards' imperial scheme. The basic units of Aztec and Incan society, the *calpulli* of Mexico and the *ayllu* of Peru, still played their organizational roles. The descendants of the ruling classes collaborated with the Spaniards to retain their privileges. In Mexico the heirs of Moctezuma held the post of *gobernador* (governor) until 1565, while in Peru, Huayna Capac's sons served as puppet emperors.

The conquest was fairly rapid but did meet with opposition, especially in the Andes and on the Mexican and Peruvian frontiers. An Incan revolt began in the Andes under the leadership of Manco Capac, one of the Inca's sons, who was succeeded by Titu Cusi. The Inca revolt was associated with the millenial movement known as *Taqui Ongo*. Frontier groups including the Chiriguanos, the Araucanians in Chile, and the Chichimecas in northern Mexico fomented rebellion. Not all resistance was armed; Guamán Poma de Ayala fought Spanish domination through literature. Wachtel cites Poma as an example of how an indigenous writer adapted Western ideas to Incan concepts and in so doing, resisted the white man: "Although Poma wrote in Spanish (albeit incorrectly) and practiced Christianity, he continued to see the colonial world through the spatial and temporal categories which had shaped the organization of the Incan empire."[44]

Proselytization and Assimilation

Parallel with the military conquest of the indigenous peoples, the Spanish supported a spiritual conquest to fulfill their duty to the Pope, who had ordered evangelization of the new lands, and as an important means to assimilate the natives into Spanish culture. Missionary activity began in 1493 with Columbus's second voyage. The mendicant orders – Franciscans, Dominicans and Augustinians –

carried out the work of evangelization with the first missionaries, the Franciscans, arriving in Mexico in 1524. The Franciscans, influenced by a millenialism rooted in Christian humanism and the medieval apocalyptic mysticism of Joachim of Flora, zealously undertook the conversion of the Indians to hasten, as they believed, the ending of the world and the second coming of Christ.[45] To improve the quality of the indigenous conversions, the friars studied the native languages and recorded many aspects of Indian life, thus producing the first ethnographic studies of the native populations.

Conversion occurred rapidly and in great numbers in Mexico. Evangelization was much slower in Peru due to the unsettled situation. In parts of the former Incan empire the process could not begin until the seventeenth century. A primary goal of the missionaries was the uprooting of Indian religious practices, in particular human sacrifice, which the missionaries viewed as diabolical.[46] Among segments of the native population, fidelity to native religious traditions was one way to rebel against the conquerors, but the rejection was not uniform in all the conquered lands. In Mexico the Indians embraced Christianity almost wholeheartedly during the early years of colonization, while in Peru, worship of the *huacas*, the local gods, persisted. In both regions, native spiritual belief and practices often continued under cover of Catholic ritual. The Spaniards contributed to a syncretism of Christian and native religious practices by erecting crosses and churches on Indian religious locations.[47] The missionaries were merely following a time-honored principle used in the early days of Christianizing peoples in Europe, even going back to the building of Christian churches on the sites of Roman temples. During the Reconquest in Spain the precedent was set for converting Moorish mosques into churches, an outstanding example being the Cathedral of Córdoba. The backfiring of the syncretism was, however, something the Spanish missionaries did not anticipate.

The props supporting the official religions, such as temples, priests, festivals, and sacred literature preserved in Mexican codices or Incan *quipus* came under attack from the missionaries, and their destruction hastened the demise of the indigenous religions. To escape a world devoid of meaning, many Indians turned to drinking. Prior to the conquest, alcoholic beverages were consumed within the context of a religious celebration as a means to commune with the divine.[48] In the Andes, along with drinking, the Indians chewed the coca leaf. The Spaniards exhibited an ambiguous attitude toward the Indians' alcoholism, condemning it as immoral but also selling wine to the natives. Religious conversion was not the only significant means of acculturation of the Indian populations; another was learning the conquerors' language. The rate of acculturation depended upon class; Indian nobles soon adopted the Spaniards' language and customs while also using their indigenous languages. The commoners remained faithful to Indian traditions, especially in retaining native languages and dress, although the latter sometimes became a hybrid of Indian and Spanish articles of clothing.

Africans in the New World merit mention also. Compared with the Indians, Africans in the Americas did not receive much attention in scholarship until the second half of this century.[49] Also an exploited people, they were, unlike the Indians, not native to the region but imported specifically for slavery. Africans came in small numbers as the slaves of Spaniards on the early voyages of exploration and conquest, and larger numbers began to arrive in the last quarter of the sixteenth century, many passing through Cartagena in Colombia, the major slaving port. They came to work in gold mining, sugar plantations, and domestic service. The Portuguese initially monopolized the trade, but following the union of Spain and Portugal in 1580, Spain had easier access to slaves and the business became profitable to Spain itself. From 1521 to 1550 about 500 slaves came each year for a total of 15,000; in the latter half of the sixteenth century the annual average was 810 for a total of 36,300. The trade in slaves and their presence in the New World posed a moral problem for the missionaries and other Christians.

Dealing in the slave trade with large numbers of people bothered some Europeans; nevertheless, they justified the trade, placing the blame on the African leaders who sold their people into slavery. The Europeans ignored the possibility that Africans would not have sold their own people if there were no demand for such labor. The missionaries were concerned that the growing number of superficially converted Africans might "contaminate" the new Indian Christians.[50] Conversion was used to justify enslavement of the African much as it had been to subjugate the Indians. The missionaries encountered obstacles to the conversion of the Africans in the New World, such as the many languages and different cultures they represented. After imparting the rudiments of the faith, not well understood by the Africans, the missionaries became indifferent to the spiritual formation of the slaves, a curious contrast to their zealous attitude toward the conversion of the Indians.

Women's Presence in the Colonies

It was not long after the conquest until Spanish women began to arrive in the New World. According to Asunción Lavrin, the first Spanish women to come to the New World "helped to shape the cultural transfer and to form the biological nucleus of a social elite"[51] (321). They carried to America the pattern of Spanish home life as well as religious and social values. In the first two decades of the sixteenth century women constituted between 5-17 percent of immigrants; the numbers reached 28.5 percent between 1560 and 1579. Like many of the conquistadors, the women came from Andalusia and headed for Mexico and Peru.[52] Although early laws encouraged the emigration of families, the first group of women were single, and they came to marry, settle, and improve their economic situation. Socioeconomic expectations of Spanish women immigrants in the sixteenth century were high, but their fortunes varied; one-sixth of all female immigrants between 1560 and 1579 came as servants, but owing to the availability of Indian women for domestic work, the Spanish women soon moved up the socioeconomic ladder. By the end of the sixteenth century, however, Spanish women were destitute – widows and daughters of conquistadors and settlers. To remedy the situation, wealthy Spaniards established shelter homes called *recogimientos*.

Indian women are an often overlooked group in Spanish colonial America. They played an important role during the conquest, serving as interpreters and concubines or wives of the Spaniards. According to Lavrin, in precolumbian times Indian women were bound by moral rules as strict as those of Roman Catholicism – premarital virginity was prized, adultery of both men and women was severely punished – so that adaptation to postconquest norms was not that sudden a change for them (346). Spanish men often married Indian women of the nobility to gain power in the Indian community. Indian women in towns and cities, particularly in the role of servants, interacted more often with the Spanish and were in a position to transmit Spanish culture to their fellow Indians.

Culture and Education

Two aspects of cultural life – education and books – affected various segments of the colonial population in the sixteenth century.[53] Separate and unequal systems of education arose to meet the needs of the settlers and their children and those of the Indians. Schools and *colegios* (private academies) offered a European education to the boys and young men from the Spanish and Creole elite. Universities were created by the mendicant orders in the sixteenth century: Santo Tomás in Santo Domingo in 1538, San Marcos in Lima in 1551, and the Royal and Pontifical University in Mexico City in 1553. These and similar institutions offered ambitious Creoles an opportunity to advance in commerce and public administration. Higher education, however, was marred by social discrimination that allowed Spaniards, Creoles, and Indian nobles to enroll but made access difficult, if not impossible, for mestizos, blacks, and mulattoes. Spanish cultural policy undertook the assimilation of Indians through efforts to convert them, as already seen, and teach them Spanish. The missionaries taught the conquerors' language in addition to Christian doctrine and established colleges where young Indians learned Latin, music, and some technical subjects, such as agriculture. The Franciscans founded the College of Santa Cruz de Tlatelolco near Mexico City in 1536 as the first residential college for Indians. Several decades later the Jesuits, who favored the development of a native clergy, founded their own Indian colleges. Unfortunately, Indian colleges died out by the end of the sixteenth century. As cultural assimilation progressed the missionaries began to fear that the Indians were being morally contaminated by the questionable behavior of some Spaniards and began to segregate the Indians into separate communities inspired by utopian ideas, derived in part from Thomas More's *Utopia.*[54] The Franciscans in Mexico, under the bishop of Michoacán, Vasco de Quiroga, set up special villages, or *pueblos hospitales*, for their Indian flocks. The Jesuits later established their famous communities, or *reducciones*, in Paraguay and California.

Intellectual life was also advanced by the reading of books. The first books, including the popular novels of chivalry, were brought to the New World by some of the conquistadors. Missionaries brought or had imported religious books, breviaries, missals, and bibles. The

crown and its administrators in the New World encouraged the importation and publication of books, although under considerable
control. The exportation from Spain of works of fiction was prohibited because the crown and its advisors feared that the newly converted Indians might read material in which they would not be able
to distinguish Revelation from fiction. The Inquisition played a role
in controlling what colonists read by censoring manuscripts and
searching ships for prohibited books. The industrious colonists,
however, found ways to circumvent the prohibition through smug-
gling and bribing customs officials. American private libraries and
catalogues of booksellers included titles by Erasmus and other humanists as well as books of chivalry. By the mid-1530s Juan
Cromberger had set up the first printing press in America in Mexico
City. Lima's first printer, Ricciardi, was operating in 1583. The first
colonial publications were mainly preaching manuals and catechisms
in keeping with the missionary activity of the time, but gradually
books on other topics – mining, medicine, history, law, geography,
and poetry – began to appear.

In addition to controlling the book trade, the crown directly or
indirectly influenced reading material that affected views of the
newly discovered world. The administration in Spain encouraged the
writing of official and unofficial accounts of the New World that
would support its policies and attempts to counter the dynastic
claims of the descendants of Columbus and other conquistadors.[55]
By order of the crown, documentation was made available to
chroniclers like Pedro Mártir de Anglería and José de Acosta to aid
them in writing their histories. In 1526 the office of royal cosmographer and chronicler of the Indies was created, with Gonzalo Fernández de Oviedo as the official chronicler. Books recording the
discovery and conquest became the foundation of colonial literary
culture. These accounts were prepared while the events were taking
place or shortly thereafter. Some were written under the obligation
to report to the crown, some to present legal demands for services
rendered, and some to describe the fauna and flora of the new lands,
while others documented the languages, customs, and histories of
America's original inhabitants. With few exceptions, the chronicles
presented the conquerors' perspective of the events and contributed
to the hegemony of European values throughout the colonial period.

Chapter Two

Discovery

The most famous discoverer and major chronicler of his voyages is Christopher Columbus, but others who accompanied him on some part of his four voyages also reported on their experiences. Columbus and most participants in these and later discoveries wrote to fulfill an obligation to report to authorities in Spain or to promote their enterprises. As a result, the ship's log and letters are the predominant discourses in this group. Columbus's son Hernando, a participant on his father's fourth voyage, chose the discourse of biography. Amerigo Vespucci, working for the Portuguese and Spanish crowns, reported his voyages in letters written in Italian.

Columbus was born to Domenico Colombo and Susanna Fontanarossa between 26 August and 31 October 1451 in Genoa. His family were wool-weavers. There is little evidence available of his early life, but he claims he went to sea at a young age.[1] Columbus wrote in Spanish and very little in Latin. Menéndez Pidal believes that Columbus learned Spanish in the years he spent in Portugal, because his Spanish is filled with Portuguese influences affecting his Castilian grammar and vocabulary.[2] Some scholars have held that Columbus was from a Spanish-Jewish family that had settled in Genoa to escape the pogrom unleashed throughout Spain in 1391.[3]

Columbus developed a plan to sail to the Orient by a westward route. Various elements came together to generate this plan in the mind and fantasy of the Genoese: contacts in Lisbon; his sailing experience in the South Atlantic for the Portuguese; his reading of Pierre d'Ailly, Marco Polo, Ptolemy, Pliny, Toscanelli; and biblical prophecies, especially the apocryphal second book of Esdras.[4]

Columbus annotated his reading in *apostillas*, marginal notes to a series of books. The notes are among his early writings and are helpful to understand Columbus's mentality and details of his biography. Among the annotated books preserved in the Biblioteca Colombina at Seville are Pierre d'Ailly's *Imago mundi* (Image of the

World), Pius II's *Historia rerum ubique gestarum*, (History of Deeds Everywhere), Marco Polo, and Pliny's *Historia natural* (Natural History). A question exists as to whether Columbus or his brother Bartholomew made the annotations. Varela concludes that the notes are attributable to Christopher Columbus because they form a homogeneous block showing the same way of thinking, the same language, and common handwriting habits.[5] The marginal notes contain Columbus's remarks on observations made during visits or stays in Ireland, the Portuguese fortress at La Mina in Africa, and Lisbon. They concern the habitability of the torrid zone; the biblical Tharsis, which he claimed was on Hispaniola; the growing of parsley, and the age of the world according to biblical computation.

In formulating his plan, Columbus also relied on information he received in letters from Florentine physician and astronomer Paolo da Pozzi Toscanelli. Two letters, whose authenticity was once disputed but is now accepted, are important for supporting the feasibility of Columbus's proposed voyage and for the vision of wealth, fabulous cities, and large populations he would find in the East.[6] The letter to Martins concerns a shorter sea route to the spice lands to be found by sailing westward and covers such topics as the region's dense population; many cities; the one prince; the Great Khan; the interest of the Khan's ancestors in learning about Christianity; the immense wealth in gold, silver, gems, and spices; and philosophers and astrologers.

Columbus's First Voyage

Columbus wrote the *Diario de abordo* (*Diary*) of the first voyage while making that voyage.[7] When he returned to Spain and met the Catholic monarchs in Barcelona, he gave the original to Queen Isabella; she had a copy made for Columbus. Both the original and the copy are lost, so we have to rely on an abstract of the *Diary* with glosses made by Bartolomé de las Casas in his *Historia de las Indias* (*History of the Indies*).[8] Las Casas gained access to Columbus's papers through his friendship with Columbus's son Diego Colón (Colón is Spanish for Columbus), whom he met in Hispaniola. Over the years Las Casas had direct access to Columbus's papers and also could consult texts in the Dominican convent of St. Paul in Seville, where the library of Columbus's son Hernando was housed after

Hernando's death. As presented in Las Casas's *History*, the *Diary* becomes a discourse in the third person with occasional passages in the first person. In this fashion Las Casas controls Columbus's discourse and lets him be heard when Las Casas believes it is appropriate. This procedure is ironic in view of the fact that Columbus silenced the Indians in his discourse; now his copyist silences him.[9]

The *Diary* exemplifies the hybridization of discourses prevalent in chronicles dealing with the discovery and conquest of the New World. A diary insofar as it is a day-to-day record of events and a ship's log, the record is also a *carta* or letter because it has a sender, Columbus, and a receiver, the Catholic monarchs (Mignolo 1982, 60). As a *carta* it has another aspect, that of a verbal chart of the ocean and islands traveled. It may also be considered a *memoria*, or memoir, in keeping with the monarchs' orders given for Columbus's fourth voyage when they ask him to "facer memoria," to keep a record of the voyage.[10]

A prologue addressed to the Catholic monarchs introduces the *Diary*. The prologue's introduction participates in the epistolary discourse. Columbus apparently wrote the prologue as he began the voyage, as indicated by his reference to the current year of 1492. He uses the prologue to guide the monarchs' interpretation of his voyage; he tries to control their reaction to his exploration by placing the voyage within the framework of the Catholic sovereigns' mission to evangelize. He reminds them of their awards to him and mentions his plans to do a new sailing chart and to put together a book. Columbus outlines his mission in the prologue: he is to go to India to see its princes, people, and lands; he is to see how the inhabitants might be converted; and he is to go westerly by an ocean route not previously traveled. The prologue makes no specific mention of looking for gold or of establishing future trade. Columbus places his mission in the context of events occurring in 1492, especially the consolidation of the Christian faith on Spanish soil. With that accomplished, the Catholic monarchs can turn their vision outwards to undertake the task of evangelization. Columbus addresses the sovereigns as Christian monarchs and lists their Christian accomplishments: in January they concluded the centuries-long *reconquista* (reconquest) by taking the last Moorish stronghold of Granada. Furthermore, the rulers expelled all the Jews from their kingdoms and dominions. Columbus affirms that he convinced the sovereigns to send him on this voyage because they had demonstrated they were defenders of the Christian faith. Because of a report Columbus gave to the king and queen about the Great Khan of India, who along with his predecessors had been trying unsuccessfully to get Rome to send men to instruct them in the Christian faith, the king and queen decided to send Columbus to India to investigate how they might best be converted. Columbus casts the Pope in a negative light, as derelict in fulfilling his responsibility to evangelize, and he exalts the Spanish rulers.

In the prologue Columbus reminds the monarchs of the rewards they promised him when they ordered him to go to India: they raised him to the nobility calling him "don," made him grand admiral of the Ocean Sea and viceroy and perpetual governor of all the islands and lands that might be discovered in the Ocean Sea, and guaranteed that Columbus's oldest son would succeed him and that all of these awards would be handed down in Columbus's family. Toward the end of the prologue, Columbus alludes to the great labor he will expend on this voyage and the sacrifice he will have to make of not getting much sleep. This statement functions to remind the monarchs to keep their promises and reward him.

The *Diary* obeys the monarchs' orders to report on the lands, princes, people, and their possibility of conversion. The nature of a diary is evident in Columbus's intention to write down his experiences and progress each day. He plans a new sailing chart in which he will locate all of the sea and lands of the Ocean Sea in their proper places and will compose a book with paintings of what has been observed. The daily entries contain information on longitude and latitude, on winds and islands, so in a sense he composed a verbal chart. The text of the *Diary* may be divided according to the three stages of the voyage: the outbound voyage, 3 August to 12 October 1492, from Palos to the Bahamas; traveling in the New World, 12 October 1492 to 16 January 1493, from the Bahamas to Hispaniola; and the return voyage, 16 January to 15 March 1493, from Hispaniola to the Iberian Peninsula.

Columbus and his crew set sail in three caravels, the Santa María, the Niña, and the Pinta, from Palos on 3 August 1492. On 12 August they reached the Canary Islands, where they stayed before making the final departure for India on 6 September. The outbound voyage was beset with problems. The rudder of the Pinta broke, and

Columbus believed it was sabotaged by two members of the crew, Cristóbal Quintero and Gómez Rascón. The episode highlights the relationship between Martín Alonso Pinzón, second in command, and Columbus, a relationship that was favorable at the start but would change later. The Portuguese threatened to capture the caravels, and Columbus surmises that the king of Portugal is envious that Columbus went to Castile for help for this voyage. The sailors were depressed over compass markings. On another occasion, they worried about winds for returning to Spain. The wind problem was solved by nature, but Columbus described the solution as a miracle. He saw it as a sign that had occurred only once before in history, in the time of Moses when the Jews were leaving Egypt. Columbus establishes an analogy between himself and Moses; Columbus's men complain about him as the Jews did about Moses, but divine favor aided Moses and now Columbus.

Another problem was the false hope of sighting land, resulting in the sailors' disillusionment, which continued for quite a while; the first sighting, which turned out to be false, was 25 September, but it was not until the night of 11-12 October that they actually saw land. Pinzón, who comes across as an intelligent and stable figure whom Columbus can trust, played an important role in the sighting – a role that Columbus prefers not to acknowledge and that is a source of the growing tension between them.[11] Pinzón advised steering southwest by west; at first Columbus does not accept this advice; then, the next day, he follows Pinzón's advice but justifies it because he saw migrating birds from north to southwest; the Portuguese had discovered lands by following the migrating birds. This explanation permits Columbus to save his pride. As the men's discontent grows, Columbus encourages them by offering hope of benefits they will receive if their journey succeeds. Throughout the problems and complaints of the outbound voyage Columbus persists in his purpose of reaching India, and he will permit no delay.

In his encounter with the New World, Columbus faced a twofold problem: the recognition of new objects and experiences and the communication of the newly acquired knowledge to his European audience. Las Casas, in his transcription and summary of several Columban documents, expressed doubts about certain reports.[12] Columbus sees and expresses what he saw. But there are problems with this seeing and saying. Columbus is capable of manipulating what he sees to produce a certain reaction in the reader. For the consumption of his sailors, Columbus admits that he manipulated the record of the mileage covered each day on the outbound voyage. He recorded less mileage than the ships actually accrued in a day's time out of concern that his men would be afraid if they learned they were going far from Spain. On the return voyage Columbus says he did not write down the correct route that he took so that other voyagers and discoverers would not retrace his path. Even his report of the arrival on Portuguese soil may have been an attempt to manipulate an appropriate response from his readers and Spanish backers; he says residents of a Portuguese village received the news of his discovery with joy.

Perspectives on the *Diary*

A reading of Columbus's *Diary* of the first voyage shows that he was aware of the problem of perception and expression. He confesses ignorance concerning the meaning of statues of female figures and whether their purpose is as objects of art or of worship. He laments not knowing some spice trees or trees he thinks are spice-bearing. He was especially concerned that his readers would have trouble believing him. Columbus begs the king and queen not to think he is exaggerating in his descriptions; rather, he is telling only a hundredth part of the reality and one must see it to believe it. Columbus apologizes for constantly describing things in superlative terms; he must have realized that excessive hyperbole would make his readers wonder what was true. Perhaps it is most useful to look at the entry of his *Diary* that captures Columbus's first perceptions, reactions, and his recording of what he saw. That crucial first day can serve as a measure against which to compare what he saw on the rest of his first voyage.

Columbus first sights land but does not describe it. At dawn on 12 October, as they draw near to land, the first thing the Spaniards see are naked people. After taking official possession of the land in the name of Ferdinand and Isabella, Columbus devotes the rest of the day's entry to his impressions of the people and his relating to them. The entry for the second day also deals mainly with the people, while he writes briefly and, as it were parenthetically, about the land. Finally, Columbus reveals his consuming interest in gold. Of the three elements – land, people, and gold – mentioned in the entries for the first two days in the New World, the most interesting comments concern the inhabitants. Generally, throughout the *Diary* of the first voyage, more is written about the inhabitants of the New World than about nature or gold, showing Columbus's fascination with the Indians.

Columbus describes the natural elements briefly and in general terms. Columbus wants to make the unseen known to his readers in Spain. Plants, trees, and climate are made recognizable to them: the trees are like those in Castile or Andalusia in April or May; they resemble those described by Pliny that Columbus has seen on the island of Chios. The fish are "very different from ours," he says, "so that it is a marvel." One passage describes gold-speckled stones in a river, and he recalls seeing the same thing in the river Tagus, the implication being that since stones in the Tagus were evidence of gold, there must be gold in this New World river. Columbus's haste to discover sources of gold affects his perception; he is constantly moving on and admits that many things might be missed, but he does not want to delay his search for gold. Columbus's brief descriptions of natural elements, devoid of detail, have a monotonous quality. The reader can predict how the next landscape encountered will be described. The natural elements are often Eden-like. The air is described as gentle and warm to show that the region was habitable. Recalling Asia as described by Marco Polo, the lands are described according to their extension, their greenery, fertility, abundance of water, and the presence of mountains. E. W. Palm affirms that Columbus used images from medieval literature, for example, from the "dolce stil nuovo" (136). The use of literary imagery does not mean, though, that Columbus was writing belle lettristic literature. His primary task, as Mignolo has pointed out, was to discover; he wrote as an obligation to report to his monarchs (Mignolo 1982, 59). Primary interests include how the land and its products can be colonized and exploited for commerce and what may be suitable locations for ports and defenses. Columbus mentions few animals; those he does observe are exotic to a European: parrots, monkeys, strange fish. Tropical vegetation is judged essentially on the basis of its potential to yield spices. Rivers, streams, and coastal waters are scrutinized for traces of gold and pearls.

The inhabitants receive more detailed description than nature, yet there is a predictable pattern, with certain aspects singled out: the Indians' physical features, moral attributes (peaceful, generous), and intellectual qualities (docile and quick to learn). Their learning ability is gauged by Columbus on the basis of their repeating what the Spaniards say, not on whether they can think for themselves. As Columbus proceeds from island to island, he notes similarities and differences among the natives of the region and evaluates the degree of civilization they demonstrate. The comparison between indigenous peoples and the revision of his earlier opinions, although not done consistently, contrasts with Columbus's monotonous characterization of nature. For Beatriz Pastor, Columbus characterizes the native Caribbean population in terms of lacks: they were not clothed, not rich, not traders, and did not possess weapons (37). Originally perceived in a state of Eden-like innocence, they go naked like Adam and Eve, not needing wealth and weapons. Columbus's characterization of innocence highlights is conducive to their exploitation.

In Columbus's description of the natives and his dealings with them during these first two days, two traits predominate and intertwine: evangelization and commerce; commerce wins out. Attention to evangelization fulfills one of the charges of Columbus's mission as outlined in the prologue to the *Diary*. The natives' first approach to the Spaniards suggests how best to evangelize them. Columbus gives them gifts to make them friendly because, he reasons, they would be better converted to Christianity by love than by force. The Indians offer parrots, balls of cotton thread, javelins, and other items in exchange, giving the impression that the Indians looked upon the transaction as barter. Columbus may well have included this detail to show the possibility of future trade and that the Indians could be given articles of little value and still be pleased. One note of disappointment sounds in all of this; Columbus concludes rather quickly and realistically that the natives are very poor.

Enhancing prospects of both evangelization and commerce is the Indians' defenselessness: they do not bear arms and are so ignorant of them that they cut themselves when handling the Spaniards' swords. Not only does Columbus link evangelization and trade, but he appears to link slavery and evangelization in the same utterance. On this second day, Columbus is already planning to take some of the Indians back to Spain so "they could learn to speak," ostensibly to learn Christian doctrine, return to the islands, and help with the evangelization of the other natives.

Columbus undermines his argument that the Indians are peaceful by mentioning their giving javelins to the Spaniards. Perhaps he dismisses the javelins – like sticks with a hook on the tip – as weapons in comparison with the European arms, but self-contradiction occurs on other occasions in the *Diary*, particularly in relation to trusting the Indians and the language spoken by them. Columbus boasted about the innocence of the Indians, but builds a fortress and justifies it in these terms: "they are naked and without arms and very cowardly, beyond hope of cure. But it is right that this tower should be built, and it is as it should be, being so far from Your Highnesses, and that they may recognize the skill of Your Highnesses' subjects, and what they can do, so that they may serve them with love and fear" (26 December). Reading between the lines we can see that he does not trust the natives and even lacks respect for them, calling them cowardly. Elsewhere Columbus undercuts his earlier presentation of the idyllic, tame Indian when he admits that some are warlike. The Christians wound two Indians and the rest flee even though they outnumbered the Spaniards 50 to 7, possibly an exaggeration to enhance the powers of the Christians. Columbus refers to the Spanish here as Christians in opposition to the Indians, who appear as infidels like the Moors whom the Christian Spaniards fought for several centuries.

Columbus suspects the Indians do know of gold and are trying to prevent him from locating it. One Indian told Columbus about lands "in which there was endless gold; which names the Admiral wrote down, and when a brother of the king knew what he had said, he scolded him, as the Admiral gathered. On other occasions also the Admiral understood that the king endeavored that he shouldn't know whence the gold came or was collected, because he did not wish him to barter or buy elsewhere" (Morison, *Journals*, 140).

Throughout the journey Columbus postulates a single language among the Indians so that their conversion should be easy, but he contradicts himself by observing different words for things. Despite Columbus's not understanding the Indians well he jumps to conclusions regarding the existence of gold in a certain area. When he meets an Indian, believed to be a man-eating Carib, and the man tells him about gold, Columbus shows his awareness of language differences among the natives of the different islands. The Spanish had to resort to sign language to communicate with the Indians. In what Pastor calls the "systematic erasure of native voices," Columbus does not let the Indians speak in the *Diary* without filtering what they say by his use of qualifiers, such as "I felt that," "I understood that he said to me."[13]

Toward the end of the return voyage, when Columbus fears that he and his ship may be lost during a storm, he puts information about the voyage on a parchment within a barrel dropped into the sea, hoping that one day it will reach the Spanish monarchs. The message on the parchment would, in Columbus's words, "show that he had told the truth in what he said and professed to reveal" (14 February). This refers to his pre-voyage arguments, the project he commended to the Spanish monarchs, and he now believes he has proven that what he encountered on this voyage has confirmed his project.

A Postscript: Columbus's Letter on the First Voyage

Columbus's letter to the sovereigns on the first voyage is in keeping with the practice of Spanish captains to write such letters during the final homeward bound voyage.[14] Columbus offers a summary of the first voyage: "This is what has been done, though in brief." The letter, written before 10 February 1493 on board the Niña, was dated 15 February off the Azores. The postscript was written 4 March near Lisbon. Although entitled "Letter to the Sovereigns," the account is addressed to "Luis de Santángel, Keeper of the Privy Purse," a friend of Columbus. A similar letter was sent to Gabriel Sánchez, treasurer of the Kingdom of Aragon, enclosed in another letter to the king and queen, now lost. Morison speculates the cover letter to the monarchs followed a formula of asking the king and queen to read the letter and to command him to come to the court to render an account of the voyage just completed (Morison, *Journals*, 180). The letter was very popular as a source of knowledge on the discovery. Since the letter was written toward the end of his first voyage, Columbus sees events from hindsight. The nautical information so evident in the *Diary* of the first voyage is missing from the letter.

The opening paragraph briefly recounts Columbus's accomplishments: he found many islands with a numerous population, he took possession of them for the Spanish monarchs, and he named the islands.[15] Following a hierarchical order, Columbus gives credit for his accomplishment first to the Heavenly King and then to the earthly king and queen, Ferdinand and Isabella. In naming the islands Columbus also followed a definite hierarchy: the first island for Christ, San Salvador; the second for the Virgin Mary, Isla de Santa María de la Concepción; the third for Ferdinand, Fernandina; the fourth for Isabella, La Isla Bella; the fifth for the royal couple's daughter, Juana.

The letter reiterates themes mentioned at the end of the *Diary* of the first voyage. Columbus sees his voyage as a triumph given by God and himself as God's instrument for this discovery. Columbus, who earned divine favor because he walked in God's way, now savors victory in the wake of years of struggle to convince the monarchs of the desirability of his plan and the obstacles to overcome. The letter's ending includes the king and queen as also being given the triumph by God, and the joy and material benefits of the enterprise extend to all Christendom.

The letter intends to demonstrate the success of the voyage. To that end, Columbus gives a different explanation here than in the *Diary* of why he founded Navidad, omits the destruction of the Santa María, but implies that he consciously and purposely founded the settlement because of its strategic location for gold and trade between Spain and the New World. Descriptions of the land and people in the letter support Columbus's argument that the voyage was successful: incredible harbors can be used in future trade; most rivers and streams contain gold and there are great mines of gold and other metals; there are many spices. Columbus stresses that these things cannot be believed without seeing them.

In the letter, for the first time, the natives of this hemisphere are called Indians. Columbus presents the Indians as well-built and handsome, innocent, timid, and peaceful in temperament. Columbus actually misjudged the Indians' friendship and peacefulness, especially of their chief Guacanagari. When he returns on his second voyage, he discovers the settlement at Navidad has been destroyed. The natives are free with their possessions and delighted with worthless objects they receive from the Spaniards. They go about naked and have no weapons of iron or steel. Some of Columbus's information on the Indians is of ethnographic interest: he observed monogamy among the people but polygamy for the king; women work more than the men; Columbus was not sure that the Indians respected private property, but he did see an example of communitarian living in the sharing of meals. They belong to no sect and practice no idolatry; they have the simple religious belief that the sky is the source of all power and goodness. Columbus attributes their belief that Columbus, his men, and ships have come from the sky not to a lack of intelligence but to never having seen clothed people or European ships.

Emphasis on the unity of appearance, customs, and language among these people is meant to convince the Spanish king and queen that it will be easy to convert them to Christianity. In an attempt at linguistic imperialism, Columbus captures some Indians so they can learn Castilian and give information to the Spanish, while the *Diary* affirms that some Spanish mariners attempted to learn the Indians' language to communicate with them. Columbus portrays himself as the generous defender of the Indians who forbade his men to give the natives worthless objects, while he gave them "good and pleasant things." Columbus's gifts, he admits, are intended to win the natives over so they will be kind to the Spaniards, become Christians, and lovingly serve Their Majesties. Naturally he wants the Indians to give things that they have in abundance on the islands and that are needed by the Spanish. Contradictions appear in his self-portrait, however, as when some Indians are taken captive, although he proposes enslaving only the Indians who persist in their idolatry.

Although Columbus has a prior mental model of this new world, his empirical approach renders him open to revising preconceived notions, as seen in his statement that in these islands he has found no human monstrosities, "as many expected." He has heard that there are some people with tails in two provinces that he has not yet visited, but he reserves judgment. On the other hand, he mentions cannibals and Amazon-like women, although he has not seen them.

Columbus ends the letter arguing for more help from the sovereigns. This voyage was hasty and the ships were not serviceable. Previous talk and writing about these lands was all conjecture, because those people did not see the lands as Columbus did. The ending attempts to justify limited accomplishments on this voyage, especially the paucity of material goods, particularly gold and spices. He promises great wealth in various forms: gold, precious stones, spices, and slaves.

The Second Voyage

Columbus's second voyage to the New World began on 25 September 1493. No journal or abstract of this voyage has survived, but some writings by Columbus and others exist, including Columbus's memorial to the sovereigns, of April 1493, outlining his ideas on colonizing Hispaniola with a series of trading posts, and the Torres memorandum of 30 January 1494, which was Columbus's official report on the colonization of Hispaniola and a request for people and things he needed. The gaps left by the disappearance of Columbus's journal can be filled by minor chronicles of the second voyage: Michele de Cuneo, Niccolò Syllacio, and Diego Alvarez Chanca.

Before undertaking the second voyage, Columbus set down his colonial policy in a memorial to the sovereigns dated April 1493, a document considered by Morison "as the beginning of Spanish, and indeed European, colonial policy in the New World."[16] The memorial was sent from Seville in early April 1493, before Columbus left for Barcelona, to be received by the Catholic monarchs after his first voyage. In it, Columbus states his ideas for the settlement and government of Hispaniola and the other islands discovered and to be discovered. He recommends that 2,000 colonists to be settled in three or four towns should be sent to secure the island and facilitate trade. Each town should have its magistrate and notary and a church with clergy to administer the sacraments and convert the Indians. Most of the memorial deals with rules about gold, again showing Columbus's great preoccupation with it while implying for benefit of the monarchs that gold is so abundant that its acquisition and sharing must be regulated by numerous rules. Governmental and spiritual matters are made dependent upon gold; for example, magistrates and notaries should be paid for their services, and one percent of gold should be reserved for building churches and supporting priests.

The minor chronicles offer revealing details of the second voyage. Michele de Cuneo, from a noble family of Savona and probably a boyhood friend of Columbus, went on Columbus's second voyage as a volunteer. Back in Savona, Cuneo put his American experience in a letter to his friend Hieronymo Annari.[17] The letter, written in literary Italian with some Genoese dialectal expressions, is dated 15 October 1495 from Savona and responds to Annari's request to learn about Columbus's second voyage. Some of the content of Cuneo's letter is determined by questions posed by Annari. The body of the letter reports on the voyage from Cádiz to Hispaniola, the exploration of the Cibao, on fauna and flora, the Indians, the voyage along the south coast of Cuba and the discovery of Jamaica, and the capture of Indians, some of whom are brought to Spain.

Cuneo's often unflattering report contrasts with Columbus's versions of his expeditions. As an interesting biographical detail, Cuneo recalls Columbus's amorous involvement with the lady of Gomera, Doña Beatriz de Peraza. Cuneo has Columbus say that the desire for gold is the main reason he undertook the dangerous voyage. The men, motivated by greed for gold, kept themselves in top physical shape, despite bad weather and poor food. In violation of the rules, they bartered gold in secret and robbed the Indians. On the island of Santa María la Gallante, 11 men organized a group to plunder the area but were lost in the wilderness. Cuneo does not criticize their intention to rob. This chronicler reports that on Guadeloupe, when Caribs fled, the Spaniards entered their houses and took whatever they desired, enslaving the Indians and carrying the best off to Spain while permitting the colonists to choose slaves from among the remainder. Neither is Cuneo shy in describing his sexual treatment of a beautiful Carib woman whom he beat into submission. He boasts of his lust and his abuse. Upon taking possession of an island granted him by Columbus, Cuneo cleared a plot of ground and simultaneously set up the cross and the gallows, thus offering both salvation and punishment to the natives.

On the second voyage, Columbus insisted that Cuba was the mainland. An abbot and most of the men, including Cuneo, disagreed. Columbus, to prevent discordant opinions affecting the future of the enterprise, did not wish to let the abbot return with the crew to Spain. Still, despite criticism of Columbus, Cuneo ends the letter praising him for his magnanimity and skills as a navigator.

The letter undermines positive impressions of the place and people that Columbus tried to convey in his writing on the first voyage. When Columbus founded Navidad, he praised its location, yet

Cuneo describes the place as unhealthy because of its marshes, while the streams yielded not a bit of gold. The slaves on the ship became sick and could not work. Cuneo views the Indians as beasts who sleep on the ground, eat when they like, have sex openly, and practice sodomy. He does credit them with not being jealous.

Two letters concerning the second voyage are more favorable than Cuneo's to Columbus and his enterprise. The texts of Guillermo Coma and Diego Alvarez Chanca have the same objective, an exaggerated glorification of Columbus, the discoverer.[18] Guillermo Coma, a Spanish physician, went on Columbus's second voyage. Coma's friend, the Sicilian Niccolò Syllacio, a lecturer on philosophy at the University of Pavia, translated Coma's Spanish letter into Latin, putting it in the style of Lucian.[19] The Coma-Syllacio letter is, according to Morison, the earliest printed report on the New World after Columbus's letter on his first voyage (229). Syllacio's translation, with a dedication to the Duke of Milan, Ludovico Maria Sforza, was published at Pavia as a pamphlet in 1494 or early 1495. Morison speculates that the purpose of the pamphlet was diplomatic (*Journals*, 229). The Duke, then in conflict with Charles VIII of France, was seeking Spanish support, hence, the compliments to Ferdinand and Isabella found in the letter.

Syllacio's humanistic studies exert their influence on his translation, which recasts the New World in terms of classical antiquity. The influence of Virgil and Apuleius is evident, and Gaius Pliny is frequently cited as an authority on natural history. He views the cannibals' devouring of the children of their captives as fiction – the story of Saturn eating his sons – being transformed into fact. Syllacio describes the rescue from a storm on spiritual and scientific levels, and the spiritual interpretation is further nuanced into pagan mythology and Christian hagiography. When all on board the ship had prayed for rescue, a god appeared. The god, speculates Syllacio, could have been the twin offspring of Leda who come to the aid of ships, or fiery humors that dissolved the storm cloud. Syllacio decides it was St. Elmo who heeds the prayers of sailors. As Columbus did in the *Diary* of his first voyage, Syllacio casts him in the role of a new Moses, who in the midst of his men's suffering from thirst, promises them a new land flowing with fountains and streams.

Syllacio stresses that the settlement at Navidad was intended to garrison the fortress, trade with the people, and civilize them. The letter blames the destruction of the Spaniards at Navidad on the licentious conduct of the men towards the Indian women, each Spaniard taking five. Syllacio mitigates the charge by commenting that the Spaniards' behavior was doubtless for the sake of progeny. The Indian men are portrayed as human in their emotions, banding together to avenge the insult to their honor.

The letter contains little on the search for gold, although Syllacio with some hesitation relates a tale he heard from a credible witness that in the region there was a rock that gushed forth gold when struck with a club, a variant of the story of Moses striking a rock and water flowing out. Syllacio speaks instead of farmers colonizing the lush and fertile land. Descriptions of the new *factoría* at Isabela constitute an idealistic projection rather than a realistic view. Syllacio foresees the city in a few years as the rival of any in Spain, with a large population and magnificent buildings, a broad avenue running through the town, and a mighty fortress on a hill. In preparation for future visits by the Spanish monarchs, Columbus's residence is called the royal palace.

Diego Alvarez Chanca reported his experience during Columbus's second voyage in a letter to the Town Council of Seville.[20] Alvarez Chanca, a native of Seville, requested to go on the second voyage as physician. Gold is the prime concern for Chanca, as it was for Columbus. Pedro Mártir reports that Chanca was greedy for gold. Columbus's reaction after discovering the massacre at Navidad is typical of this man obsessed with gold. He commanded that the ground be searched where the fortification had been in case gold had been buried there, as he had previously ordered. To encourage future expeditions, Chanca assures his readers that gold is so abundant that the Spanish sovereigns can consider themselves the richest rulers in the world.

Some Indians were more civilized than those of other islands, but the Caribs are described as living in degradation worse than beasts. Their choosing unsuitable locations for their dwellings and their diet of snakes and insects are adduced as evidence of low intelligence. The vocabulary of the letter betrays the Spaniards' attitude toward the Indians, who are referred to as heads of cattle. On the destruction of Navidad, Chanca implies the Indians' culpability when he reports the Indians as not approaching the Spaniards on their return to Navidad on the second voyage, as if they had something to hide. He has a mixed opinion on the natives' capacity for conversion; they imitate what the Spaniards do, but they also keep idols in their huts.

Columbus's Third Voyage

The third Columbine voyage left Sanlúcar de Barrameda in May of 1498. The three principal sources for this voyage include Las Casas's abstract of Columbus's lost diary made during the outbound voyage, Columbus's letter to the sovereigns of 18 October 1498 and his letter to Doña Juana Torres of 1500.

Compared with the *Diary* of the first voyage, the abstract of the third voyage is less detailed, but it does have the texture of a journal, with the days spent on the voyage given not as headings but embedded in the text.[21] As in his diary of the first voyage, Columbus addresses Ferdinand and Isabella, again producing a hybrid of ship's log and letter. From the abstract it seems that Columbus's lost diary of the third voyage was written as a propaganda piece directed to the sovereigns and not primarily as the customary ship's log. Columbus states that his purpose on the third voyage was to discover new lands and islands south of the equator. He wants to test the theory that there were more lands to the west, a theory propounded by the Portuguese king John II and corroborated by the Indians of Hispaniola, who spoke of black people south and southeast of Hispaniola. But in his concern for the people he left on Hispaniola, he sent three caravels directly there with supplies.

Throughout the text Columbus seeks to convince the king and queen to continue their support for the enterprise in the face of disparagers and opponents. During the outbound voyage on the Cape Verde Islands, Columbus compares the lands won by the Portuguese unfavorably with those he has discovered for Spain. The Cape Verde Islands, he says, are dry, sterile, and a haven for lepers. The sovereigns are meant to compare the Cape Verdes with the lands Columbus discovered so they will appreciate what he had discovered for them. He also compares the great amounts spent by the Portuguese on their African discoveries and the poor results with the greater rewards to come from lands in the New World, despite the little spent by Castile. Columbus also informs the sovereigns that he

is well aware of the impact of his first discoveries: their fame re-
sounds throughout the world.

Columbus and his crew suffered a great deal on this voyage, ex-
periencing heat so intense they feared they would burn to death. Divine intervention, in Columbus's thinking, granted a respite. Here
again Columbus infers that he is divinely chosen for a mission, so the
rain storms and cloudy weather are sent by God. They were also rescued from being engulfed by a great tidal wave in the Gulf of Paria.
In addition to mortal threats from nature, Columbus personally suffered from gout, insomnia and eye trouble.

The third expedition encountered people of a new cultural area
that ran from eastern Venezuela to Honduras. These inhabitants
were skilled in fishing, weaving and metallurgy. As proof that the climate was mild and the area habitable, Columbus cites people living
near the equator who were lighter in color than expected, with
flowing hair. These heavily armed people used embroidered articles
woven from cotton. Columbus notices the similarity in the workman-
ship of these articles and those of Guinea, but he then dismisses a
connection. More civilized than those on Hispaniola, these people
have attractive houses and are willing to please and extend hospitality. Evidence of gold in the region appears in the people's wearing of
objects that look like golden eyes around their necks. There is also
evidence of pearls.

A theme that runs through the rest of the narrative is the haste to
return to Hispaniola because the provisions for which Columbus
paid dearly were spoiling. Columbus gives several reasons for has-
tening back to Hispaniola, some of which seem legitimate, but one
wonders if some are excuses for not continuing to explore this new
continent he claims is so near. Among the legitimate reasons,
Columbus has not heard from Hispaniola in some time, supplies
were badly needed there, and those he was carrying were quickly
spoiling. He also claims he has almost lost his eyesight from continual watches in the night. Among Columbus's more questionable reasons for not staying in the area to make more discoveries is that his
men had not come prepared to make discoveries (he did not tell
them before leaving Castile of his intention because he feared they
would create obstacles and ask for more pay). The vessels, he
argues, were too big for discovery. These reasons are suspicious

because at the beginning of the abstract Columbus indicates that the purpose of his voyage is discovery.

Columbus frequently reminds the sovereigns of what he has accomplished for them, asking them not to pay attention to those who speak against the undertaking. He balances what the sovereigns have spent against what they will reap, expressing fears that the enterprise might be abandoned. They should not abandon the undertaking, he argues, but proceed and give Columbus aid. Contrasting what the Portuguese spent on behalf of their possessions in Guinea, he stresses the opportunity for Ferdinand and Isabella to be the first Spanish rulers to gain land outside of Spain. Columbus speaks of the regions he has discovered as "another world," and concludes from the abundance of sweet water in the gulf coming from the great river Orinoco and from his reading of the biblical Esdras, book 4, chapter 6, that he is near a continent previously unknown.

Toward the end of the abstract, Columbus stresses his spiritual bent. His renunciation of material for spiritual gain could be his way of exhorting the monarchs not to put too much emphasis on getting gold and spices from the enterprise but to be happy with contributing to the service of God. He has not endured the sufferings of this voyage to enrich himself, for he knows that everything in this world is vain except what is done for God. With the implication that the sovereigns are wavering in their support, Columbus reminds them that he has demonstrated the existence of gold in these lands. He mentions both the new continent and the earthly paradise at the end of the abstract when summarizing his case with the sovereigns for their continued support.

The letter to the sovereigns of 18 October 1498 was written not long after Columbus arrived on Santo Domingo, 31 August 1498, but it was sent along with a painting in October.[22] The letter stands in relation to the abstract of the third voyage as the letter to Santángel does to the diary of the first voyage. It is much longer than the letter on the first voyage, but it too has a propagandistic objective.

Columbus's tone is not depressed, despite the opposition he knows exists at Court. As he has been doing all along, he views the enterprise of the Indies as divinely inspired and himself as having a divine mission, believing the enterprise to have been foretold by the prophet Isaiah. Insisting that something of value will come of his journeys, he argues that his critics put their trust only in material gain (which he renounced toward the end of the abstract of the third voyage to defuse criticism of the lack of material returns from the undertaking). Concerning opposition to the initial project, Columbus recalls that he was supported by two friars and the monarchs. Placing origins of his defamation during the second voyage, Columbus acknowledges the main complaint that he did not send quantities of gold immediately, having been hindered by the brevity of time and other obstacles. He cites as proof of his success, nonetheless, the many peoples to be saved, the service of these peoples as subjects of the Spanish crown, plus evidence of the existence of gold, copper, and many spices. Columbus appeals indirectly to the pride and ambition of Ferdinand and Isabella, alleging that his disparagers could not be swayed by the achievements of great princes in the past and referring to the competition of the Portuguese, who colonized Guinea. He reiterates that he has discovered another world, different from that of the Greeks and Romans.

Columbus makes several points about the New World in the third letter. One hundred leagues west of the Azores he observed a considerable change in the sky, the stars, and the temperature. It seemed as if a hill were there and he was ascending. Columbus revises the opinion of authorities that the world is spherical, emphasizing that their theory was the result of speculation on their own hemisphere, while he had first-hand knowledge of the Western Hemisphere. Holy Scripture testifies that there is an earthly paradise containing the tree of life and a fountain. Columbus believes that beneath the equinoctial line, at the summit of the earth, which is shaped like the stalk of a pear, is the location of the earthly paradise, but no one can go there if God does not will it. Columbus also disputes accepted belief about the earthly paradise; he does not believe it is a rugged mountain. To support his opinion that the earth is mainly land, not water, Columbus cites authorities such as Pliny, Petrus Comestor, Nicholas of Lyra, Aristotle, Averroes, and Pierre d'Ailly. The contrary position was held by Ptolemy and his disciples. From Columbus's own experience he knows that the climate is increasingly mild, the trees are green as in Valencia in April, and the people, of lighter color, with long smooth hair, are more intelligent and are not cowardly.

Toward the end of the letter, to strengthen his case with the monarchs, Columbus again reports on the process of evangelization among the natives, which he joins to political allegiance, so that by making them Christians he also makes them subjects of their majesties. He ends the letter by praying for the forgiveness of his calumniators.

Columbus's Letter to Doña Juana Torres

Columbus wrote his letter to Doña Juana Torres, dated 1500, while being returned to Spain as a prisoner, or possibly upon landing.[23] He wrote to Doña Juana because she was the queen's confidante. Doña Juana had been the governess of Isabella's son, the Infante Don Juan, now dead, and Columbus had met her at Court where his two sons had served as pages to Don Juan. The letter attempts to justify what Columbus has done on the third voyage and to plead for Doña Juana's mediation with the Catholic monarchs, especially with the queen, to stop slanders by his opponents, to remind the sovereigns of their promises to him, and, if they feel he still needs to be judged, to send two honorable persons to the Indies to see that they can obtain gold in a matter of hours.

This letter, written by a man in chains, so to speak, differs markedly in tone from the more triumphant letter to the sovereigns on the third voyage. Columbus, using the medieval motif of the world versus God, represents the world as having mistreated him and employs biblical imagery of the depths to convey his experience. The world oppresses him, but God, who has saved him recently from great distress, will do the same again. In that recent experience Columbus heard a voice saying "O man of little faith, arise, for it is I; fear not" (Morison, *Journals*, 290-91). Columbus then summarizes the background of his voyages. Reading between the lines, it seems that Columbus was criticized for not coming up with sufficient gold to justify his mission. To make matters worse, rumor circulates that Columbus's patron Queen Isabella is dead.

Frequent references to spiritual matters may constitute Columbus's appeal to the spiritually inclined Queen Isabella, then grieving over the loss of her son, the Infante Don Juan. Columbus equates the new world he has discovered with the New Heaven and the New Earth described in the biblical books of Isaiah and the Apocalypse and claims that God made him the messenger of these new lands. Attributing the undertaking solely to the initiative and support of

Queen Isabella, and not mentioning King Ferdinand until much later, Columbus portrays the queen as chosen by God, who gave her the spirit of understanding and great courage. God made Isabella the heiress of all as his well-beloved daughter (an idea that reflects the biblical relationship between God the Father and Christ His Son). Columbus equates himself with St. Peter and the Apostles who, inspired by the Holy Spirit, struggled in the world but finally triumphed. When Columbus's alleged misdeeds are investigated by Bobadilla, sent by the monarchs, Columbus takes courage from his belief that God, who delivered Daniel and the three youths from the lions' den, will likewise deliver him from this oppression. Now Columbus is reviled and would gladly renounce the whole enterprise were it not for his dedication to the queen. Columbus declares he undertook the mission partly to assuage the queen's grief at the death of her son.

Criticized for not delivering enough gold, Columbus hoped on the third voyage to bring back pearls and gold. But he ran into problems: half the population of Hispaniola was in rebellion against him, and he was harassed by Alonso de Hojeda. Columbus is resigned to the monarchs' decision to send Bobadilla, but he criticizes Bobadilla for issuing the colonists a large number of permits to seek gold. The permits are not in the best interest of the monarchs because the settlers want to grab what they can and leave Hispaniola. Columbus, through Doña Juana, begs redress of what he considers wrongs done to him by calumniators and especially by Bobadilla, reminding the monarchs of their promises to him at the outset of all his voyages.

Columbus speculates he may have given the impression that he was fleeing, and so Bobadilla arrested him and his brothers. Columbus says he does not understand why he was imprisoned. Attributing greed for gold to Bobadilla, Columbus criticizes the way he has been judged: he should be judged not as the governor of a long-established territory, such as Sicily, but as a captain who must contend with the entirely different situation of the conquest. As a captain, he ought to be judged by men of arms, not by men of letters.

Columbus's discovery of an extensive gold mine is a miraculous event announced by a prophetic message. He heard, he claims, a message from Christ on Christmas Day when he was suffering from the attacks of Christians and Indians. About to abandon everything, he received the divine message to be of good cheer: all shall be provided for him and he will receive relief. That very day, he learned there were mines over 80 leagues of land; later it was clarified that there was one massive mine.

Columbus finally admits to having committed errors, arguing that he did not commit them maliciously but through ignorance and necessity. He expects the monarchs to be more charitable toward someone who has rendered them so much service. He hopes they will not want to judge him, but he hedges his bets by requesting that they order an inquiry into his affairs by two honorable persons at Columbus's expense; he is confident they will find a considerable amount of gold in four hours. One of Columbus's greatest complaints against Bobadilla is for his seizing of Columbus's records, thus giving Columbus no way to clear himself. The final words of the letter affirm his belief in God's power to punish ingratitude and injuries.

The Fourth and Final Voyage

Columbus, in chains, arrived in Spain in October 1500. While the crown was considering his case, minor voyages of exploration were undertaken. In 1501 the monarchs named Nicolás de Ovando governor of the Indies. Columbus, finally freed, prepared for his fourth voyage and left Spain in May 1502. Arias Pérez, who made the fourth voyage with Columbus, said that Columbus "always called this, his Fourth and last expedition, *el alto viaje*."[24]

This "high voyage" was the most dangerous of the four voyages, and Columbus returned to Spain a defeated man. He poured out his sentiments in the *Lettera Rarissima* to the sovereign, 7 July 1503. Internal evidence, according to Morison, shows that Columbus wrote the opening sentences on Dominica, but really began writing the letter in Belén and finished it shortly after his arrival in Jamaica (371). Columbus entrusted the completed epistle to Diego Méndez for delivery to Spain. It was written in Spanish, but the Spanish text has since been lost. The earliest source is an Italian translation published by Simone de Lovere at Venice in May 1505, known as the *Lettera Rarissima*, the name under which it was reprinted by a librarian of the Biblioteca Marciana in Venice in 1810.[25]

When Columbus arrived off Hispaniola, he was told in the name of the sovereigns that he was prohibited from going ashore. The people with Columbus, including his son Ferdinand and his brother Diego, became discouraged. Many horrendous storms follow, becoming progressively worse, so that Columbus likens them to the biblical deluge. Columbus attributes to his brother Diego the salvation of one of the ships. His people were exhausted and depressed from the storms and prepared themselves for death at any moment. Columbus was especially concerned for the sufferings of his son, but the youth proved to be courageous and picked up the spirits of his fellow crewmen.

Columbus complains of ingratitude when he reviews his life of service amidst great hardships; now he has no roof over his head, no money to pay his bills; his son Diego, left behind in Spain, has been dispossessed of honor and his father's estate. Columbus's only hope is in the king and queen whom he calls just and grateful several times in the letter, so it becomes a motif, part of the plea for justice and gratitude.

Columbus reports gold in the province of Veragua, but it is all hearsay. He decides not to return to the mines, which he considers already won, and thereby creates in the sovereigns the expectation of gold, the certitude that it is there. Unfortunately, no one can say where Veragua is or how they got there because the weather and the currents drove them. More indications of gold exist, but the Indians give incorrect directions at the order of their leader, Quibián, who wants to deceive the Spaniards and keep gold. Columbus's brother Diego and others do go in search of gold and bring back a great quantity, says Columbus.

When Columbus tries to leave the island, the condition of his ships and the weather prevent his departure. Suffering from a high fever and exhaustion, Columbus feels hopeless. He cries out to the monarchs' captains and they do not answer. Only God answers his cry cast to the winds by means of a voice, not the voice of God, but of His messenger. Columbus is asleep, as if he were in a swoon in keeping with the mystical nature of the event, when he hears the voice.

The voice chides Columbus for his doubts, recounting what God has done for Columbus and implying that He did not do more for Moses and David – again, Columbus equates himself with biblical figures of the chosen. Columbus has been special since his birth, and now in his manhood God made him world famous by his discoveries. The voice, saying that God gave the Indies to Columbus, confirms Columbus's claim. God also gave Columbus the keys to the limits of the Ocean Sea.[26] Citing biblical precedents of Abraham and Sarah, the voice prophesies that Columbus will accomplish more in his old age. As Columbus did in his letter to Doña Juana, the voice blames the world and not God for afflicting Columbus. In a transparent reminder to the sovereigns, the voice says: "The privileges and promises which God bestows, He doth not revoke; nor doth He say, after having received service, that that was not His intention, and that it is to be understood differently. Nor doth He mete out suffering to show His might. Whatever He promises He fulfills with interest; that is His way." The voice states that God has revealed a portion of the rewards Columbus will receive, but the voice does not say exactly what they are. The voice's last words are "'Fear not, but have trust. All these tribulations are written on tablets of marble, and not without cause" (Morison, *Journals*, 378-79).

The people of Cariai and the surrounding region practice sorcery, and they attempt to cast a spell on Columbus with magic powder. Columbus paints a different picture of natives this time: instead of the unity of language he claimed on the first voyage, the multiplicity of languages makes it difficult for Spaniards to get information (a potential justification for not getting the information).

In the letter, Columbus mentions his desire to undertake a new project, the rebuilding of Jerusalem and the conversion of the people of the East. His discussion of gold leads him into declaring this intention. Columbus cites Josephus, who says Solomon obtained his gold in Aurea. Columbus claims that the gold mines of Aurea are part of the mines in Veragua. Now the Spanish monarchs can give orders to collect gold from the same source used by Solomon and David. It is not clear for which mission Columbus is volunteering, for rebuilding Jerusalem or for carrying the Christian gospel to Cathay. He believes that Joachim of Flora has prophesied that a man from Spain will rebuild Jerusalem. Joachim, however, did not mention a Spaniard for this task. At this point, Columbus has reached the depths: he is bankrupt materially and spiritually; he asks whoever has charity, truth, and justice to weep for him. He asks the sovereigns to help him go on a pilgrimage to Rome and other places, if they transfer him from Jamaica.

The Biography by Columbus's Son

A work that merits inclusion in the category of chronicle of the Indies is Ferdinand Columbus's (1488-1539) biography of his father. What makes it unique is that Ferdinand participated in one of the voyages, the fourth, made by his father to the New World, and Ferdinand also drew on his father's writings and letters, some of which have been lost. Ferdinand, the son of Columbus's mistress, Beatriz Enríquez, was of a scholarly bent and a bibliophile amassing more than 15,000 books before his death. According to his will, Ferdinand's books became the property of the Cathedral Chapter of Seville; later they constituted the Biblioteca Colombina. Unfortunately, most of the books were lost or destroyed. Ferdinand wrote the biography toward the end of his life, and it was not published in his lifetime. It was issued in Italian, not in the original Spanish.

The Life of the Admiral Christopher Columbus by His Son Ferdinand consists of a dedication to Baliano de Fornari, the author's foreword, and 108 chapters.[27] The early chapters (1 through 15) are polemical in their consideration of Columbus's origins; the refutation of Giustiniani's false account of Columbus's early occupation; Columbus's education; his activities before he came to Spain; his three principal reasons for believing he could discover the Indies; the refutation of Gonzalo de Oviedo's claim that Spain in an earlier time was in possession of the Indies; Columbus's disillusionment upon not receiving support from the Portuguese king; and his eventual turning to Ferdinand and Isabella. The remaining chapters narrate Columbus's four voyages; the last chapter briefly recounts the last days of Columbus and his death in Valladolid.

The Italian translation is dedicated to Baliano de Fornari, a wealthy physician of Genoa, by Giuseppe Moleto, a Sicilian mathematician and professor at the University of Padua, who helped Giovanni Battista di Marini with the task of publishing the Italian edition. The dedication does not mention that the Italian translation was done by Alfonso de Ulloa. The dedication echoes a notion repeated with some frequency by Ferdinand in the biography, that Columbus is a man chosen by divine providence to reveal hidden knowledge beneficial to humankind.

In his foreword Ferdinand Columbus states it was fitting for him to write the history of his father's life and discovery of the New World and the Indies because he had sailed with his father. When he saw that other historians had been uneven in their treatment of his father's life so that the truth had not been told, he decided to write his own version. He promises to tell the story of his father's life using as sources Columbus's writings and letters and his own observations. Later, Ferdinand confesses that his knowledge of his father's voyages and early days is imperfect because his father died before he could question him about certain matters.

In his attempt to honor the memory of his father, Ferdinand deals with questions of Columbus's parentage and ancestry, because those who were born in great cities and of noble parents are the ones who receive honor. Ferdinand states that some people wanted him to write of the noble origins of his family, descended from a Roman hero, Colonnus, and including among their ancestors two Coloni, who, according to Sabelicus, won a victory over the Venetians. Ferdinand rejects the position that honor derived from birthplace and ancestry is paramount and promulgates a notion of honor based on deeds. His father earned honor by his illustrious deeds. Ferdinand sidesteps the issue of his father's noble birth by introducing the notion of providentialism and portraying him as chosen by Christ to be His apostle to carry His name to distant lands. Columbus is compared with Christ, who was content to come from obscure parents. Columbus himself chose to leave in obscurity his birthplace and family. The truly important issue is that Columbus had the qualities his great task required. Columbus's parents, says Ferdinand, were persons of worth but reduced to poverty by wars in Lombardy.

Having sidestepped the issue of his father's origins, Ferdinand compensates by explaining the etymology of Columbus's name, allegedly changed from Colombo to Colón to conform to the country he came to live in and to relate it to Colonnus. The latter intention demonstrates that Columbus was still concerned with positing a noble ancestry for himself. The etymological interpretation of the mystery of Columbus's name is part of Ferdinand's providential reading of his father's life. The name foretold the role he was to play.

The surname Columbus means "dove" because Columbus brought the grace of the Holy Spirit to the New World. The combination Christopher and Colón, the Spanish version of Colonnus, which, says Ferdinand, means "member" in Greek, represents Columbus as a member of Christ. Christophorus Colonnus, like St. Christopher, "crossed over with his company that the Indian nations might become dwellers in the triumphant Church of Heaven" (*Life of Columbus by His Son*, 4). Ultimately, Ferdinand argues that one should not inquire about Columbus's ancestry or parentage, since he is the source of his own glory, a concept prevalent in Spanish Golden Age authors, like Cervantes. Despite insisting on ignoring his father's ancestry and emphasizing his father as source of his own glory, Ferdinand himself claims glory from his father's deeds.

A point that, according to Ferdinand, undermines his father's honor is the claim by the historian and Bishop of Nebbio in Corsica, Agostino Giustiniani, that Columbus, before he became an admiral, practiced manual skills. Giustiniani made his claim in his *Polyglot Psalter* (1516). Ferdinand takes pains to disprove the charge because, he says, manual labor did not correspond to the greatness of his deeds. Ferdinand refutes Giustiniani's claim by citing the bishop himself who, says Ferdinand, contradicts himself in a statement in the *Psalter* outlining the early days of Columbus's career but making no mention that he practiced manual arts. To further discount Giustiniani's artisan claim, Ferdinand says his father studied at the University of Pavia, but there is no evidence for it, and lists the sciences Columbus learned through reading – geography, astronomy, geometry, and map making. As further refutation of the claim of manual labor, Ferdinand in chapter 4 cites examples of Columbus's navigational experience in many lands before becoming an admiral.

For Ferdinand, Giustiniani is a "false historian and an inconsiderate, prejudicial, and malicious compatriot" (*Life of Columbus by His Son*, 6). Ferdinand further maintains that Giustiniani told more than 12 falsehoods about Columbus's navigation and discovery. Ferdinand briefly refutes these falsehoods, such as that Columbus did not learn geography from his brother in Lisbon but taught his brother, that Ferdinand and Isabella did not immediately accept Columbus's proposals, but he had to wait seven years for that acceptance, that Columbus did not travel with two ships but three, that he did not discover Hispaniola first but Guanahaní (San Salvador).

Ferdinand takes up the three reasons that persuaded Columbus to undertake the discovery of the Indies to show the weak foundation of the project and to satisfy the many persons who wish to know the exact reasons. Columbus based his project on natural reason, the authority of writers, and the testimony of sailors.

To defend his father, who was censured for naming the lands he discovered the Indies, Ferdinand offers two explanations: the lands were the eastern part of India beyond the Ganges, and he hoped the name India, with its associations of wealth, would attract the interest of the Catholic sovereigns who had doubts about the enterprise.

Ferdinand also argued against claims made by Gonzalo Fernández de Oviedo that prejudice Columbus's honor and glory. Oviedo maintained that there was an earlier discoverer of the sea route to the Indies and that Spain had earlier possessed the Indies. Chapter 10 is devoted to demonstrating the falsehood of Fernández de Oviedo's claim, which was presented in book 2, chapter 3, of his *Historia general y natural de las Indias* (General and Natural History of the Indies) of 1535. Ferdinand says that Oviedo did not know Latin, that he used a translation that altered the Latin text of Aristotle; Ferdinand believes that Aristotle was referring to the Azores.

Ferdinand's life of his father has always attracted interest because the author went on the fourth voyage. In one of his documents on the voyage Columbus praised the bravery of his young son, then 13 years old, which inspired the others on the voyage and consoled his father. In Ferdinand's account of the voyage, he does not mention himself as a hero or in any special way. Ferdinand places himself in the "we" of the crew; he is an observer and, like the other men, suffers the brunt of storms and the deprivation of food. Ferdinand uses the third-person narrative when writing about his father. Ferdinand himself recedes into the background of the group, the "we" and "us"; occasionally, the "I" emerges to comment or explain a point. Ferdinand's position is in keeping with his concept of historiography as practiced in the Renaissance, where the center of the narration is the hero.

Isabella had died in 1504 to the great grief of Columbus; she had aided and favored him while Ferdinand was unsympathetic to his projects. Now King Ferdinand wanted to rescind all Columbus's rights and privileges, but was deterred, says Ferdinand, by his sense of shame, which governs noble souls. Even if Ulloa or someone else added the end section on the epitaph to Columbus's tomb in Seville, the epitaph, "To Castille and Leon / Columbus gave a New World," and last paragraph correspond to the thesis of Ferdinand Columbus's *The Life of the Admiral*, that Columbus rightly deserves honor and glory for being the discoverer of the West Indies.

The Accounts of Vespucci

The Italian merchant and navigator Amerigo Vespucci, a contemporary of Columbus, was born in 1454 in Florence and died in 1512 in Seville. He was a man of commerce and an explorer whose writings report his participation in early voyages to the New World. His name has been handed down to posterity – America – for the newly discovered lands in the Western Hemisphere. Unlike Columbus, Vespucci was from a documented noble and cultured family with ties to the Medici. Also unlike the self-taught Admiral of the Ocean Seas, Vespucci had received a formal humanistic education from his uncle, the Dominican friar Giorgio Antonio. That humanistic education most likely accounts for Vespucci's intellectual curiosity, his willingness to question the established authority of the philosophers and to contradict them when he had the evidence. Vespucci's empirical approach is more pronounced than that of Columbus, who reached many of his theories from his reading of scripture.

In 1484, Vespucci entered the service of Lorenzo Pier Francesco de Medici, to whom he addressed several of his letters. His work for Lorenzo brought him to Seville for the first time in 1489; the Medici's agent there, Berardi, was involved in outfitting fleets. At Berardi's death, Vespucci managed the agency. Vespucci met Columbus during preparations for Columbus's third voyage. Vespucci himself turned to voyages of discovery for a period between 1497 and 1504. In 1508, Vespucci's navigational skills and experience were recognized when he was appointed chief navigator for the Casa de Contratación (House of Trade) in Seville, a position of great responsibility that entailed examinations for marine licenses and the preparation of official maps of the newly discovered lands.

The letter of 18 July 1500 from Seville to Lorenzo Pier Francesco de Medici recounts Vespucci's explorations in service to the Catholic monarchs.[28] The discourse employed is, as he states, an account by letter. To round out the written account of his voyage he, like

Columbus, has also made plans and descriptions of the world that he will send to Pier Francesco. Vespucci says the letter of 1502 may be considered a schedule or *capita rerum* of the things he observed. Discovery and observation are paramount to Vespucci, for whom these explorations were genuine voyages of discovery, unlike those made two years earlier by a fleet sent out by the king of Portugal to make discoveries by way of Guinea. Vespucci says the Portuguese went to lands already discovered and by a route described in cosmographical authors. Vespucci stresses that his third voyage was made solely for the purpose of discovery, not to look for profit. Although they found nothing of value while exploring, he is unwilling to concede the absence of wealth. Vespucci admits he is a doubting Thomas – his own words – when natives tell him of gold and other metals to be found in the region. Vespucci has to see it before he will believe.

In his voyages and letters, Vespucci's motivation is to achieve fame. In the letter of 4 June 1501 he prays that it may not be pride, since he dedicates each task to God's service, yet there is not the insistence on spiritual concerns evident in Columbus's writings. In another letter, of 18 July 1500, Vespucci seeks recognition for having designated the polar star of the meridian. However, he was not able to achieve his goal, blaming bad nights and faulty instruments. A letter on Vespucci's third voyage gathers together the most notable occurrences of this expedition. Vespucci hoped to expand that work in leisure time and to achieve by it fame after death. The case of the polar star illustrates Vespucci's humanist-inspired attitude toward authorities and experience. The polar star, he believed, was described by Dante in Purgatory, Canto 1. Vespucci was guided partly by authorities, but what he learned through experience overrode accepted authority. In this letter, Vespucci disproves the theory of most philosophers, who held that the Torrid Zone was uninhabitable because of the great heat there. Vespucci found reality to be very different. For him, practical experience was of more value than theory.

Vespucci's letter of 18 July concerns navigation in the South and West, his observations of the country discovered, along with its inhabitants and animals. Empirical observation is evident as Vespucci described the purpose of his mission to a group of natives that he and his crew were men of peace out to see the world. Vespucci at one point imagined himself in a terrestrial paradise because of the beautiful and sweet-smelling trees. Later in the letter on his third voyage – believed to be written in 1502 – he conjectures he must be near the terrestrial paradise because of the abundance of trees, birds, herbs, and fruits. Vespucci, unlike Columbus, mentions but does not give importance to the terrestrial paradise. Columbus had stressed the generosity of the natives encountered in his earlier voyages. A difference from Columbus's presentation of the natives is that they gave more out of fear than affection. Vespucci believes that the land he found was bounded by the eastern part of Asia. Opportunities for material gain were listed matter-of-factly (unlike in Columbus's writings). Vespucci does not have to make a case for the economic potential of the areas explored. The crew brought back gold, pearls, and precious stones, and sold many slaves when they reached Cádiz, although Vespucci offers no explanation or justification for taking and selling slaves.

The letter of 4 June 1501, addressed to Lorenzo Di Pier Francesco de Medici from Cape Verde, was written from the high seas at the beginning of Vespucci's third voyage and presents information on India that Vespucci learned from one Gaspar, a crew member on one of two Portuguese ships returning home. The letter is more a report about the two ships' experience in India than about Vespucci's own third voyage. Gaspar's account of the visit to a kingdom in the interior of India rich in gold, pearls, and gems is reminiscent of the lands Columbus sought. Vespucci's catalog of the Portuguese treasure from India notes the good business and great riches of the king of Portugal. His references to Indian place names, as Vespucci is aware, do not coincide with the names recorded by the writers of antiquity. In a similar situation Columbus would force a relationship between the ancient name and what he heard in the Caribbean, as in the case of Saba, the place of origin of the three wise kings of the Gospels, attributing the discrepancy to the natives' poor pronunciation. Vespucci, by contrast, conjectures that the names have been changed, as with place names in Europe.

The continuation and termination of Vespucci's third voyage is recounted in an undated letter, which Letellier believes was written in 1502 from Lisbon and addressed to Lorenzo. Vespucci's description of the natives encountered on this voyage contains Utopian elements: there is no private property, but they hold everything in common; there are no boundaries of kingdom or province; and they obey no king or lord, since each is his own master. The Indians have no religious belief but live according to the laws of nature. Vespucci, unlike Columbus, does not conclude from these data that it would be easy to convert them to the Christian faith. The idealistic life of the Indians is disturbed, however, by war, whose only cause, so far as Vespucci was able to learn, was to avenge the murder of ancestors.

The report on the third voyage posed some questions that Vespucci attempted to answer in the fragmentary letter (1502?), in a response to several questions raised by Lorenzo and others whom Vespucci calls slanderers and malicious and envious persons. He stands by his statement in the earlier letter that the people in the Torrid Zone were not black, but white, even though this contradicts the philosophers' opinions. Vespucci chides the recipient of his letter for not answering his accusers. In his defense of the letter to which objections were raised, Vespucci explains that it was in the style of a familiar letter. He hopes eventually to write something with the help of a learned person that he can leave behind, which will give him fame.

Vespucci's most famous letter has received the Latin title *Mundus novus* (New World). Probably written between September 1502 and May 1503, it is addressed to Lorenzo Pietro de Medici. In it, Vespucci identifies the new lands as a new world and declares that his last voyage has exposed two beliefs as erroneous: the ancients who said there was no continent to the south beyond the equator, and others who said there was a continent but claimed that it was uninhabitable. The purpose of the journey was to seek new regions toward the south. Vespucci describes the route of the voyage that, he claims, sailed over a fourth of the world. Like Columbus on several occasions, Vespucci and his crew suffered many violent storms and often feared for their lives. To his earlier descriptions of the natives, Vespucci adds that they are more epicureans than stoics, and there are no merchants among them which would seem to give the Europeans an advantage in future commercial enterprises. Again, there is no mention of converting the natives, but Vespucci's men tried to dissuade the natives from their depraved customs. Among the details observed in these lands: the climate is temperate and good; there is no illness caused by corrupt air; there are no fruits similar to the European varieties; there are no metals except gold, which is abundant but not valued by the natives; and the region is rich in pearls. Finally, Vespucci believes that if the terrestrial paradise is to be found anywhere, it surely must be in these lands. The inclusion of descriptions and diagrams of the stellar formations he observed during the journey adds another dimension to the discourse of the letter. In addition, Vespucci claims he has prepared a little book, now in possession of the Portuguese king, in which he has diagrammed the movements of the stars.

The last text attributed to Vespucci provides a summation of the four voyages he claims to have made. The *Lettera di Amerigo Vespucci delle isole nuovamente trovate in quattro suoi viaggi* (Amerigo Vespucci's Letter about the Islands Recently Discovered on His Four Voyages), usually cited as the *Lettera*, is addressed from Lisbon on 4 September 1504 to Pier Soderini, gonfalonier of Florence. The recapitulation of the four voyages is introduced by a prologue and followed by a brief conclusion. Vespucci calls his account a "prolix letter" to Soderini, who is a very busy man with affairs of state. The contents of the long letter, he observes with feigned modesty, are not befitting a man of Soderini's rank, for they are presented in a barbarous style devoid of learning. These defects are counterbalanced by Vespucci's confidence in Soderini's virtues and in the truth of the account that deals with things that the ancients never wrote about. Vespucci says he wrote the letter to Soderini at the insistence of Benvenuto Benvenuti, a fellow Florentine and friend of both men.

Common to all of the foregoing accounts is a certain measure of clearly perceptible self-interest that could bias the reporting. Since that bias is abundantly evident, however, readers may allow for it and discount certain passages accordingly, thereby reducing the skewing of the narration. These diaries and letters are remarkable, not only for their recording of one of the great moments of history but for what they tell us (inadvertently as well as deliberately) about their writers, their cultures, and the spirit of the age.

Chapter Three

Conquest

The writings of the discoverers at the end of the fifteenth century and beginning of the sixteenth record their impressions of the New World. Although Columbus was primarily involved in discovery, he did begin the conquest by claiming land, taking captives and slaves, and making the first settlements. A variety of discourse types were used to record the conquest, with the *carta* (letter) and the *relación* (account of services) predominant. The areas of the conquest were New Spain (Mexico), Guatemala and Yucatan, New Granada (Colombia) and Venezuela, Peru, Chile, and Río de la Plata (Argentina, Uruguay), but the two major focuses of conquest were Mexico and Peru because of the size of their empires, their wealth, populations, and cultures.

The Accounts of Cortés

Chronicles about the conquest of New Spain were written by both participants and nonparticipants.[1] Cortés recorded his participation as leader of the conquest of New Spain in five letters known as *cartas de relación* or letters of information. Cortés was born in 1485 in the town of Medellín in Extremadura, and died in 1547 at Castilleja de la Cuesta near Seville. This controversial figure has been called, as Anthony Pagden notes, "soldier-scholar of the Renaissance, a bandy-legged syphilitic liar and, most improbable of all, a humane idealist aiding an oppressed people against tyranny."[2] His parents were noble but poor. His early biographer, Gómara, says Cortés attended the University of Salamanca but did not finish the program of study, much to his parents' disappointment.[3] Some Latin phrases and legal formulas appear in his letters, as well as citations of popular *romances* or ballads. Pagden credits Cortés with a passing knowledge of Latin and legal literature, which appears in conventional formulas in the opening paragraphs of his letters (Pagden, xlvii). Cortés could have learned Latin phrases and legal formulas while working for notaries in Spain and on Hispaniola.

Cortés was a discoverer and conqueror, not a man of letters. Writing was for him an obligation.[4] Furthermore it was a means to justify his rebellion, usurpation of power, and conquests.[5] His letters received the name *cartas de relación* (letters of information) with Jacob Cromberger's printing of Cortés's second letter in 1522. The contents span the years 1519-26 and cover the territories of Cuba, Mexico, and Guatemala. The letters constitute a hybrid discourse comprising letter, official report (relation), and diary.[6] As a captain of the Spanish crown, Cortés had an obligation to send a *relación* or report to the king, and Cortés refers to his writings as *relaciones* in the text of some of the letters. Cortés's relations differ from the conventional relation in that they are longer, have a narrative structure, and are written in epistolary form (Pagden, xxxix).[7]

The first letter, written sometime in July 1519 from Vera Cruz, the first town founded by Cortés and his men, is lost. The *Carta de la Justicia y Regimiento de la Rica Villa de la Veracruz a la Reina doña Juana y al Emperador Carlos V, su hijo, en 10 de julio de 1519* (English title in Pagden's translation: "The First Letter Sent to the Queen Doña Juana and to the Emperor, Charles V, Her Son, by the Justiciary and Municipal Council of the Muy Rica Villa de la Vera Cruz on the Tenth Day of July, 1519") takes the place of the lost first letter in editions of Cortés's letters.[8] Cortés himself referred to the letter in his second letter; Bernal Díaz del Castillo mentions that Cortés told his men he wrote the letter, but he did not show it to them. Gómara mentions the letter and gives a summary of it. Two other historians, Cervantes de Salazar and Fray José de Sigüenza (who claims he had a copy of it), also attest to its existence.[9] According to Esteve Barba, both the lost letter and the letter from the *cabildo* (town council) tried to justify Cortés's conduct toward Diego Velázquez but the lost letter, in Gómara's summary, emphasized Cortés's problems with Velázquez's relatives and supporters who were in Cortés's band; Cortés did not mention the previous expeditions to the region carried out by Francisco Hernández de Córdoba and Juan de Grijalba for fear those expeditions would undermine Cortés's claim to the discovery (Esteve Barba, 139).

The town council's letter was written to counter the false account of the discovery of Yucatan in letters sent to the crown by Diego Velázquez. J. H. Elliott says you can see Cortés's hand in the town council's letter.[10] The council's report claims to be the true version of events. The letter proposes to render an account of the discovery of the land up to the present, what the land and its people – their way of life, their religion, and customs – are like and the profit to be gained. The general thrust of the opening pages is that the letter writers are those who truly served their royal highnesses. Diego Velázquez, the governor of Cuba, is depicted as motivated by cupidity in sending the first two expeditions led by Hernández de Córdoba and Juan de Grijalba. The writers of the letter claim they paid for almost all the provisions of the fleet and risked their own lives. They went to trade with Indians for gold but met with some hostility. This expedition did not learn anything of the land. Diego Velázquez was vexed that the Grijalba expedition produced little gold.

The town council details the genesis of Cortés's expedition and contrasts Velázquez and Cortés, with Cortés portrayed as better serving the crown and putting up more of his own fortune than Velázquez had done previously. Cortés's expedition is contrasted with the two previous expeditions. Cortés came to evangelize and to make Indians vassals of the Spanish crown. The previous voyages were essentially for barter. Cortés's negative view of Grijalba's report of his expedition aims at exalting his own expedition. Cortés thinks the report is a fiction and that no Spaniards had landed on the coast. His criticism is undercut, however, when a canoe appears later with a Spaniard, Aguilar, who had been living there. Cortés, desiring a true account of these lands, wanted to take the time to explore the Grijalba River and its towns, rumored to be wealthy. Cortés's band did not always get gold items of much value, however. Praise is accorded Cortés's treatment of the Indians so that Spaniards will be well received for future settlements. As a confirmation of the divine favor on this expedition, the writers cite the case of 400 Spaniards who triumph in a battle with more than 40,000 natives.

The men of the band take authority into their own hands and renounce the jurisdiction of Diego Velázquez in a collective action emanating from the troops themselves, who stress their noble lineage and their intention to serve God and the monarchs. They urge

Cortés not to carry out Velázquez's orders. This collective action re-
moves responsibility for disobedience from Cortés. The men fear the
monarchs will not receive the wealth that is rightfully theirs. To
soften the act of insubordination, they urge the establishment of
legitimate structures for a settlement in the form of a town and a
court of justice under the sovereignty of the crown. The authors of
the letter give the impression that they are putting the sovereigns'
rights above all else; they also remind the monarchs to favor them in
the future. They report that they drafted a petition to Cortés that he
cease trading and settle the land to prevent its destruction and ap-
point officials for the town to be founded. Otherwise, they threaten
Cortés, they would "protest against him." Cortés responds that he is
devoted to the sovereigns and has disregarded his own interests in
continuing to barter. He founded the town of Rica Villa de la Vera
Cruz and appointed *alcaldes* (mayors) and *regidores* (city council-
lors). When it was discovered that Cortés no longer had any authority, the newly established town council appointed Cortés in the name
of their majesties as chief justice and *alcalde mayor* to be in effect
until the monarchs should decide otherwise. The town's officials decided to write to the monarchs and send gold, silver, and jewels
above the royal fifth. Following the close of the letter comes an in-
ventory of the gold, jewels, precious stones, articles of featherwork,
and cotton clothing sent with the bearers of the letter to their
majesties.

The authors return to the letter's purpose announced at the beginning, to give an account of the land, its people, and their customs
and wealth. They create the impression that they are more scrupu-
lous regarding the truth than are reporters from earlier expeditions.
They deduce that there must be much gold, silver, and precious
stones in these lands; express horror at the Indians' practice of human sacrifice, in which they take out the living victim's heart and en-
trails; and report having heard that the natives are all sodomites.
Asking their majesties to put an end to such evil practices, they allege
a providential design in the discovery of these lands because the discovery gives the monarchs an opportunity to earn divine reward for
bringing these natives to the true faith. These people are more suited
to conversion than natives they have come upon elsewhere because
their lifestyle is more civilized and reasonable. The monarchs should
beseech the pope to authorize that after the natives have been cate-

chized they may be punished as enemies of the faith if they remain rebellious. The writers beg the monarchs not to award Diego Velázquez grants of *adelantamiento* or governorship in perpetuity; any such concessions already granted should be revoked, and Cortés should be allowed to govern them for as long as the crown sees fit.

Conquest of the Mexican Capital

The second letter was sent to the emperor Charles on 30 October 1520 from the town of Segura de la Frontera, the headquarters where Cortés was preparing the reconquest of the Aztec capital.[11] Following the usual format, Cortés recapitulates the main points reported in a previous letter. Cortés wanted to inform the emperor of events transpiring since the lost first letter. An important purpose of Cortés is to make the monarch as proud of New Spain as he is of the Holy Roman Empire. The thesis of the letter, according to J. H. Elliott, was that Charles was the legal emperor of the new empire and that Cortés would recover it for the emperor (Pagden, xxvii). In his attempt to glorify Charles's new empire, Cortés recounts his impression of the city of Tascalteca: he considers the city almost unbelievable; he compares it with the familiar, to Granada; and he stresses the civilized nature of the people and their government, recalling one of the Italian city states. Cortés describes Tenochtitlán not in the chronological order of when he came upon it but only after the Aztecs' transfer of authority to the Spanish. He describes the location of the city on the salt lake, the many squares with their markets and produce, the numerous temples, and the priests.

Cortés suffers continual problems with his own men and with other Spaniards. Plagued by the disloyalty of Velázquez's men and others in his own band, he arranges the scuttling of the ships. Despite the fear of Cortés's men and their desires to return to Cuba, he encourages them to continue with the expedition. He reasons that they are morally obliged to fight the enemies of the Christian faith and to win glory here and in the next world. More trouble comes from emissaries of Francisco de Garay, who claims he discovered the land and wanted to colonize it. A major problem is posed for Cortés by the arrival of Pánfilo de Narváez with ships sent by Diego Velázquez. Narváez claims he has brought royal decrees making him governor in this area. Cortés learns the ships came on a mission to kill him. Cortés depicts himself as the only one acting to serve the emperor. In a letter to Narváez, Cortés described Narváez's move as a "grave disservice" to His Majesty. The land belonged to His Majesty, it was colonized by his vassals, and legal and municipal institutions were in place. Narváez should be instated by royal decree to assume the titles he was claiming. Narváez is eventually captured.

In his relations with the Mexican Indians Cortés employs the woman Malinche as interpreter and as his concubine.[12] He plays the subjugated Indian vassals against the Aztec emperor Moctezuma, using to his advantage the animosity between the people of Tascalteca and Moctezuma. In his welcoming speech to Cortés, most likely heavily edited by Cortés himself, Moctezuma expresses the belief that the Spanish emperor is the natural lord of the Aztecs foretold by their traditions, namely, that descendants of their founders would return one day to make them their vassals. They would come from the East. He accepts Cortés as supreme representative of the Spanish monarch. Cortés's reply is intended to make Moctezuma believe that the Spanish monarch is the one they were expecting. Moctezuma's speech to his chieftains about submission to the Spaniards repeats that the Spaniards are descendants of the region's founders and asks his chiefs to obey the Spanish king, to render tributes and services previously rendered to him to the king, through Cortés. This was not a joyful submission because Moctezuma wept as he spoke and his men wept as they listened. Even the Spaniards were moved to pity Moctezuma. The chiefs accepted the submission, recorded by a notary public and witnessed by many Spaniards. The problem, however, is, as Cortés indicates at the beginning of the letter, that all the documents containing agreements made with the Indians have been lost.

In a violent attempt at introducing Christianity in these lands, Cortés has the most important idols thrown down the steps of the temples and the temples cleansed of the blood of the victims. Images of the Virgin Mary and the saints are then placed there.

During Cortés's absence dealing with the Narváez threat, the natives in the region of Tenochtitlán rose up against the Spaniards. When Moctezuma tried to address his captains from the fortress roof in order to stop fighting, he was struck in the head by a stone, dying three days later. The "Noche triste" episode follows, in which the Spanish must flee the city under a bloody attack from the Aztecs.

The third letter, addressed to the emperor Charles 15 May 1522, is written from Cuyoacán, where Cortés oversees the pacification and government of New Spain. The main subject is Cortés's reconquest of the Aztec capital Tenochtitlán and its provinces. The reconquest is prepared with the building of 13 bergantines to retake the Aztec capital. Cortés's speech encouraging his men to initiate the retaking of Tenochtitlán is meant to appeal equally to the emperor, because Cortés stresses that the Spaniards serve God and the emperor by this undertaking. Cortés offers several reasons why the men should fight to recapture the capital: to spread the Christian faith, to serve the emperor, and to protect their lives; he also says they will be helped by their Indian allies. Emphasis falls on the victories gradually won by the Spaniards as they progress toward the capital. Cortés, concerned with the suffering of the Aztecs, attempts repeatedly to no avail to get the Aztecs to make peace. The Spaniards' Indian allies demonstrate cruelty toward the Aztecs, going so far as to dine on the flesh of their enemies. Cortés claims he reprimanded them for their savagery. The allies are of great help in the reconquest, but Cortés is unwilling to give them the complete credit they deserve. Cortés is almost captured twice by the Aztecs. A conspiracy is plotted among supporters of Narváez to kill Cortés. In April 1522, they begin the siege of Tenochtitlán. Sixty Spanish soldiers are captured and sacrificed by the Indians, a scene watched with horror from the distance by Alvarado and his men. Cortés initiates a strategy of destroying everything in sight as his troops slowly advance to the capital. The city surrendered on 13 August 1521 with the capture of Cuauhtémoc. The defeated Aztec leader asks to be killed, but Cortés spares him graciously. Cortés, recognizing the achievements of his men in the defeat of Tenochtitlán, commends them to the attention of the emperor. Cortés decides to rebuild Tenochtitlán to guarantee peace and security for the region and to preserve it, as it is a famous and important city.

Cristóbal de Tapia arrives in Vera Cruz, claiming to bring royal decrees. Cortés feigns willingness to comply with the orders, but does not obey, citing as justification that the pacification of the lands was not yet completed and the natives might rebel. The town council likewise offered lip service "accepting" the decrees but not putting them into effect until advised by Cortés. The disobedience is similar to what happened at the time of the founding of Vera Cruz.

With Tenochtitlán captured and pacification under way, Cortés could turn his attention to other matters. Toward the end of the third letter, plans for the discovery and exploration of the Southern Sea are introduced. Cortés had heard reports of the existence of the sea, and he considers it a route to gold, pearls, precious stones, and spices. He sent Spaniards to the coast, and they took possession of the Southern Sea. Now Cortés is having caravels built to explore the sea. Cortés exalts the discovery of the Southern Sea as the greatest achievement and the most beneficial to the emperor since the discovery of the Indies.

The Process of Colonization

Cortés faced a moral dilemma in coming to terms with solving economic problems in the colony. The conquerors and settlers need help to support themselves. A possible solution would be enslaving the natives, but they are very intelligent and show signs that they can conduct themselves as citizens. Consequently, it seemed a serious matter to enslave them. The emperor's expenses have also been considerable. So with the advice of unnamed knowledgeable persons, instead of enslaving the natives Cortés set up the *encomienda* system. He now awaits the emperor's decision on the *encomienda*. A postscript to the letter by three officials, Julián Alderete, Alonso de Grado, and Bernardino Vázquez, endorses Cortés's third letter as their official report to the crown.

The fourth letter was sent to the emperor from Tenochtitlán on 15 October 1524. The letter reports the building of the colony of Medellín and the conquest of the provinces of Guatusco, Tustepeque, and Guasaca. Bishop Juan de Fonseca caused trouble for Cortés. The Bishop is portrayed as hiding the truth from the emperor and as responsible for disturbing the settlers. Cortés tells his people that the Spanish monarch had no knowledge of Fonseca's doings. Cortés asks the monarch to reward the conquistadors. Further threats came from Velázquez, Diego Colón, and Francisco de Garay. Cortés is saved from Garay by the arrival of letters from Vera Cruz with a decree from the king prohibiting Garay from interfering in Cortés's territories. Garay attempts reconciliation with Cortés, proposing the marriage of his son to Cortés's daughter. Garay dies from illness and grief at a rebellion he believes he caused.

Cortés devotes much of the letter to discussing his expenses in the emperor's service, most likely prompted by the arrival of officials sent by the emperor to take charge of the crown's revenues and property and to audit the accounts. After spending all he owned, Cortés used monies from the royal revenues. He wants some of what he paid for expeditions refunded. Cortés attributes not sending more expeditions to discover other parts of New Spain to the disturbances caused by fleets sent by his enemies. The delay in sending expeditions cost the royal treasury a fortune that has not been collected. Cortés promises to restore all that has been lost. The expedition to Las Hibueras (Honduras) is promising but will cost Cortés considerable expense in ships and salaries for the men.

Evangelization is a concern of Cortés now that he is engaged in the work of pacification. Instead of the bishops sought in a previous letter, Cortés now requests members of religious orders to direct the conversion of the Indians. Tithes should be given for building houses and monasteries for the missionaries. Cortés changed his mind about the bishops because their greed would cause the natives to lose respect for the Christian religion. He prefers members of the Franciscan and Dominican orders, who are more observant of chastity and honesty than the secular clergy.

Cortés's interest in the colonization of New Spain involves shipping animals and plants to the colony and issuing ordinances governing the settlement of the land.[13] He complains that the royal officials on Hispaniola have prohibited sending mares and breeding animals to New Spain. The Mexican colony has to buy horses and cattle at excessive prices from those officials. Cortés complains that the islands have benefitted at the expense of New Spain and asks the emperor to send a royal warrant to the islands permitting anyone so disposed to export animals to New Spain. He also asks that the Casa de la Contratación in Seville authorize every ship coming to the territory to bring plants. Cortés does not want Mexico to be exploited, destroyed, and abandoned as happened in the islands. He promotes a permanent settlement and issues ordinances regulating colonization. Cortés ends with his view about ordinances for the new lands. He reserves to himself the right to add ordinances as he sees fit because new circumstances require new considerations and decisions. In the future, if Cortés seems to contradict past rules, the emperor should know that "a new fact elicits a new opinion."

In the fifth letter, addressed to the emperor from Tenochtitlán
on 3 September 1526, Cortés provides an account of his expedition
to Honduras to suppress the rebellion of Cristóbal de Olid, Francisco de las Casas, and Gil González de Avila and to bring the inhabitants of that region into the emperor's service and the Christian faith.
Cortés complains that for too long he had been idle with a wound in
his arm and was determined to undertake new adventures. During
the expedition Cuauhtémoc was executed by hanging because he
had planned a rebellion of the Indians accompanying the Spaniards.

The Spaniards Cortés sought were terrorizing the natives and
seizing their merchandise. Cortés experienced great joy when he
heard the lost Spaniards were nearby. He found them in dire straits,
sick and hungry. The unexpected arrival of a ship (not intended for
Cortés) from the islands solves some of their problems. Cortés buys
the ship with its provisions. Cortés learned that Cristóbal de Olid had
died. Olid had fallen in with Diego Velázquez's servants and urged
the Spaniards to disobey royal authority, Cortés claims, and he
threatened death to Cortés and his band. Cortés pardons Olid's men,
confirming them in the offices awarded earlier.

During Cortés's absence from Tenochtitlán, natives in previously
subjugated provinces rebelled because of mistreatment by the
Spaniards. At Cortés's return to the capital he was welcomed with
rejoicing by Spaniard and Indian alike. Cortés went to the monastery
of San Francisco to thank God and confess his sins. Cortés learns of
the arrival in Vera Cruz of the royal judge, Luis Ponce, to investigate
civil disturbances that had occurred. Cortés claims he was pleased
with the monarch's decision to hold the inquiry, but Luis Ponce died
suddenly from an illness within a few days after his arrival in the
capital.

Cortés uses a strategy that worked well for him in the first stage
of the conquest. The municipal council of this city and the represen-
tatives of the towns ask Cortés again to take charge of the government and administration of justice in the name of the emperor.
Cortés beseeches the emperor to make public both his good and bad
deeds to clear his honor. Rivals and enemies have levelled two
charges against him, the crime of stating that he is not bound to obey
the royal commands, and that of excessive self-enrichment. The ac-
cusation is that Cortés has kept most of the natives as his slaves and
has obtained a great quantity of gold and silver from the Indians. He

admits that he has slaves and some gold and silver but affirms that he is still poor and in debt because of expenses in expanding the emperor's domains in these parts. He asks to serve at Court. Because he was an eyewitness, he will be better able to advise the emperor about policy in New Spain. There his words would carry greater weight than the letters he writes from Mexico. If the emperor does not want him at Court, Cortés asks permission to keep in perpetuity all he now possesses. He mentions the new church he foresees for New Spain – a Franciscan-inspired millenial idea – where God may be better served than in the rest of the world.

Cortés describes the Chichimecas of the northern Pacific coast as a barbarous people who are not as intelligent as the natives encountered elsewhere in New Spain. The Spaniards are to make war on the Chichimecas and reduce them to slavery, if they cannot be converted. It seems like a pretext to use the Chichimecas for economic purposes. Making slaves of the Chichimecas will serve the emperor, and the Spaniards will benefit greatly from the Indians' work in the gold mines; and, as a secondary consideration, some of the Chichimecas may be saved by living among the Christians.

Ships are ready to begin the voyage to discover a route to the Spice Islands. Cortés asks that he be granted all he asked to undertake the enterprise. Cortés is sure that eventually the emperor will recognize his services, but if he does not, Cortés will be content knowing that the world knows of his services and loyalty. This reputation will constitute his children's inheritance.

Other Chroniclers of the Conquest of Mexico

Francisco López de Gómara's *History* comes chronologically between Cortés's *Cartas de relación* and Bernal Díaz's *Historia Verdadera* (True History). Gómara's work is a history, not a series of first-hand accounts, as in Cortés's letters. Francisco López de Gómara was chaplain to Cortés and later to Cortés's son Martín. His work dealing with America is *Historia victrix* (Victorious History), or *Historia general de las Indias* (General History of the Indies), of 1552. Gómara will also be discussed in chapter 5 on the general histories. The second part of his history, dedicated to Martín Cortés, concerns Cortés and the conquest of Mexico.[14] Gómara wrote as if the conquest were solely the work of Cortés. This emphasis provoked the reaction of Bernal Díaz del Castillo. Bernal accused Gómara of getting money from the Cortés family. Las Casas accused Gómara of being Cortés's servant. Bernal Díaz del Castillo criticizes Gómara and other humanist historians such as Illescas and Jovio essentially for using rhetorical style as a substitute for the truth, exaggerating the numbers of Mexican warriors and of the dead, carrying out unequal distribution of merits among the conquistadors, and giving Cortés total credit for the enterprise.

Bernal Díaz del Castillo

The common soldier's account of the conquest of New Spain is set forth by Bernal Díaz del Castillo in his *Historia verdadera de la conquista de la Nueva España* (True History of the Conquest of New Spain). The history differs from Cortés's version because it purports to be a history, not letters of relation, and it is written some time after the events rather than close to them or while they were occurring, as was the case with Cortés's letters. Bernal was both soldier and chronicler, and his work provides a different perspective on the conquest, the perspective not of a leader but of a soldier in the ranks.

Bernal Díaz was born between 1495 and 1496 in the Castillian town of Medina del Campo to Francisco Díaz and María Díez Rejón. The reader learns of Bernal's life and early adventures from his history.[15] Bernal selects the information he wants the reader to know for a certain purpose. He wants his audience to consider him as a man who comes from a tradition of service to the Spanish crown and who wants to gain glory for the monarch and glory and wealth for himself. The presentation of family background is in keeping with Gómara's history, where part 2, chapter 1, is devoted to Cortés's early years. Bernal, however, uses a paragraph while Gómara fills a short chapter. He was born in a family he describes as dedicated to the service of the crown. The family was of modest lineage but of some prestige in the town. Later Bernal assumed noble airs when he added del Castillo to his surname.[16] Like his father, Bernal will end his days in 1584 as *regidor*, or town councillor, in Guatemala. Bernal says nothing about his education, while Gómara reports Cortés's attempt at learning for a few years in Salamanca. Like other Spaniards of his time, Bernal may have read the popular romances of chivalry, which would later influence his vision of New Spain and the form and style of his history.[17]

The commonly held opinion is that the publication of Gómara's book was the cause of Bernal's writing his history. This opinion is now questioned as the sole reason. Bernal also criticizes two other humanist historians, Jovio and Illescas, but they do not receive the brunt of his attack. Bernal claims he was already at work on the book when the works of Gómara, Jovio, and Illescas came to his attention. Essentially, Bernal is trying to defend his own and his fellow conquistadors' rights to reward for their services to the crown during and after the conquest. He also desires glory for himself and for his children, for whom the book is their inheritance. Bernal echoes Cortés's statement at the end of his fifth letter that their father's service is his children's boast of glory. The idea of the glory of one's deeds as his descendants' inheritance might be implicit in Cortés, but not the idea of the book memorializing them.

The subjects of the history are Cortés, Bernal, the conquistadors, and the conquest itself: its benefits to God and crown. The providential nature of the enterprise is evoked. Bernal used several types of discourse to communicate his subject and purpose: the memorial, forensic rhetoric, history, and the *relación*.[18] The purpose of history for Bernal is to perpetuate the deeds of men. Bernal raises himself to the level of Julius Caesar when he asks rhetorically, if Caesar could write about his deeds, why not Bernal? One of Bernal's boasts is that, unlike some historians, he writes about what he learned as an eyewitness. But is everything in his history what he experienced and witnessed? Apparently not, because he was out of action for a while in 1519; and he reports events occurring in places where he was not present. Since Bernal wrote his history (at least, most of it) with many years separating him from the events narrated, the question arises about how trustworthy is his memory. When he recalls past events he says it is as if he sees them as present to him. That is part of Juan Luis Vives's definition of history. Of course, it is also Bernal's claim that he has a vivid memory. Why did he not write about these events earlier? In Bernal's response, there may be a dig at Cortés, who wrote his famous letter while involved in the events.

Bernal's history is structured according to several main divisions: a brief prologue, then chapters grouped around expeditions to or in the area of what became New Spain – two expeditions preliminary to Cortés's, which constitutes the heart of the history; events after the final taking of the Mexica capital Tenochtitlán; expeditions of pacification to Guatemala and Honduras; and, finally, chapters that deal with three issues or concerns – the further and declining affairs of Cortés, treatment of the newly conquered Indians, and Bernal's claims to the rights and privileges of a conquistador.

From another perspective, the history comprises two major divisions: from the beginning to the definitive capture of Tenochtitlán the work is the record (biography) of an individual, Bernal, and of a collective hero, Bernal's fellow conquistadors. The remainder of the history, while still keeping Bernal present, deals with the establishment of the new colonial society.[19]

The prologue is brief. Bernal was aware of how famous chroniclers compose a prologue to their histories; they manipulate language to give luster and credibility to their accounts. Bernal is not a scholar; therefore, he will not write such a prologue. He lacks the eloquence and rhetoric needed to do justice to the history he will narrate, but the plainness of his presentation, his quality as an eyewitness of the events, and his unscrupulous honesty are his strengths. Bernal identifies the collective protagonist of the history – the valiant conquistadors in the company of Cortés – and the subject – the heroic deeds performed during the conquest of New Spain and its provinces. At the time he wrote the introductory note, Bernal says he was 84 years old, blind, and deaf and with no wealth other than his true story to bequeath to his descendants. He stresses that his history is true.

Bernal lists the captains and soldiers who accompanied Cortés from the start of his expedition to New Spain and paints verbal portraits of some of them. He discusses the merits of the true conquistadors and reports on his participation in 1550 at the Court held in Spain at Valladolid, where he defended the perpetual *repartimiento* for the old or original conquistadors. Finally, to ensure that he receives proper recognition, Bernal presents a *memoria* (report) of the battles and skirmishes in which he took part.

Bernal's attitude toward Cortés is mixed. The conquest of Mexico was not the accomplishment of Cortés alone. Bernal does not deny Cortés's accomplishments, but balances them with the participation of the soldiers. Where Gómara repeats "Cortés did," "Cortés conquered," "Cortés decided," Bernal writes "we did" "we conquered." Some passages where Bernal exalts Cortés also serve as an opportunity to praise the soldiers: to say Cortés was obeyed swiftly and with respect is to exalt the soldiers' devotion; the same is true when he says they would give their lives for Cortés. In chapter 212 Bernal expresses his gratitude to Cortés for supporting Bernal's claims to recompense from the Spanish crown. Bernal insists that he and other conquistadors footed the bill.. Various events are presented as the ideas and plans of soldiers, with Cortés going along, as in, for example, the withdrawal from Velázquez's authority.

Minor Chroniclers of the Conquest of Mexico

A different kind of historian who wrote about the conquest of New Spain is the humanist Francisco Cervantes de Salazar.[20] Born around 1518 in Toledo, he studied humanities in Salamanca, and later he traveled to Italy and Flanders as Latin secretary to Cardinal García de Loaysa, president of the Council of the Indies. The connection to Loaysa, as well as his friendship with Hernán Cortés and his son Martín, may account for his interest in the New World. Cervantes de Salazar held the chair of rhetoric at the newly founded university in Mexico, later becoming its rector. Cervantes de Salazar is known for his seven Latin dialogues of 1554, the last three written in Mexico and having Mexican settings and topics.[21] He began writing his history, *La Crónica de la Nueva España* (Chronicle of New Spain) from 1557.[22] In 1560 the city government of Mexico made him city chronicler, but he wanted the king to name him official chronicler. Among his sources for the history were his own observations, information from participants in the conquest, and the accounts of Jerónimo Ruiz de la Mota, Alonso de la Mata, Alonso de Hojeda, and Gómara. He relied heavily on Gómara's history but insisted on correcting Gómara, as did Bernal Díaz. He contradicts Gómara, challenging facts and changing numbers, dates, and names. Unlike Gómara, Cervantes composed his history in Mexico. Cervantes does not condemn the conquest, which he sees as the normal expansion of Spain which, in turn, benefits the conquered.

The *De rebus gestis Ferdinandi Cortesii* (About the Deeds of Hernando Cortés) is a fragment by an anonymous author of a Latin history. The author of the fragment is very favorable to Cortés. There appear to be similarities with Gómara's history, of which Gómara was

finishing a Latin version. Esteve Barba places its composition be-
tween 1548 and 1560 (167).[23] Alonso (or Francisco) de Aguilar,
Andrés de Tapia, Bernardino Vázquez de Tapia, and the Anonymous
Conquistador are minor chroniclers of the conquest of Mexico. Jorge
Gurría Lacroix calls them "soldier chroniclers," including among
them Cortés and Bernal Díaz del Castillo.[24] All were soldiers in the
conquest of Mexico, so their accounts are those of eyewitnesses.
Some of what they relate they learned from other participants.

Alonso de Aguilar (1479-1571) assumed the name Francisco
when he entered the Dominican order.[25] Aguilar underwent a drastic
change in his life's direction at the age of 50, from conquistador and
wealthy innkeeper and holder of a *repartimiento* of Indians to a
Dominican friar. His account is titled *Relación breve de la conquista
de la Nueva España* (Brief Account of the Conquest of New Spain).
Aguilar's short introduction states that he was more than 80 when he
wrote his *Relación* at the request of fellow Dominicans who wanted
his account of the conquest. He wrote as an eyewitness, with brevity,
to the point, and the truth of his version compensates for a lack of
rhetorical flourish. The work is divided into eight *jornadas*, or
stages, in which the conquest unfolded. Gurría alleges that Aguilar's
Relación is a panegyric to Cortés (46). Cortés, however, does not escape criticism. Aguilar defends the rights of the conquistadors to
payment, especially the rights of the least among the conquistadors.
He criticizes Cortés for not allotting towns and land to those who
aided him in the conquest instead of to some who never participated
in it. Toward the end of the eighth *jornada*, Aguilar reports on the
different provinces of New Spain, their inhabitants, agricultural
products, and religion. Aguilar mentions that in some provinces the
number of Indians and towns has declined since the conquest. For
Aguilar, the Indian religion is the most abominable he has ever read
of or seen. Aguilar's concept of history is providentialist: God puts a
hill in a certain spot for the Spaniards to use as a fort. God punished
Cortés and the men were punished when they boasted of their feats
instead of thanking God. Healings were worked through two Italians.

Andrés de Tapia, another conquistador who recorded aspects of
the conquest of Mexico, authored *Relación de algunas cosas de las
que acaecieron al Muy Ilustre Señor Don Hernando Cortés*
(Account of Some Things that Happened to the Very Illustrious Hernando Cortés). The title makes obvious that de Tapia's account, lim-

ited to the deeds of Cortés, differs in focus and spirit from Bernal's.[26] From de Tapia's description of the scuttling of the ships, Cortés emerges as cagey – he said he would leave one ship for those who wanted to return to Cuba, but also scuttled that ship after those men stepped forward. De Tapia's version resembles López de Gómara's in being laudatory of Cortés. At times de Tapia was a severe critic of Cortés in the *residencia*, or legal inquiry, held for Cortés.

Bernardino Vázquez de Tapia's chronicle is *Relación de méritos y servicios del conquistador Bernardino Vázquez de Tapia: vecino y regidor de esta gran ciudad de Tenustitlán, México* (Account of the Merits and Services of the Conquistador Bernardino Vázquez de Tapia: Resident and Regidor of This Great City of Tenustitlán, Mexico).[27] Vázquez de Tapia wrote his *relación* circa 1544 (between 1542 and 1546) to protest changes in the laws regulating *encomiendas* and *repartimientos*. The text's style shows it is more than a list of services. Although it uses legal language, it is written in a straightforward fashion and flows along.[28]

The Anonymous Conquistador's original Spanish text is lost. His chronicle gives special attention to customs of the Mexican Indians, providing more detail on these matters than Bernal.[29] Speculation has attributed the authorship to Francisco de Terrazas, Cortés's majordomo, or Alonso de Ulloa.

Pedro de Alvarado (1486?-1541) authored two extant letters of *relación*, written to fulfill an obligation to Cortés, who sent him to Guatemala as captain general. Alvarado reports to Cortés, while Cortés wrote to the king. Alvarado wrote at least three letters; the first was lost.[30] The subjects covered in the first letter include the conquest of towns, the founding of Santiago de los Caballeros, minerals in the sierras, and Indian customs. In the second letter (28 July 1524) Alvarado complains to Cortés that he has not received the rewards his services merit because Cortés has not reported Alvarado's services to the king. Alvarado asks Cortés to report to the king who he is, what he has conquered, and what are his wounds. Alvarado also speaks on behalf of the men in his company.[31]

Chroniclers of El Dorado and Other Lands

The conquistadors in Nueva Granada (Colombia) and Venezuela were mainly seeking El Dorado, the legendary land of wealth.[32] Gonzalo Jiménez de Quesada, the conquistador of Nueva Granada, is credited with a *relación* about the conquest now lost, but the *relación* is available in Herrera's *Decades*, volumes 5 and 6. Pedro de Heredia wrote letters about Cartagena.[33] An anonymous author penned a *relación* on the discovery and settlement of the province of Santa María. Antonio de Lebrija and Juan de San Martín wrote about Santa Fe.

Peru was a second important center of Spain's discoveries and conquests.[34] Pedrarias Dávila wrote a letter of April 1525 announcing the existence of the land, but without calling it Peru.[35] He wrote to the king that he had sent a fleet under the command of Captain Pizarro to a region in the West of which he had heard news of great wealth. Pedrarias gives credit to Fray Fernando de Luque, Pizarro, and Diego de Almagro for their financial help in making the expedition possible. Pascual de Andagoya is noteworthy for referring to the region as Birú and Perú. Because of his injuries he had to let Luque, Pizarro, and Almagro explore the new region.[36] Hernando Pizarro (1502-78), brother of Francisco Pizarro, wrote a letter dated 23 November 1533 to the Audiencia of Santo Domingo about seizing the gold in the temple of Pachacamac.[37]

An anonymous chronicle was published in Seville in 1534 with the title *La conquista del Perú llamada la Nueva Castilla* (The Conquest of Peru Called New Castile). Porras Barrenechea believes the author was Cristóbal de Mena.[38] Mena expresses his discontent over the division of the ransom taken for Atahualpa, a complaint common to many conquistadors here and in other regions of the New World.

Francisco de Xerez (Jerez) was chosen by Pizarro as his scribe and later as secretary. His chronicle, written at Pizarro's request to record the true account of events, is *Verdadera relación de la conquista del Perú* (True Account of the Conquest of Peru).[39] Pedro Sancho de Hoz, Pizarro's secretary, continued the chronicle at Pizarro's request.[40] Miguel de Estete participated in the conquest in the cavalry and witnessed the meeting with Atahualpa and his imprisonment. He inserted in Jerez's chronicle a report on the journey to seize the treasure in the temple at Pachacamac.

Pedro Pizarro, cousin of Francisco Pizarro, participated in the siege of Cuzco and later in the civil wars. He finished his account (*relación*) in Arequipa, 7 February 1571, dedicating it to Philip II.

His position on other chroniclers recalls Bernal's charge against those who wrote what they had not witnessed. Pedro Pizarro accuses Cieza de León of getting his information from persons who participated in the civil wars. Pizarro does not record the chronology of events. The short title of his account is *Relación del descubrimiento y conquista del Perú* (Account of the Discovery and Conquest of Peru).[41] Diego de Trujillo was an average soldier in the conquest and among the few surviving conquistadors at the time of his writing, April 1571. Like Bernal, Trujillo complained that the new arrivals in Peru were receiving favors, while the real conquistadors were overlooked. The abbreviated title of his chronicle is *Relación del descubrimiento del Reyno del Perú* (Account of the Discovery of the Kingdom of Peru).[42]

Cieza de León

Pedro Cieza de León (1518?-60) was appointed chronicler of the Indies by President La Gasca.[43] Cieza's renown as a chronicler rests with his *Crónica del Perú*, dedicated to Philip II.[44] In the dedication the author outlines the purpose of his writing, expresses the typical false modesty of Renaissance writers, and summarizes the material of the chronicle, which discusses nature, geography, political divisions, anthropology and ethnography, fauna and flora, and the great deeds of the few Spaniards who participated in the enterprise in Peru. Some elements recall the content of other chronicles, for example, the substitute first letter of Cortés, which presented material required by the crown as part of the usual *relación*. To obtain the king's good will, Cieza states that he wrote while enduring hardships. His service to the king in the wars came first. In the prologue, Cieza states as one reason for writing the chronicle that others who see the great services rendered to the crown will be motivated to imitate them. This purpose is in keeping with one of the concepts of humanistic historiography enunciated, for example, by Juan Luis Vives, that history does more than inform, it should lead to action inspiring readers to imitate the heroic deeds of the conquerors of Peru.

Cieza's prologue outlines the division of the *Crónica* into four parts; in the prologue he does not title the first three, but the second part is the "Señorío de los Incas" (The Rule of the Incas), and the third part concerns the discovery and conquest of Peru. Part 4, "Las guerras civiles de Perú" (The Civil Wars in Peru), is divided into five books dealing with the wars in Las Salinas, Arupa, Quito, and elsewhere. Cieza traveled to gather information on the Indians, their cities, customs, and monuments. The first part of the chronicle was published in 1553; the second and third parts were not published for a long time afterward. Like Bernal and other chroniclers, Cieza in the prologue uses the historiographical topos that his work is truthful, a virtue more important than the surface adornment. He offers his chronicle to two kinds of readers: the learned and virtuous, and others who presumably are not. Only the first group – learned and virtuous – should judge it. This certainly is an attempt to protect himself and his work from criticism.

Cieza de León reports the discovery and conquest of Peru in the third part of his chronicle, which consists of 97 chapters.[45] Sanz de Santa María adds five chapters from Antonio de Herrera that make up for Cieza's lost chapters. The preface to the third part sets out the topics to be covered. Cieza praises the tenacity of Marquis Don Francisco Pizarro and mentions the many trials of the 13 Spaniards who discovered Peru along with Pizarro. Pizarro, appointed governor by the king, conquered Peru with the aid of only 160 Spaniards. The Incan emperor Atahualpa was taken prisoner. The Adelantado Don Pedro de Alvarado arrived and Francisco Pizarro made agreements with him. Cieza calls the war waged by the Indians against the Spaniards in Cuzco cruel and relentless. At the end of the third part the Adelantado Don Diego de Almagro returns from Chile and takes Cuzco by force of arms while Captain Hernando Pizarro was serving high justice there.

Cieza sees the killing of the Indians as permitted by divine providence to punish the Indians, and not because the Spaniards merited it. Order and harmony characterize the Inca empire before the Spaniards arrive; the Spaniards disrupted that harmony. The Christians, the Spaniards, are the instruments of evangelization on the one hand but destroyers of the order and harmony of the Inca system on the other (by their sin of greed). Cieza is possibly making a case for the order and organization of the Incan empire as a providential preparation for their conversion to Christianity, analogous to the situation of the Roman Empire at the time of the birth of Christ.

Juan Ruiz de Arce participated in the conquest under Francisco Pizarro. Unlike most chronicles, his work is addressed to his children so they might imitate him and his ancestors; this is in keeping with one of the purposes of humanistic history, to give an example to be imitated.[46]

Alonso Enríquez de Guzmán's chronicle is called by Esteve Barba a novel of his life, in the manner of a picaresque novel (411). The chronicle evolved as he lived. Enríquez intercalated official letters and royal letters of patent in an attempt to give the account credibility. He was in Almagro's camp, but later turned against him. He was sent back to Spain and imprisoned for a time.[47]

Agustín de Zárate's *Historia del descubrimiento y conquista del Perú, con las cosas naturales que señaladamente allí se hallan y los sucesos que ha habido* (History of the Discovery and Conquest of Peru, with the Natural Things Especially Found There and the Events Which Took Place) was published by order of Prince Philip in 1555. It consists of seven books, apparently written while Zárate was in prison in Valladolid between 1546 and 1553. Zárate arrived in Peru to witness the civil conflicts. He wrote about them, but then decided to broaden his research to include the discovery and conquest of Peru because these explained later events. He feared for his life in Peru, so he returned to Spain with documents to use in writing his chronicle. He relied on accounts by Rodrigo Lozano and La Gasca as well as Gómara's history.[48] Zárate calls his discourse a *relación* and a history. He used "memoriales" (reports) and diaries in its elaboration.

The Conquest of Chile and La Plata

Pedro de Valdivia (1497-1553), according to Carmen Pumar Martínez, was neither discoverer nor conqueror of Chile, but the founder of cities and the one who conceived the idea of a greater Chile ("el gran Chile").[49] Diego de Almagro, with 500 men was the discoverer; the conquerors were many, with García Hurtado de Mendoza standing out.[50] Valdivia's letters deal with different aspects of the conquest of Chile. Letters were addressed to the emperor, Hernando Pizarro, Prince Philip, and Gonzalo Pizarro, sometimes repeating information given in earlier letters. At times letters were sent to two people simultaneously with the same information. Valdivia's style blends naturalness and respect for the monarch with familiar language and popular expressions. According to Rodolfo

Oroz, Valdivia uses Roman history for comparisons of events and demonstrates a knowledge of Latin (540).

Alonso de Góngora Marmolejo's text is the *Historia de Chile desde su descubrimiento hasta el año de 1575* (History of Chile from Its Discovery until the Year 1575).[51] Góngora Marmolejo took the idea for his history from Ercilla's poem *La Araucana*. His history, finished in 1575, emphasizes the experience of conquest by Spaniards in Chile, alleging more hardships than elsewhere in the Indies because the natives were more warlike. He claims he is the first one to write about the events in prose. Ercilla wrote some things, but not enough to do justice to all the events in Chile. Góngora observes that he does not expect much credit for the care he put into writing the history; such has been the experience of other authors. While reticent about himself, he occasionally voices a complaint common to other conquistadors: no remuneration for the hardships endured.

Pedro Mariño de Lobera told Jesuit Father Bartolomé de Escobar that he would like his chronicle shortened and put in correct language and style.[52] Escobar's reworking cut down on the naturalness of Mariño's original. Escobar also eliminated passages.

Ulrich Schmidel's chronicle, originally written in German, offers information on the conquest of the Río de la Plata region. For 20 years he participated in events from Río de la Plata and Asunción to the sierras of Peru.[53] His account of these can be read in conjunction with Núñez's *Commentaries*. Ulrich Schmidel, native of Bavaria, was a commercial traveler for the house of Welzer and Niedhart.[54] Schmidel's chronicle spans the years 1535 to 1552. In the Río de la Plata region Schmidel served under Martínez de Irala. Schmidel's work, written 12 years after Núñez's *Commentaries*, contradicts Núñez's version of events. Luis Domínguez believes Schmidel wrote to refute the *Commentaries* while defending Martínez de Irala (xvii). Another German adventurer of the time was Hans Stade, whose field of operation was in Brazil.

The chroniclers of the several conquests were participants, both leaders and common soldiers, and nonparticipants, who were often learned men. The chroniclers employed a variety of discourse types, depending on the individual writer's purpose and audience. Cortés addressed letters to the emperor to fulfill an obligation to report events, to justify his deeds, and to enumerate his future plans for the development of the territory newly acquired for the crown. Bernal Díaz del Castillo, a soldier in the ranks and, later, a land holder, addressed authorities in Spain in an attempt to redress what he considered wrongs committed against him and his fellow true conquerors, who did not get their due for their labor in the conquest. Bernal employed the discourse of history, but broke with the Renaissance mold by incorporating and highlighting the deeds of the common soldiers. López de Gómara was neither a participant nor an immediate observer of the conquest of Mexico, since he never set foot in the New World. His purpose was to write a classical history of events using the discourse of Renaissance historiography. The accounts of Cortés and Bernal Díaz are more vivid and interesting than those of López de Gómara's and Cervantes de Salazar, the latter a professional rhetorician writing from New Spain. Numerous minor chroniclers of the conquest of Mexico reveal different attitudes toward Cortés. Some of these chroniclers wrote for self-advancement, and the majority complained that the conquistadors were not getting their due from greedy leaders. Cieza de León is the most important of the Peruvian chroniclers. Cieza wrote to inspire his readers to heroic action in imitation of the conquerors. Whether chronicle, memoir, biography, apologia, or exemplary, hortatory discourse, these texts retain the flavor of authenticity imparted by eyewitness accounts and the benefits of contemporaneity.

Chapter Four

Exploration

Voyage chronicles focus on the long ocean voyages and explorations of lands and rivers that were an important facet of the conquest in general. These chronicles record the excitement, incredible dangers, and difficulties that befell explorers and conquerors, portraying the expeditions and the conditions of the regions explored. Expeditions are reported and discussed in many kinds of chronicle, but an identifiable body of chronicles concentrates specifically on expeditions. Expeditions were made throughout the new lands: New Spain, Guatemala and Yucatan, New Granada and Venezuela, the Amazon, and Peru. Some of these territories served as bases for expeditions to other areas.

The Yucatan was an early target of exploratory expeditions emanating from Cuba. Francisco Hernández de Córdoba had reached the area first in 1517. The second expedition to the Yucatan was led by Juan de Grijalva in 1518. Bernal Díaz del Castillo claims he participated in the Grijalva expedition. Events of the expedition are chronicled in the work known as the "Itinerario" (Journey).[1] Like several chronicles of expeditions, it was not written by the leader but by someone else, in this case by Juan Díaz, the expedition's chaplain, who briefly records successes and defeats as the group advances through the Yucatan. Grijalva and his men are portrayed in a positive light often as overeager explorers.

Cabeza de Vaca: Exploration in North and South America

With New Spain as a base, some expeditions and discoveries centered on Florida and the southeastern United States. Florida was discovered by Juan Ponce de León in 1513. The first major chronicle about Florida would appear in 1542, written by Alvar Núñez Cabeza de Vaca. This traveler and explorer, first in North America and later in South America in the Río de la Plata region, was born around 1490 in Jerez de la Frontera.[2] Among his famous ancestors, a thirteenth-century forebear facilitated the decisive victory of Christians over the Moors in the battle of Las Navas de Tolosa (1212), and Cabeza de Vaca's maternal grandfather, Pedro de Vera, took part in the conquest of the Canary Islands. Cabeza de Vaca cites his grandfather's accomplishments at the end of the *Naufragios*, when he lists himself among members of the Florida expedition, indicating his pride in that family connection. He refers to a similar idea in the prologue. He was motivated to excel in service to the crown, in part because of his illustrious background. He made his first mark on history as treasurer and "alguacil mayor" (provincial governor) in Pánfilo de Narváez's expedition to Florida.

Cabeza de Vaca left the record of his and his companions' odyssey of suffering and hardships in Florida and the Southwest first in an account drafted shortly after he and his companions returned to New Spain and years later in the text now commonly known as the *Naufragios* (Shipwrecks). The first account Trinidad Barrera reports as *Relación del viaje de Pánfilo de Narváez al Río de las Palmas hasta la punta de la Florida, hecha por el tesorero Cabeza de Vaca (año 1527)* (Account of the Voyage of Pánfilo de Narváez to Río de las Palmas and the Tip of Florida, Written by the Treasurer Cabeza de Vaca [in the year 1527]).[3] The date, however, does not square with the 1536 report that Cyclone Covey calls the *Joint Account*, written by the three survivors Alvar Núñez, Castillo, and Dorantes in Mexico City in 1536 and intended for the Audiencia of Santo Domingo.[4] A fourth survivor, the black slave Estebanico, was not a party to the report. Covey believes that Castillo actually wrote the *Joint Report* (Covey, 16). Gonzalo Fernández de Oviedo incorporated a version of the report in his *Historia general y natural de las Indias* (General and Natural History of the Indies), volume 3, book 35. The first edition, titled *La Relación* (The Account), was published at Zamora in 1542. A second edition with a title change came out in 1555. Since then, the text has been popularly known as the *Naufragios*.

The text is divided into 39 chapters preceded by a prologue addressed to the Emperor Charles V. The prologue indicates what Cabeza de Vaca will narrate in the chronicle, offering a brief summary of the contents: Cabeza de Vaca wandered for 10 years, lost

and naked in many strange lands. He gathered information about
geography, location of lands and provinces, the distances between
them, food supplies, animals, the inhabitants and their customs.
Cabeza de Vaca defines his purpose for writing as service to the emperor. Service to the prince is an imperative for his subjects. The
Naufragios are offered as service in lieu of the actual conquest.
Cabeza de Vaca hopes that the information gathered will be of service to the emperor and helpful to those who go there in the future,
especially missionaries. The failed conquest is thus converted into a
missionary success.[5]

Concerning the discourse type of the *Naufragios*, Trinidad Barrera says the text represents "an account, history and fiction" (19).
Cabeza de Vaca was also conscious of writing history because he
stresses the social utility of the text. He did not intend to write fictional literature, but this did not prevent him from using literary devices to convey his message. He employed elements from the travel
narrative, the Byzantine novel, and the picaresque novel. Cabeza de
Vaca relied on his experience and observation, making his eyewitness testimony a guarantee of the veracity of the narrative. What he
learned by hearsay from the Indians and other Spaniards provided
further information.

The work is organized in episodes according to a linear
chronology. On another plane the text is circular; the prophecy of
the Moorish woman placed at the very end of the text foretold all
that was to happen, and, so, at the end of the account the text has
come full circle. Luisa Pranzetti considers the narrative to be structured according to four macrosequences, "choque, encuentro, inte-
gración y retorno" (shock, encounter, integration, and return).[6]
Trinidad Barrera also perceives a fourfold structure (43). The
rhetorical device of "presagio" (foretelling) is used to create sus-
pense. The Moorish woman's prophecy, funeral boxes, magic
amulets, and the sinister monster, Mala Cosa, portend disaster.

The theme of shipwreck has various meanings, including the notion of all the calamities that beset the survivors. Other themes include turning failure into success, demythifying the conquest and the
conquistador.[7] In demythifying the New World, Cabeza de Vaca presents a threatening geography and a scarcity of food plants. He describes the inhabitants' physical and moral natures, presenting the
Indians as innocent at some times and very cruel at others. Cabeza

de Vaca advocated avoidance of force and use of peaceful means in the conversion of the Indians.

Alvar Núñez Cabeza de Vaca is both protagonist and author of his chronicle. Pranzetti sees the "I" versus the "other" opposition repeated in various combinations in the narrative. Maura reads a Christ figure into Cabeza de Vaca's self-portrait. Cabeza is critical of Pánfilo Narváez, the expedition's original leader, casting him in the role of antagonist, while his companions Dorantes, Castillo Maldonado, and Estebanico, the black slave, receive attention from the author as his accomplices in performing healings for the Indians. The Indians' favorite at first is Castillo; later Dorantes becomes favorite, but ultimately Cabeza de Vaca dominates the scene (Covey, 11-12).

After the Florida expedition, Cabeza de Vaca returned to Spain and was appointed "adelantado" (governor of a frontier province) of Río de la Plata. In 1540 he sailed to South America, where he succeeded Don Pedro de Mendoza as governor of Río de la Plata. Cabeza's term of office in Río de la Plata lasted from 1541 to 1544. Captain Domingo Martínez de Irala, accusing the new governor of crimes, led a mutiny against him. Cabeza de Vaca was sent in chains to Spain where he had to wait eight years for a decision on his case. Eventually he was acquitted, but he did not recover his governorship. His second major chronicle, the *Commentaries*, came out of his South American experience. The *Commentaries* were published along with the *Naufragios* in 1555.[8] Domínguez believes Núñez wrote the *Commentaries* "to justify himself before the world" (xvii).

The king's license to print the *Naufragios* and *Commentaries* together indicates that Cabeza de Vaca wrote the *Naufragios* but that he had the *Commentaries* composed. Pedro Lastra believes that Cabeza de Vaca wrote the *Commentaries'* prologue in the first person and signed his name, but he transferred the act of writing the text to Pero Hernández whose role was limited to scribe and possibly adviser to Alvar Núñez. To justify his failure in Río de la Plata region Cabeza de Vaca could not write effectively using the first person narrative, so he had Pero Hernández write for him (Lastra, 154, 157). According to the license, the *Commentaries* are useful to those going to the Río de la Plata region because they contain information not found in most accounts of the land and customs of the people. The license sees the two works as forming a unit, but it does not explain how they do.

Cabeza de Vaca dedicated the *Commentaries'* prologue to Prince Charles, son of the emperor Charles V. In the prologue, Alvar Núñez states he was sent to Río de la Plata to help people in trouble there and to continue Pedro de Mendoza's discovery. He wrote the chronicle because pleasure is to be gained from reading about events and changes of fortune; it offers testimony to God's benefits to the author. A third reason emerges in chapter 1 and is repeated in the last chapter. He wrote to redress the wrong done to him: he was not paid as promised for what he spent on the adventure. In the first chapter, Cabeza de Vaca relates how he came to South America, to Río de la Plata. He came to aid and relieve Spaniards in trouble there. Prior to the voyage, Charles V made arrangements with him drawn up in a capitulation listing Cabeza de Vaca's expenditures and his recompense in the form of being named governor, "adelantado," and recipient of the twelfth part of all business done in the region. The last chapter is linked to the first chapter. After Núñez's acquittal, he lost the governorship and received no compensation for his expenses in relieving the Spaniards and on his voyage of discovery.

The meaning of the word *commentaries* in the title is, according to Lastra, "memoirs" and a commentary and gloss on a document of services rendered to the crown written by Alvar Núñez in 1545, whose brief title is *Relación General* (General Account) (158). For Lastra, the *Relación General* is the subtext of the *Commentaries*. The "I" of the *Naufragios* becomes "he" in the *Commentaries* (Lastra, 163). Lastra says the change was necessary for Alvar Núñez's credibility. The *Commentaries*, much longer than the *Naufragios*, recount Cabeza de Vaca's voyage to Asunción and his experience in the Río de la Plata region. Cabeza de Vaca details the land expeditions he practiced in the North American adventure. He and his men suffered numerous privations. A fictional-sounding episode in the *Commentaries*, chapter 2, mentions the song of crickets saving his crew from shipwreck on rocks. From Cabeza de Vaca's perspective, he and his followers treated the Indians well while Martínez de Irala and his band mistreated them. The good treatment of the Indians led to difficulties with his men and other colonists. A later chapter of the text depicts the rebels' permitting the Indians to kill and eat humans in exchange for their military help in the rebellion.

On the return voyage to Spain, as reported in the last chapter, Cabeza de Vaca was poisoned with arsenic three times. Fortunately, he had an antidote. A violent four-day storm arose, which was interpreted as punishment for wrongs done to Cabeza de Vaca. The storm subsided when chains were removed from the prisoner. The storm led some officers to acknowledge they had made false statements against Cabeza de Vaca. His enemies were motivated by malice and jealousy when they saw that Cabeza de Vaca discovered a country and route in three days while others there for 12 years had not accomplished anything comparable. Further "divine" retributions befall Cabeza de Vaca's enemies. García de Vanegas, who had arrested Núñez, died a sudden and terrible death, and his eyes fell out of his head. Alonso Cabrera, an accomplice, went mad and killed his wife. The friars involved in the revolt likewise died suddenly.

Chronicles Based on De Soto's Explorations

De Soto's expedition was next in time. Cabeza de Vaca's account may have served as an inspiration or incentive to further exploration. Hernando de Soto, of noble birth, had already distinguished himself in the conquest of Peru and had returned to Spain with a large fortune. Seeking new challenges, he asked to be named governor of Florida. The Spanish monarch also put de Soto in charge of Cuba. De Soto became governor of Florida in April 1537; he set sail from Sanlúcar de Barrameda in 1538 and landed at Tampa Bay in May 1539. De Soto was looking for the fountain of youth.[9] Highlights of De Soto's expedition include the battle of Mobile between de Soto's forces and those of the Indian chief Tascaluza, his crossing the Mississippi on 15 June 1541, and his travel through northwest Arkansas. De Soto died 21 May 1542. The survivors of de Soto's expedition landed in Pánuco on 10 September 1543.

The Hidalgo de Elvas (Gentleman of Elvas) wrote a *relación* about the de Soto expedition composed in Portuguese and published at Evora, Portugal, in 1557 with the title *Relaçam verdadeira dos trabalhos que ho governador dom Fernando de Souto e certos fidalgos portugueses pasarom no descobrimiento da provincia da Frolida* (True Relation of the Vicissitudes that Attended the Governor Don Hernando de Soto and Some Nobles of Portugal in the Discovery of the Province of Florida).[10] Theodore H. Lewis suggests that one unnamed "hidalgo" is Alvaro Fernández (130). The author, who participated in the de Soto expedition, had to rely on his memory to write the report after the events occurred. The relation records the discovery and navigation of the Mississippi River, de Soto's death, the building of boats, the first voyage down the river, and the arrival in Mexico of the expedition's survivors. Noteworthy is the emphasis on the sufferings rather than the triumphs of de Soto. The author also gives attention to Portuguese participation in the exploration of Florida. The third-person narrative focuses on de Soto and his companions, not on the "hidalgo" himself. The poet Fernando da Silveira, in an epigram at the beginning of the text, offers an early reader's opinion of the small book's value. It is a pleasing story, despite the absence of fabulous material, contains useful information on new lands and peoples, and is a record of achievements and wars that both delight and cause fear. A modern reader, however, questions whether there is not some fabulous material. For Lewis, the lengthy speeches of the caciques are more fiction than history "manufactured for the occasion" (130). Other fabulous elements include the episode of hundreds of Indians remaining in a lagoon for more than a day and a lake dyed in blood in the battle of Mobile.

Two other chronicles of de Soto's expedition are by Luis Hernández de Biedma and Rodrigo de Rangel. Hernández de Biedma was a participant in the adventure. His chronicle is titled *Relación de la isla de la Florida* (Account of the Island of Florida).[11] Rodrigo Rangel gave his journal to Gonzalo Fernández de Oviedo for use in preparing the section on Florida in his General History.[12] Pedro Menéndez de Avilés wrote a collection of letters as chronicling Spanish activity in Florida. As "adelantado" of Florida, he was charged with combatting incursions of French Protestants in the Florida peninsula. His services and geographic descriptions were detailed in seven letters to the king between August 1565 and January 1566.[13]

The Search for La Cibola

Chronicles were also generated based on expeditions looking for the Seven Cities. The legend of the Seven Cities originated in the Middle Ages. Seven bishops with a large number of faithful fleeing from the Moorish invasion set sail from Lisbon. After many days of sailing, they allegedly reached an island they called Antilia, where they built seven beautiful cities. Later, navigators sailing west either claimed that they came upon the island with its Seven Cities or were on the lookout for it. When the New World was discovered, the location of the Seven Cities was placed somewhere in America.

The Viceroy Mendoza wanted someone to get information on the region of the Seven Cities. He finally persuaded Fray Marcos to lead the fact-finding expedition. He was to report on the region's climate, people, fauna, flora, and metals. Fray Marcos de Niza was attracted by Estebanico's fabulous tales. Estebanico spoke about a region rich in gold and precious stones whose inhabitants lived in Seven Cities made of stone. Germán Vázquez says Estebanico mixed the Spanish legends with Aztec myths and tales from the Arabian nights.[14] Fray Marcos de Niza, a native of Portugal, came to Mexico in 1537 from Peru, where he was superior of the Franciscan order. Fray Marcos started out looking for the Seven Cities of Cibola on 7 March 1539 from San Miguel de Culiacán. He was accompanied by another friar, Fray Honorato, by several Indians, and by Estebanico, who had accompanied Cabeza de Vaca on part of his wanderings.

The Indians received them with respect and friendship. These Indians wore necklaces of shells and pearls. They pointed to the location of rich Indians farther on, but indicated the name of the cities was Cibola, not Antilia as in the legend. Fray Marcos sent Estebanico ahead to explore. The system of communication determined sounds like a fictional element. Estebanico would send a messenger with a cross, the size of which indicated the result of the exploration. In an echo of Cabeza de Vaca's journey, Estebanico pretends he is a famous healer. Wearing luxurious robes, he would bless the Indians, demand gifts, and threaten them with his greyhounds. Fray Marcos reached the outskirts of Cibola, naming it "Nuevo Reino de San Francisco," the New Kingdom of Saint Francis – with its implication of Franciscan millenarism – and took possession of the land in the name of the emperor, Charles. Fray Marcos learned that the people of Cibola, fed up with Estebanico's abusive treatment, had killed him and his companions. Fray Marcos did not proceed further; he observed the city from a distance, terming it a city larger and better than any he had seen, including Mexico City. He may have seen Zuñi pueblos southwest of Santa Fe, New Mexico. Niza returned to Compostela and then went on to Mexico City to make his report.[15]

Fray Marcos's account, in turn, inspired another search for the
Seven Cities of Cibola, this time led by Francisco Vázquez Coronado.
The viceroy of New Spain, Antonio de Mendoza, received the right of
exploration from the emperor. Mendoza sent an expedition headed
by 30-year-old Francisco Vázquez de Coronado. Pedro Castañeda de
Nájera, who wrote about Coronado's expedition, was a soldier in
it.[16] Many years later, he composed his account, *Relación de la jornada de Cibola* (Relation of the Journey to Cibola), a brief report of
what happened, and what he heard and saw during the expedition.[17]
Castañeda's additional purpose for writing his *relación* some 20
years after the event was to correct erroneous geographical notions,
for example, that the area was contiguous with Florida. Castañeda
narrates the discovery of the territory and covers geographical descriptions, ethnography, elements of natural history, and the final
abandonment of the undertaking. Castañeda, aware of the issue of
historical reality versus imaginative elements, asserts he is not writing
fables like those in books of chivalry. The Spaniards' deeds in this
region surpass accounts in the books of chivalry and even those
about the 12 peers of France. The entire episode resulted in disillusionment; the journey was harsh, the so-called fabulous city of
Cibola was not as big as the explorers expected, and they received a
hostile reception from the Zunis. The greatest disappointment was
finding no gold. Fray Marcos, now the Franciscan provincial accompanying Coronado's expedition, became the butt of insults and returned to New Spain. Coronado decided to continue the expedition
so as not to return empty-handed. As in so many relations, the expedition is motivated to advance by rumors of wealthy lands still ahead.

As revealed in Cortés's later letters, the two goals of Spanish expansion were the search for the northwest passage and the discovery
of new lands in the ocean. Among several minor chroniclers, Francisco de Alarcón wrote a *relación* concerning his sea expedition
along the California coast. Preciado was the chronicler of Francisco
de Ulloa's expedition. Juan Rodríguez Cabrillo continued exploring
the coasts of California to find a strait to the north. His expedition is
recorded in a chronicle by an unknown author, perhaps Paéz.[18] Another chronicle exists for a different kind of expedition in Guatemala
and Yucatan. Fray Alonso Ponce was a traveling missionary whose
chronicle in the form of a journal is the result of travels he was required to make as commissary general of the Franciscans to visit

monasteries. He kept a daily record over a four-year period in which he noted the geographic and ethnographic aspects of the area.[19]

Chronicles of Exploration of the Amazon River Region

Vicente Yáñez Pinzón, captain of the Niña on Columbus's voyage, discovered the outlet of the Amazon. Fray Gaspar de Carvajal is a realistic observer and narrator of the events in which he participated, but at times his *The Discovery of the Amazon* is distorted by the legends, myths, and fables that circulated among the conquistadors. Toribio de Ortiguera, a native of Asturias and later a resident of Quito, wrote a chronicle entitled *Jornada del río Marañón* (Journey to the Marañon River) about the expedition of Pedro de Ursúa.[20] He was not an eyewitness to events.

An expedition was organized in 1559 by Viceroy Marqués de Cañete under the command of Pedro de Ursúa to look for El Dorado and the land of Omagua. One of the members of the expedition, Lope de Aguirre, rebelled and killed the governor Ursúa on New Year's Eve of 1561. He became the leader of a group of rebels called the "marañones."[21] Pedro de Munguía, a captain in Lope de Aguirre's guard, deserted Aguirre's band, and wrote a *relación* detailing Aguirre's atrocities. Francisco Vázquez and Pedrarias de Almesto supply information on Aguirre's behavior. Vázquez's *relación* gives considerable information about Aguirre's life in Peru. Pedrarias de Almesto copied Vázquez's manuscript and added to it, highlighting his own contributions to the expedition. Pedrarias's *relación* is favorable to Ursúa, stating he tried to guard Ursúa.[22] The poet Diego de Aguilar y Córdoba wrote a chronicle titled *El Marañón*, narrating the civil wars in Peru and Pedro de Ursúa's journey to Marañón. Aguilar began to write in 1578 and retouched his work in 1593, sending the completed account to his uncle Andrés Fernández de Córdoba in Italy. The account follows Vázquez's *relación*. An interesting adjunct to Aguilar's chronicle is the account he gives of several poets who wrote in the colonial period.

Voyage chronicles, written primarily by members and not leaders of expeditions, break with previous types of chronicles by portraying failure along with success. Alvar Núñez Cabeza de Vaca's chronicle is the most noteworthy and interesting of this group. For him, history has a social utility offering information helpful for the ruler back in Spain and for missionaries who will labor in the region. Cabeza de Vaca figuratively changes failure into success through his mixed discourse employing report, history, and fiction. He uses literary devices effectively to convey his message, while the episodical nature of voyage discourse maintains the reader's interest. The *Naufragios* marks a noticeable change from other types of chronicles in reporting geography, nature, and people as sinister phenomena. An engrossing aspect of the narrative is the Europeans' encounter with the new and the "other" in the region. The participants pass from initial shock through adaptation to integration in the new culture before returning to their own culture. The discourse of Cabeza de Vaca's second chronicle, The *Commentaries*, is noteworthy as a lengthy gloss of a document of service. The *Commentaries*, like the *Naufragios*, also stress useful information, while drawing attention to the text as a source of aesthetic pleasure. Like Bernal Díaz and other conquistador-chroniclers, Cabeza de Vaca also wants to be properly paid for his services. His *Naufragios* inspired expeditions to the American Southwest in search of the mythical Seven Cities, such as De Soto's expedition, which spawned several minor chronicles, among them the Gentleman of Elvas's engaging narrative. Whether travel narrative, memoir, fiction, or a blend of several types of discourse, these writings, too, are remarkable for their record of the human response to one of history's greatest adventures.

Chapter Five

General Chronicles

General chronicles include natural history, ethnography, and on occasion historical events. Some general chroniclers made direct observations of the New World. Others wrote in Spain, using reports sent to them or to government agencies. Some chroniclers' direct observation of American nature forced them to reexamine the writings of the ancients and to challenge medieval and renaissance scientific ideas. One type of general chronicle is the official chronicle. The official chronicle is typically general in scope. Official chroniclers were appointed by the Spanish crown to develop an encyclopedic chronicle of the Indies.

An Epistolary Chronicler: Pedro Mártir

The earliest general chronicle on the Indies was an ongoing project of Pedro Mártir de Anglería (1455-1526), a native of Anghiera in Italy. His chronicle was somewhat official in that ecclesiastical figures and statesmen requested information on the New World from Pedro Mártir, who wrote his letters while the events detailed were happening; they are among the first reports of the New World. His connection with Spain began in Rome, where he developed a friendship with the Spanish ambassador to the Holy See. Going to Spain, he became a war correspondent during the Granada campaign. He was a priest, master of nobility, and chaplain to Queen Isabella. Named Spanish ambassador to the sultan of Egypt, he wrote *Legatio Babylonica* (Embassy to Babylon) and became a member of the Council of the Indies, later serving as chronicler.

Pedro Mártir intended to be a historian in order to pass on his name to posterity. He believed glory would accrue to him as a consequence of writing history. He chose the letter as his particular discourse for the chronicle. His collections of letters formed part of the discourse popular at the time. Pedro Mártir's collection of letters in Latin, the *Opus epistolarum*, contains 813 epistles. Although the *Opus epistolarum* is not exclusively a chronicle on America, some of its letters allude to the New World. Anglería's first news of America on Columbus's return from his initial voyage is in letter 130 of 14 May 1493. The collection of letters was published in Amsterdam in 1530, four years after Anglería's death. The general subject matter covered events in Spain and elsewhere.

The *De Orbe Novo*, written in Latin and commonly known as the *Decades*, is really Pedro Mártir's chronicle on America.[1] Pedro Mártir announced that he was beginning such a collection on the discovery in letter 162 of the *Opus epistolarum*, addressed to Count Borromeo. Mártir intended to include all that is worthy of memory. There are eight *Decades*, each one containing 10 books in epistolary format. Since he never went to America, his sources included information he heard from navigators and discoverers. In the manner of a modern-day reporter, he questioned such figures as Columbus, Cabot, and Vespucci. He began the *Decades* in 1494 and finished the eighth in 1526. The *Decades* are addressed to illustrious recipients, among them Cardinal Ascanio Sforza, Viscount Francesco Maria Sforza, and several to Pope Leo X and Pope Clement VII. The descriptions are so convincing that they give the impression that Pedro Mártir describes things he actually saw.

The writing of the *Decades*, caused by impulses from outside the author, is an ongoing topic in the text, prompted by an exchange of letters or the reading of sections that have been sent out. At the beginning of book 1 the role of letter writing undergirding the *Decades* is present as a theme. The Vicount Ascanio Sforza had asked in a letter for information on the newly discovered lands, and books 1 and 2 of the first *Decade* is Pedro Mártir's response. Pedro Mártir had stopped writing about the New World after completing the second *Decade*, when he then received letters requesting him to continue his narrative of events dealing with that region.

Mártir's previous writing of the *Decades* had thus been favorably received to the extent that readers wanted him to continue his narrative to bring them up to date. The Augustinian Egidio Antonini commanded Mártir in the name of the pope to add to his three previously written *Decades*. He attempts to lend authority to his writing by invoking detailed reports, trustworthy men, legal depositions, and, above all, the aura of authority lent by three popes and several princes.

The first three *Decades* span the years 1492 to 1516. The first *Decade* is the only one that has an epilogue, book 10, an "Epilogue to the Decade," addressed to Iñigo López Mendoza, Count of Tendilla, Viceroy of Granada. Pedro Mártir pays tribute to the discoverers of new lands and the sovereigns who inspired and supported their undertakings. In ancient times, he points out, such heroes would be worshipped as gods. He narrates events chronologically from the beginning in an attempt to avoid excluding anyone who played a role in the discoveries. Occasionally Pedro Mártir lets himself be sidetracked to supply background information on an event; for example, he recalls the discovery and settlement of the Canaries, but he quickly resumes the primary narrative thread.

The second *Decade*, book 1, has as its subject matter the discoveries of coasts, the leaders of chief expeditions, and the promise the newly discovered lands offer. His approach is to relate what is noteworthy and in summary fashion. In the second *Decade* Pedro Mártir complains that his first *Decade*, which he calls the Ocean Decade, was printed and circulated without his permission. Mártir's friend, Lucio Marineo Siculo, was responsible for that Spanish edition published in 1511 (*De Orbe Novo*, 190n1). In this *Decade* he justifies forcing Indians into slavery when they behave with cruelty and do not receive the Spaniards with hospitality. Yet, Mártir calls the natives defenseless, in an apparent criticism of Alonso Hojeda's policy.

The sources for the third *Decade* include correspondence from the discoverers and leaders of expeditions, among them Vasco Núñez de Balboa. In book 1 of the third *Decade*, Pedro Mártir attributes the lack of frequent communication among the Indians to the lack of an economic base. Since they are naked and have no money they have very few wants to communicate. The fourth *Decade*, with an introduction addressed to Pope Leo X, focuses on Yucatan, Cozumel, and Hispaniola, and narrates the rivalry between Diego Velázquez and Hernán Cortés. Book 1 of this *Decade* tells the strange story of how some fugitives who landed in Darien were astonished to see Pedro Mártir's books in that region. Apparently, if we are to believe him, Mártir's books have reached such a distribution that they are found in unexpected corners of the New World.

The fifth Decade's subject matter contains events reported by Hernán Cortés. Pedro Mártir affirms that the letters about Cortés contain new and extraordinary matters that meet the writer's criterion for reporting matters that satisfy his readers' desire for marvels. He believes his unpolished style is counterbalanced by the great attraction of the writing – the novelty of the matters presented. The sixth *Decade* reports Gil Gonzalez's exploration of the southern coasts of the continent. The seventh *Decade* concerns the islands off the coast of Cuba, given the name Lucayas. Many details of natural history are presented. Pedro Mártir criticizes the Spaniards' greed for gold as the cause of the destruction of the islands' population. He is not keen on the proposal of the Dominicans to assign Indians to certain nobles for protection. The subject matter of the eighth *Decade* is very ambitious in scope, including a mix of historical events, natural history, and ethnography, with special attention paid to New Spain: incidents in the lives of captains, quadrupeds, birds, insects, trees, herbs, ceremonies, manners, and superstitions of the natives, as well as the fleets on the high seas.

The purpose of these writings, or of learning more about these happenings, is to demonstrate that the human race has become more illustrious thanks to events in the Indies and the church on earth has been increased. In the seventh *Decade* there is a statement that one profit to be gained from reading the *Decades* is diversion; yet Mártir also includes less amusing material, such as Sforza's sufferings and trials. Sometimes he admits that his sources are not helpful. Mártir explains his delay in writing by blaming the poor quality of the letters received by the Royal Council of the Indies. He points out that some of the letters deal in trivialities, like the discovery of a human finger. Some letter writers exaggerate the importance of their discoveries, believing that they surpass the first discoverers of the New World.[2]

The Chronicle as an Ongoing Process

Gonzalo Fernández de Oviedo y Valdés (1478-1557) was born in Madrid. Not much is known about his family, leading to speculation that the family was hiding something, such as Jewish ancestry or his father's being on the political side of Juana La Beltraneja.[3] Oviedo was raised in an aristocratic environment and followed a career of royal service. Oviedo began writing early, taking notes of what he witnessed. His works fall into several categories: fiction, genealogy, moral and spiritual life, politics, court life, translations from the Italian, and history.

In Spain at age 13 he served as a page to the Infante don Juan, an experience that would result in a book of guidance, the *Libro de cámara del príncipe don Juan.* At age 19 he went to Italy, where he served various royal figures. Returning to Spain he worked as secretary and scribe for the Inquisition; then he became a scribe and notary public in Madrid. In 1519 he published a novel of chivalry, *Libro del muy esforzado e invencible caballero de fortuna propiamente llamado Don Claribalte* (Book of the Very Brave and Invincible Don Claribalte).[4] He went to the Indies nine times, where he filled several positions that included secretary of the Council of the Indies and of the office of branding slaves and Indians. He was named official chronicler in 1532. As "alcaide," or warden, of the fortress at Santo Domingo he had the opportunity to meet important figures of the conquest. Oviedo formed his notes on nature taken for the general history into the *Sumario de la natural historia de las Indias* (*Natural History of the West Indies*) at the request of Charles V in 1526.[5] He completed the summary in the city of Toledo on 15 February 1526. In the dedication to Charles V, Oviedo sets forth his definitions of history and the historian based on those of the Roman scholar Pliny the Elder. Oviedo will imitate Pliny's procedure in his brief summary. History, which preserves the work of nature in the memory of humanity, encompasses the works of nature. The definition does not say anything about the events of humankind. The historian is a prudent, well-traveled individual. A true and authentic history contains what the historian has actually seen and understood.

According to Pliny, the historian must cite who he heard something from, what sources he read, and what he saw as an eyewitness. Oviedo affirms that his history can be authenticated by many eyewitnesses who, now living in Spain, are even present at court. The general subject of the summary is what he has seen on the islands and mainland of the Indies. He has all of this and more written in a longer form in originals and in a chronicle he has been writing for some time, including events from 1490 down to the present. All those writings are left in Santo Domingo. The summary is a stopgap measure to give the king a compendium of information and some recreation until Oviedo is able to send him the larger chronicle. He selects material from the larger work left in Santo Domingo. The summary, he claims, does not contradict the contents of the larger chronicle.

The summary begins with Columbus's discoveries. In the dedication, Oviedo recognizes Columbus's service as one of the greatest that a vassal could render his prince. Oviedo stresses that he will narrate only some of the myriad things accomplished in the history of the Indies. He will deal specifically with the course of the voyages to the New World, fauna, flora, geology, and ethnography. The summary includes mainly natural history, with some attention paid to ethnography. In a use of the modesty topos prevalent in sixteenth-century literature, Oviedo asks the king to excuse his summary if it is not as ordered, as it is in the larger chronicle. He excuses these faults on the grounds of his haste to return to the Indies to serve the crown. The novelty of the subject compensates for any slip in order and arrangement. The newness in the summary also converts reading into a recreation.

Oviedo, comparing his summary with the standard classical work of Ptolemy and with recently published histories of the New World, concludes that his work should be held in great esteem. The things described are as true and new to Europeans as anything Ptolemy described in his cosmography and equally different from those described in other histories. The matters discussed are so strange and unusual that Oviedo considers his time and effort well spent.

Oviedo most likely began writing the general history in 1514-15 and continued until he was interrupted in 1548-49. The *Historia general* has a prologue addressed to the Emperor Charles. His model again is Pliny's book on natural history. History has a role in recording the work of nature. The general history sets down what Oviedo has seen in the Indies, although he has not seen everything he describes. The general history is divided into three parts. The first was published in Seville in 1535; a new printing of it appeared at Salamanca in 1547. Parts 2 and 3 were not published in Oviedo's lifetime, partly because of opposition from Bartolomé de las Casas.[6]

These topics are covered in the history: the route to the Indies and navigation, the people of the region, fauna and flora, the rites and ceremonies of the natives. The vocabulary of the general history incorporates new words from America. The dedicatory letter is dated from Seville, 30 September 1535. The first part of the general history is dedicated to Cardinal Fray García Jofre de Loaysa, president of the Royal Council of the Indies, who was already dead in 1548 when Oviedo put the finishing touches to part 1. Oviedo refers to "these histories" ("estas historias"), because they are general and natural histories.

Oviedo allegedly writes the history because he wanted to serve the king, to give thanks and praise to the Creator of so many wonders, to comply with the king's order to copy these materials, and, finally, to give the world news it will find pleasing. He promises a second and a third part. As a claim to authorization for his history he says persons who serve in the Council of the Indies saw and corrected the history. He ends the dedication begging Cardinal Loaysa to continue his favors to the Indies, particularly to Santo Domingo and Hispaniola, where Oviedo was procurator, and asks that the prelates sent there be chaste and virtuous and that they reside in their dioceses. The second favor requested is that a similar criterion be observed in the election of justices and officials of the Real Hacienda. Like an echo of Las Casas, who often compared the natives to sheep, Oviedo implies that the "bad" bishops and justices are wolves who attack the sheep. There is also the problem in Spain of knowing what is truly happening in America because of the great distance separating the two regions.

In a prologue to the first part of the history addressed to the emperor, Oviedo delimits the area to be covered, distinguishing between the East and West Indies. Oviedo declares he differs from some authorities, namely, some cosmographers who hold that less than a fifth of the earth is inhabited. From his own experience, he knows that there are kingdoms and people in the Indies. This differing from the ancients and other authorities will be his posture throughout the book. The European mind is overwhelmed by the contemplation of the variety and multitude among the people, flora, fauna, mountains, and other features that are found in the Indies. The keynote of the descriptions is amazement. Most important, all of these wonders are under the rule of the Spanish monarch. The general history is a bringing-up-to-date of material in the earlier summary, obeying orders by the king to send information to the Royal Council of the Indies that could be included in the emperor's ongoing project of compiling a glorious chronicle of Spain.

The history has three purposes: to contribute to the chronicle of Spain project, to make known the greatness of the lands under Spanish authority, and to give all Christian kingdoms occasion to thank God for the increase of the Catholic faith. Even nonbelievers, in learning of these wonders, will be obliged to praise the Creator.

Oviedo cites two drawbacks to his doing justice to the subject matter: his style is inadequate, and he is too young. The truth of what he tells will make up for these shortcomings. He casts doubt on the truth of the versions of other authors who wrote histories of the Indies in Latin and the vernacular. They never set foot in the region, but they attempt to make up for the truth by their style. Oviedo believes his strong point is telling the truth as an eyewitness observer. The king can order his style to be polished and smoothed out. Oviedo lists among his credentials that he came to the Indies in 1513 for the first time, participated in the conquest and "pacification" as captain and vassal, and risked his life among natural dangers in the New World.

The first five books of the first part deal with the discovery and conquest of the Antilles; book 6 is titled "Libro de los depósitos" (Book of Deposits); books 7-15 concern nature in America that was already outlined in the summary; books 16-19 treat the discovery and settlement of San Juan, Cuba, and Jamaica. Oviedo explains that the book of deposits includes matters that require only brief treatment and do not merit a separate book each, such as the Indians' dwellings, "batey" (a game), and two hurricanes that hit Hispaniola. He promises that the reader will always find something new.

The books in the second part continue in consecutive numbers from the first part. The second part follows a geographical criterion, proceeding from south to north: book 20 described Magellan's voyage and Patagonia; book 21 provides geographical description of the coasts from Tierra del Fuego to Labrador; books 22-25 recapitulate discovery and conquest of the southern part of Tierra Firme (mainland) from Río de la Plata to Venezuela; books 26-32 detail events in Central America, from Cartagena to Yucatan; book 33 concentrates on the conquest of Mexico; books 34-38 deal with North America – Nueva Galicia and Florida. The third part is dedicated to events in Peru. Book 39 describes the southern coasts; books 40-43 describe recent events in New Mexico, Guatemala, Nicaragua and Castilla del Oro; books 44-49 portray the conquest of Peru and its civil wars; and book 50 includes the "Libro de los naufragios" (Book of Shipwrecks).

The general history contains foreign and "barbarous" (that is, indigenous) words because they denote what is new. Strange words are needed to explain phenomena of the Indian cultures. Oviedo argues that the use of such words should not discredit his command of Castilian, which he validates by citing his background: he was born in Madrid, raised in the royal palace, conversed with nobles, and has read in Castilian. Furthermore, Castilian, he claims, is the best of all the vernacular languages. Oviedo responds in chapter 30 to critics in Spain who might contend that he should have written his history in Latin. Moses and David and other scriptural writers wrote the Old Testament in their own language; Saint Paul wrote the Epistle to the Hebrews in his own language so that it could be better understood by them. This is a universal rule: all the ancient writers wrote in languages in which they could be understood. These histories more generally understood by Spaniards best satisfy them when written by eyewitnesses. The truth of the works in Latin cannot be judged by those who have experience of the Indies and cannot read Latin. Their argument would be valid if Oviedo's Latin were of the quality of Cardinal Bembo's. The general history is not the narrative of a particular royal life or kingdom, but an account of a New World, or *mare magno*, to which many writers and styles can contribute now and in the future.

Oviedo is repetitious at times, for example, reiterating in slightly different words what he said in a previous passage about the dangers and privations he had to go through to gather the material. The second time he says this, his point is that readers benefit from the reading without having to actually experience the hardships. The unfolding nature of the general history means that many novelties and secrets will be discovered as time and nature reveal them.

Oviedo compares his procedure to that of Pliny: the books are divided by subject. He has not taken his subjects from the books he has read, as Pliny did, but he gathered all of his material during countless hardships, necessities, and dangers over more than 22 years. Oviedo says he owes the invention and the title to Pliny, whom he imitates not in the nature of what Pliny wrote but in his distinction among the books and their subjects. Oviedo believes he differs from Pliny because he attributes effects and works of nature

not to nature but to God. Oviedo's history also differs from Pliny's in
its inclusion of the narrative of part of the conquest of the Indies. He
is the first to give an account of their discovery, and of other things,
which, although not part of natural history, are necessary to the
prehistory in order to know the beginning of everything and to
understand how, from the beginning, God moved Ferdinand and
Isabella to order looking for these lands. The dedication to the
second part of the general and natural history emphasizes the glory
of Spain, differentiating the Spaniards from the Romans and other
ancient peoples like the Assyrians and Greeks. Reiterating the theme
of providentialism, he portrays Spain as divinely chosen. Oviedo
discusses the glories of the Goths and natives of Spain versus the
Romans because he claims the Goths and Spaniards found the
Indies.

To lend authority to his text, Oviedo acclaims the church's right
to make corrections to his history. Like Pliny and other writers, he
fears detractors. Wary of criticism from those in Europe, Africa, and
Asia, he suggests they see the Indies before they judge him. Again, he
has first-hand experience and writes at a time when other eyewitnesses are alive and available to him. Since his history is for the king,
written by royal order, and the king pays his way, he would not dare
to lie. He expects his reward from God, for being a faithful writer,
and from the king. Oviedo admits his history will have its detractors;
some people may be offended, for he has a low opinion of some who
have come to the Indies: greedy, envious, stupid, many are not of
noble blood. What Oviedo has not seen he has obtained from many
eyewitnesses, thus authorizing the truth of what he says. Plurality is
key because it is his way of achieving some objectivity among different versions of events. Oviedo has royal decrees for governors to
send him materials to consider for his use in writing his history.

Oviedo repeatedly criticizes historians in Europe who write
about these parts without having seen them. Also, informants of
events in other provinces should have their qualifications examined
before accepting their statements as true. Oviedo believes these new
books will be better than what he has already written and envisions
someone else continuing this work. At the end of his life he feels
close to the heart of the great and innumerable secrets of the second
hemisphere.

From the beginning of the history of the Indies, Christians have preyed upon other Christians. They drew most of the sufferings upon themselves. Fighting among friends is viewed as something new in these times. Oviedo lists the names of important figures involved in internecine conflicts: Diego Velázquez and Diego Colón; Diego Velázquez and Hernando Cortés; Cristóbal de Olit and Hernando Cortés; Alvarez and Cortés; Francisco de Montejo and Diego Velázquez; Vasco Núñez de Balboa and the governor Diego de Nicuesa; Francisco Pizarro and Diego de Almagro, governor Pedrarias Dávila; Francisco Pizarro and Sebastián de Benalcázar. Like brothers, Francisco Pizarro and Diego de Almagro were of one will and one heart, one man in two bodies. Both were a mirror and example of good friends. He likens them to Damon and Pythias. Pizarro's brothers came between the two friends. Pizarro and Almagro had also been Oviedo's friends. Now they are not, but he refuses to speak ill of them by lying; however, he will tell the truth, which is sufficiently damaging. Oviedo claims that throughout the history that he speaks without passion, adulation, or exception. His purpose, he says, is not to reprimand anyone but to tell what really happened. Of course, in the telling, some people will look bad. Greed is the cause of their troubles. He sees men in the Indies not conforming to the creed of one Lord, one faith, one baptism, and one God. Oviedo interprets the Lord as secular ruler, different from the meaning in Paul's Letter to the Ephesians.

Disasters and shipwrecks on the seas of the Indies, the topic of book 20 in the first part, is later transferred to the third part as book 50, the last book of the history. Such accounts let readers know how dangerous navigation is. Oviedo limits navigation to the Indies, starting in 1492. Linen for sails and wood for ships should not be blamed for ship disasters but rather men, who choose to venture out to sea. Unlike Pliny, Oviedo has experienced dangers of the sea and details some of them. Oviedo also had bad experiences at sea in areas near Spain, Italy, and Flanders. Men risk such dangers for livelihood, duties, and adventure. The purpose of this book on shipwrecks is to give glory to God, who has rescued sufferers. Also, Oviedo's advantage over other chroniclers is that he has sailed. The description of miraculous rescues meets the need to provoke amazement in the reader, a goal that from the start has been among Oviedo's purposes.

Oviedo's summary and his promise to publish a longer history is believed to have had an impact on Las Casas's decision to write his own history. Bartolomé de las Casas's general history, the *Historia de las Indias* (*History of the Indies*), is not his most famous work; it is overshadowed by the *Brevísima relación de la destrucción de las Indias* (*The Devastation of the Indies: A Brief Account*), discussed in chapter 6, yet it is still one of his most important historiographic texts. Las Casas began his *History* in 1527, the same year he founded the Dominican Convent of Puerto de Plata on Hispaniola.

The Chronicle in Defense of the Indian

Las Casas's purpose in writing the *History* was to present the true version of events in the Indies, events, he claims, not accurately presented by other historians. Ultimately, his purpose is to defend the rights of the vanquished Indians. A reading of the *History* should lead, therefore, to action to redress wrongs. Further purposes enunciated are: (1) to benefit Spain, (2) to defend the honor and royal reputation of the kings of Castile, (3) to free Spain from its error of believing that the Indians are not men but brutal beasts incapable of virtue and doctrine. Las Casas wrote his prologue in 1552, long after beginning the *History* in 1527. In the prologue he announced plans for six books, but he only completed, so far as is known today, three. Each, with the exception of book 1, covers the events of a decade: book 1 chronicles events in 1492-1500, book 2, 1500-1510, and book 3, 1510-20. Among Las Casas's credentials for undertaking the history are, he claims, that he was there, he participated, and he observed. He knew and communicated with important figures in the discovery, conquest, and colonization. Among these figures are his father and his uncle, the kings of Spain, officials of the government bureaucracy in Spain and the Indies, Columbus, Cortés, Pizarro, and Bernal Díaz del Castillo.

The discourse of Las Casas's history is hybrid, containing history, ship's diary, biography, autobiography, and letters. Like the general histories already discussed, it contains material on natural history and ethnography but not in the quantity found in Las Casas's *Apologética historia* (Apologetical History), his major work on natural history and ethnography. He originally planned a history that would include a part on the Indians, which he separated from what is today the *History of the Indies* because the ethnographic section was becoming too long. Las Casas is aware of the formula of a chronicle and seems to want to adhere to it. He admits that he does not follow a strict chronological development.

At the beginning of book 3, Las Casas recognizes the diffuse nature of his narrative, attributing it to interruptions caused by his many duties in and out of the monastery. He admits he may have altered the order of things, recording events that belong properly in one book in another. He trusts the benevolence of his readers to blame his memory and to continue reading. Truth, rather than a concern for style, has guided the composition of his *History*.

There are long commentaries on events and on political, legal, and theological issues. The commentaries often take the form of a chapter or a series of chapters. A good number of commentaries deal with Columbus: his voyages, his writings, his reasons for believing he had discovered the mainland, and the location of the earthly paradise. The section on the earthly paradise is inserted to support Columbus's conviction that he had indeed found the location of the earthly paradise. Other commentaries concern abuses against the Indians: Columbus receives divine punishment for abuses against Indians. There are digressions, for example, on the River Nile, the production of pearls, and the workings of a sugar factory.

The *History* contains much information, but readers have questioned how precise the information is. For example, are Las Casas's numbers exaggerated? In a certain extreme case, one Spaniard on horseback allegedly kills 10,000 Indians in an hour. There is much documentation from various sources and from Las Casas's own experience. Rómulo D. Carbia accused Las Casas of falsifying documents but Carbia could not prove it.[7]

Book 1 starts with the obligatory discussion of the creation of the world and humankind. The Portuguese maritime expeditions before Columbus serve to set the context of Columbus's voyages while providing an opportunity to condemn the Portuguese for their involvement in African slavery. In general the book covers the discovery of the Indies by Columbus along with voyages of discovery made by, among others, Amerigo Vespucci, Alonso de Hojeda, Juan de la Cosa, and Vicente Yáñez Pinzón. Three of the Columbian voyages are detailed in this book. The precedents of Columbus's first voyage are covered. The Columbus narrative alternates between his voyages and his stays in Spain and the Indies. The book ends with the arrival in Hispaniola of the governor Bobadilla and Columbus's imprisonment. Portuguese colonization is described. Las Casas recounts the Jesuits' praise for the good qualities of the natives of Brazil in an attempt to make his case for the unity of the Indian peoples, their shared humanity, their innocence, and the positive potential of all the natives in the New World.

Book 2 chronicles further events on Hispaniola: Bobadilla's government, the arrival of Nicolás de Ovando, and Diego Colón's rule. Las Casas enters the narrative as a participant with the documentation of his arrival. Events in Columbus's life continue with an account of his fourth voyage, his return to Spain, and his death. More expeditions are documented: Hojeda and Nicuesa to the mainland, Díaz and Vicente Yáñez Pinzón to Central America, and Ponce de León to Puerto Rico. The Indian cause is pursued, showing their victimization in wars of repression and in the first "repartimientos." As a promise of defense for the Indians, the first Dominicans arrive.

In book 3 the Dominicans vigorously pursue the defense of the Indians, notably in the sermons of Fray Antonio Montesinos. Las Casas records the civil measures taken to protect the Indians with the Junta and Laws of Burgos and of Valladolid. The Spanish empire expands into Cuba and Florida. The autobiography of Las Casas reaches its complete development. Las Casas shares an encomienda with Pedro de Rentería, but Las Casas then experiences a conversion and decides to defend the Indians. He intervenes at the Spanish Court on behalf of the Indians on several visits to Spain. Las Casas's experiment in peaceful colonization at Cumaná fails, and he enters the Dominican order. Abuses in the Indies receive Las Casas's critical judgment, focusing on such figures as Hernán Cortés and Balboa. He records the disagreements between Diego Velázquez and Hernán Cortés, considers Cortés a tyrant, and criticizes Gómara as Cortés's chronicler. Balboa is also depicted as a tyrant on Darién. There is discussion and harsh criticism of the "requerimiento" – a statement read to the Indians before attacking them, demanding that they become Christians and subjects of the Spanish king – and of the illegality of the encomienda system. Abuses led to the extermination of the Indians of Cuba and to the uprising of the Indian chieftain

Enriquillo on Hispaniola. Las Casas criticizes versions of history written by Gómara and Oviedo.

The *History* revolves around Columbus and Las Casas as the two main personages.[8] All of book 1 and half of book 2 are devoted to Columbus's enterprise. Las Casas's life emerges in book 2; but is presented mainly in book 3. Parallels are suggested between stories of Columbus's life and Las Casas's life, with Columbus the chosen caudillo, Las Casas the chosen priest and conscience. Las Casas has high regard for Columbus, yet he does not hesitate to criticize him for abuses. Las Casas, by alternating between "I" and "he," also projects himself as a historical figure. Las Casas the narrator is thus able to praise himself as Las Casas the character.[9]

In Las Casas's last will and testament, he left his papers in the care of the Dominicans at the Monastery of San Gregorio, prohibiting the reading and publication of his book for 40 years after his death. The *History* was to be published if deemed for the good of the Indians first and then of Spain, to glorify God and to reveal the truth. The truth would make known God's justice. If He decided to destroy Spain, it would be clear that it is on account of the destruction that the Spanish wrought in the Indies.

Gómara's General Chronicle

Francisco López de Gómara (1511-62) is recognized as both a general historian of the Indies and a chronicler of the conquest of Mexico.[10] López de Gómara also wrote a *Crónica de los Barbarroja* (Chronicle of the Barbarossas) and an *Annals of the Emperor Charles V*. Trained in classical literature, he wrote his history according to the precepts of classical rhetoric and the concept of the hero. The figure of Hernán Cortés is singled out while all others are presented as secondary to him. According to Esteve Barba, Gómara first wrote the conquest of New Spain and then composed his history of the Indies as an introduction to it (95). Both parts formed his major work, the *Historia de las Indias y conquista de México* (History of the Indies and Conquest of Mexico) published in Zaragoza in 1552.[11] The first part narrates the conquests and discoveries made in the Indies up to 1522, and the second part relates the conquest of Mexico. The second part has received more attention than the first part because of Bernal Díaz del Castillo's attack. Under pressure from the Inquisition, Gómara revised his work for the second edition of the *Historia*, published in Salamanca in 1568.

Gómara's history of the Indies has as preliminary material a prologue to readers, a statement addressed to translators, and a dedication to the Emperor Charles V, King of Spain, Lord of the Indies and the New World. In the prologue to the readers, Gómara presents his concept of historiography, and affirms the importance of order and good language in writing the history. His approach is to present a general survey. He points out that he follows two styles – he is brief in the first part and prolix in the second. He defines criteria used in selecting the materials, being well aware that he would be criticized. The statement to translators indicates his confidence that people will want to translate his history, and so he lays down two rules. He discourages others from translating the history into Latin, promising that he will do that. The dedication to the Emperor Charles speaks of the greatness of the discovery and its providential nature and explains the term *New World*. He points out the similarity of Europeans and Indians, recognizing the Indian as a descendant of Adam. Now they are Christians, thanks to the emperor and his predecessors. No other nation has expanded as has Spain. The work of the Spanish is discovery, subjugation, and conversion. In the scheme of providence, the discovery was for the purpose of converting the Indians, and the Spaniards were chosen as its instruments. The conquest is viewed as naturally succeeding the centuries-long "reconquista" waged against the Moors. The conquest does not consist in despoiling the Indians, but ennobles them. Why does Gómara write the history? He insists on writing in the vernacular and not in Latin. He will prepare a somewhat different version in Latin in which he will say things kept silent in the Castilian.

The first part is preceded by an introduction followed by numerous brief chapters. In the introduction, Gómara writes about knowing and understanding the world as God's creation, but claims that not all things can be known. The chapters are grouped about certain topics: about the world being one and not many, round and not flat, inhabitable and, in fact, inhabited; and about the location of the Indies. Several chapters are devoted to Columbus's discovery. After a discussion of Hispaniola, Gómara interposes several chapters dealing with ethnographic and natural history. There follow descriptions of the islands discovered by the Spanish, New Spain and

Cortés, and the discovery of the South Sea, Venezuela, Río de la Plata, and Magellan's explorations. The partition of the New World between the Spanish and the Portuguese and conquest of Peru receive much attention in several chapters. New laws and ordinances for the Indies are detailed, followed by a portrayal of Central America. The inclusion of the conquest of the Canaries seems out of place, from a chronological and geographical perspective.

The first part concludes with a tribute in praise of the Spaniards' achievements. So much land has been won in 60 years' time. No other nation has done what they have in battle, navigation, and evangelization. He emphasizes the good done for the Indians in giving them one God, one faith, and one baptism, leading them to abandon human sacrifice, cannibalism, sodomy, and polygamy. The Spaniards have taught them letters, thereby making them human, not animals. Gómara admits that while it would have been better not to have taken material objects from the Indians, the greatest evil done to them was in making them work too hard in the mines. Those responsible for the death of the Indians in the mines ended up badly, the result of God's punishment. Finally, regarding the conquest, Gómara refers the reader to the work of Sepúlveda, whom he calls the emperor's chronicler.

Chronicling Nature and Behavior

Father Joseph de Acosta (1540-1600) was born in Medina del Campo to a family of Portuguese descent.[12] He received a humanistic education at the University of Alcalá and entered the Jesuit order as did all his brothers. He taught in Spain at Segovia, Salamanca, Alcalá, and Ocaña, then went to the Indies where, after a brief stay in the Antilles, he worked as a missionary in Peru. For the purpose of evangelism he learned Aymará. Named Jesuit Provincial for Peru, he was ordered to resolve the problems of Jesuit expansion in Peru and to evangelize the Indians. The third provincial council of the Jesuits commissioned Acosta to draft a catechism and confession manuals in Castilian, Quechua, and Aymará. His observations in the New World and his missionary activity resulted in two works published together in 1589, *De natura Novi Orbis y De promulgando Evangelio apud barbaros sive de procuranda Indorum salute* (On the Nature of the New World and The Propagation of the Gospel among the Barbarians or Attempts to Save the Indians). The second title is that of a treatise about the problems and methodology of mission work.[13]

The *Historia natural y moral de las Indias* (*The Natural and Moral History of the Indies*) was written when Acosta had returned to Europe; part of it he had already set down in Latin in Peru, and for the rest he had to rely on his memory.[14] The history includes preliminary material consisting of the official *aprobación*, or approval, a dedication, and a prologue; the body of the work comprises a total of seven books divided into two major sections: four books are devoted to natural history and three books to moral history. The aprobación, testifying to the Catholic nature of the doctrine set forth in the history, was signed by the famous humanist and author Fray Luis de León.

The dedication to the Infanta Isabel Clara Eugenia, daughter of Philip II, is dated 1 March 1590 from Seville. Acosta, emphasizing that knowledge of nature and strange customs and deeds causes pleasure and delight, offers the history to the princess for her entertainment in the hope that she will recommend it to her father, the king. Acosta has one criterion in mind for the princess's reading of the text and another one for her father. The criteria reflect the sexism of the day. For the princess it is to offer pleasure and delight and to be read in her spare moments. That purpose also determined the language used, the vernacular, which is not meant as an insult to the princess, for the history is not for vulgar understandings. For the king it will offer a consideration of affairs and of people that are part of his royal responsibility. Acosta recalls that he had dedicated another book to the king, a book composed in Latin, on the conversion of the Indians. All he has written is intended ultimately to bring more help and favor to the people of the Indies.

In the prologue to the reader, Acosta explains why he wrote a book on the Indies when so many already existed. Acosta has not seen any that adequately treats the causes of the Indies' novelties and wonders of nature. He also claims – erroneously, in view of the histories we will see in chapter 6 – that he has not read any history of the Indian inhabitants. Acosta lists the sources for the first part of the history, natural history, as the experience of many friends, his own research, and conferences with prudent and knowledgeable men. For information on the Indians, he consulted with men of experience in these matters, as well as the Indians' discourses and relations on the deeds and customs of the Indians. Acosta views his history as useful in service to the Gospel. Acosta refers to his text (belonging to the discourse type of the history) in various ways as history, *relación*, and book.[15] The Indies are not a new world in the sense that much has already been written about them; but his book is a new type of discourse to which he has given the name of a natural and moral history of the Indies, for it is partly historical and partly philosophical, dealing with the works of nature and of free will, which are the deeds and customs of men.

The first book of the natural history deals with cosmography, geography, and the land and its inhabitants. Acosta's universe is earth-centered. Book 2 treats the torrid zone to correct erroneous ideas held by the ancients and to demonstrate that this region is habitable. Book 3 considers the simple elements of air, water, land, and fire in the New World. A statement in book 3 concerns three approaches to the study of nature. In ascending order these are curiosity, which is the least useful, since it is merely the desire to know new things; philosophy, which is to know the causes producing natural phenomena; and, finally, the most useful, theology, which leads to knowledge of the Creator. Book 4 presents the compounds: metals, plants, animals. Acosta considers the influence of time and environment on natural species.[16] Plants and animals are categorized as to whether they are native to the region or imported from Spain.

For the moral history, Acosta wrote a special prologue treating the inhabitants of the New World in general and the Mexicans in particular. He does not treat the Spanish because they have been discussed sufficiently by other historians. He repeats an idea stated in the prologue, that he puts his history at "the doors of the Gospel," that is, in service to evangelization and to the glorification of the Creator for drawing the Indians out of the darkness of paganism, giving them the light of the Gospel. He will study the Indians from the perspective of their religion and culture. Book 5 on the Indians' religion includes topics such as idolatry, burial practices, temples, priests, penances, sacrifices, and religious festivals. Some practices are seen as copies of Christian worship, for example, sacraments and monasteries. Acosta attributes to the work of the devil the apparent similarities. Acosta is aware that some readers question the benefit of this knowledge, since reading about the Indians seems to resemble reading books of chivalry. Knowledge of the Indians' religious practices is useful for missionaries to determine if the Indians are still practicing their superstitions openly or in secret. Such knowledge will make the Spanish grateful for their Christianity when they compare it with the satanic religions, and they will thank God for calling the Indians to Christianity.

In book 6, on the Indians' culture, Acosta's intention is to prove that the Indians possess complete powers of reason. The discussion of culture includes their method of computing time, their writing system, the government structure of the Incas and the Aztecs, war, education, and civil holidays. In considering the Indians' rationality, Acosta does not ignore censurable aspects of their life but attributes them to their social formation. Barbarity and cruelty are not unique to the Indians. The Greeks and Romans could be barbarous and, at times, surpassed the Indians in cruelty.

Book 7 deals in particular with the history of the Mexicans, treating their origin, succession of rulers, and notable deeds. Acosta narrates Mexican history from the wandering of the seven tribes to the Spanish invasion and the imprisonment of Cuauhtémoc. Miracles in New Spain favored the establishment of Christianity among the Mexicans. Unified kingdoms in Peru and Mexico and their universal languages were further aids to evangelization. Acosta argues that benefit will come from any true and well-written history because, since human beings are so similar, knowing the deeds of one group benefits others. No matter how barbarous, a people may still be praiseworthy in some respect. Because the Indians differ from the Europeans, understanding the Indians gives pleasure. The Spanish benefit also when they are a credit to their own culture. Acosta shows how the Indians should be treated, hoping to eradicate the European belief that Indians lack reason.

In the last chapter, Acosta criticizes the missionaries as cold in spirit and failing to find new peoples to convert. Merchants and soldiers moved by greed and the acquisition of power are doing that work for the churchmen. Acosta cites St. Augustine's interpretation of a prophecy by Isaiah that the church can grow by human and earthly means, in this case, men seeking the welfare of their own business. Acosta condemns abuses committed in evangelization, but he believes that God drew good out of evil by making the subjection of the Indians the means to their salvation.

The Official Chronicle

The post of cosmographer-chronicler of the Council of the Indies was established in October 1571. The Laws of the Indies prescribed the duties of the official chronicler.[17] One of the early holders of the newly created position of cosmographer-chronicler of the Council of Indies is Juan López de Velasco (1530-40 to 1598), who had already been working in the administration of Philip II. Little is known about López Velasco's early years and education. From the nature of his written works, geography was probably his major study. He finished his *Geografía y descripción universal de las Indias* (Geography and Universal Description of the Indies) in 1574.[18] He also produced works to reform the teaching of Castilian and language texts on Castilian orthography and etymology. In 1591 he was named secretary to the king and his former post was divided, since it was too much for one person.

The first part of the geography has no heading and covers topics from the boundaries of the Indies to the Royal Treasury. Within the first part are these natural divisions of topics: geographical delineation of the Indies, discovery of the Indies, and natural history – temperature, healthfulness of climate, storms, winds, fruits, trees, grains, animals, birds, fish, mines and metals. A division on ethnography provides facts on the Indians, their physical appearance, dress, dwellings, government, religion, marriage, and war making, plus, finally, a section on their conversion to Christianity and their freedom.[19] There follows a section on the Spaniards who emigrate to the Indies, those later Spaniards born in the Indies and their occupations, the Council and government of the Indies, governors, property of the deceased, and the mixed races: mulattoes (born of black and white parents), mestizos (born of parents of different races, usually white and Indian), and zambaigos (of Chinese and Indian descent). The religious life and structure of the Indies receives attention, with sections devoted to archdioceses and dioceses, jurisdiction of the prelates, construction of churches, religious orders in the Indies, and the Inquisition. The second section, titled "Hidrografía general de las Indias" (General Hydrography of the Indies), contains sections on the seas, currents, and various routes to and from the Indies, within the Indies, and even as far as the Philippines. The third main division of the work is divided into two sections: "Tabla General de las Indias del Norte" (General Table of the Indies to the North) and "Tabla General de las Indias del Mediodía" (General Table of the Indies to the South).

Antonio de Herrera y Tordesillas (1559-1625), major chronicler of the Indies, wrote the *Decades*, the short title given to his *Historia general de los hechos de los castellanos en las Islas y Tierra Firme del Mar Océano* (General History of the Deeds of the Castilians in the Islands and on the Mainland). The first and second parts were published in Madrid in 1601 and 1615, placing his history outside the primary time frame of this study, yet it merits mention both in association with the official chronicle and also because he began work on the general history in the last decade of the sixteenth century.[20] Among Herrera's numerous publications are four works of history published in the sixteenth century, dealing with Scotland, England, Portugal, France, and Milan. In the seventeenth century, a history of the world would be published, *Historia general del mundo durante el reinado de Felipe II* (General History of the World During the Reign of Philip II)(1601-1612). Herrera translated historical, political, and spiritual works.

The general history consists of eight decades, each in turn composed of 10 books. The history begins with a geographic introduction, based on López de Velasco's information, to set the stage for the historic events to be narrated. The chronicle contains the ethnographic information that we have come to expect in most of the general histories discussed. The time period covered is 1492-1554. Herrera relied quite heavily on other chronicles and viceregal documents, intending to present the Spanish side of things to counteract negative opinions about Spain circulating in Europe over such matters as the conquest.

The scope of the general chronicles discussed in this chapter corresponds to a larger definition of history which includes nature, human behavior, and ethnography in addition to purely historical events. These also enjoy some degree of official status, ranging from Pedro Mártir's letters written at the request of important ecclesiastical and political personages to the official chronicle authorized by the crown. Several chroniclers interject their personal agendas – a criticism of Spanish economic policy, advocacy of sending better secular and religious leaders to the Indies, and defense of the Indian population – while fulfilling the usual purposes of historiographical discourse.

Pedro Mártir's chronicle is interesting for its use of epistolary discourse and the division of the material into decades. Oviedo's encyclopedia-like chronicle, encompassing all manifestations of nature and ethnography he could include, offers very interesting reading, especially on the internecine struggles in the Indies, but its length may deter a modern reader. His summary, on the other hand, is more manageable, but often reads like a catalogue. Las Casas's purpose in the *History of the Indies* is to defend the rights of the vanquished Indians. Like other general histories, it contains material on natural history and ethnography but the latter is not present in the quantity found in his apologetical history. The *History* gains much interest because it revolves around Columbus and Las Casas as the two main personages. The clarity of style in Gómara's general chronicle, written in the mode of classical Renaissance history, commends it to readers. For Father Joseph de Acosta, who chronicles nature and behavior, the Indies are not a new world in the sense that much has already been written about them. His chronicle is noteworthy as a new type of discourse, partly historical and partly philosophical, dealing with the works of nature and of free will, which are the deeds and customs of men. The official chronicle written by those holding the post of cosmographer-chronicler contains much data that is of interest to statisticians and census keepers but lacks the literary imagination found in most other types of chronicle.

Chapter Six

Ecclesiastical Chronicles

Religious chronicles were written by men officially associated with the church, usually in the role of missionary. They were participants in the so-called spiritual conquest of America. The majority were Franciscans and Dominicans; other orders represented were Jesuits, Mercedarians, and Augustinians. They often wrote out of obedience to their superiors, to record the work of conversion of the Indians, to explain the native civilizations they encountered, and, above all, to advance the work of evangelization by presenting valuable information on the Indians' history, languages, and customs. Their sources varied from their own experience and study of native culture to information from other religious observers, from conquistadors, and native informants. The discourse types used were history, *relación*, and memorial.[1]

Franciscan Chroniclers of New Spain

The Franciscans in New Spain included, first of all, Fray Toribio de Motolinía (1482/91-1569), whose real name was Toribio de Paredes or Benavente. Fray Toribio was one of the first 12 Franciscan missionaries led by Fray Martín de Valencia to undertake the evangelization of New Spain. He left Sanlúcar in Spain, 25 January 1524, arriving at the port of San Juan de Ulúa in New Spain in May 1524.[2] In New Spain he began to call himself by the Indian name Motolinía, which means poor. His missionary work took him as far as Nicaragua. In 1536 he was guardian of the Franciscan convent (monastery) of Tlaxcala. He participated in conflicts with civil authorities over his defense of the Indians and in disputes between the Franciscans and Dominicans over the policy of Indian baptism. He wrote a letter to the emperor (2 January 1555) in which he attacked Bartolomé de las Casas.

The earliest mention of Motolinía's works gives the impression that he was a prolific writer.[3] His works fit into several categories of discourse: Christian doctrine and spirituality, theatrical works known as "autos," hagiographic writings, and historical writings. His historical works, the *Memoriales* (Reports) and the *Historia de los indios de la Nueva España* (*History of the Indians of New Spain*), interest us in this book.[4] Motolinía's major and definitive historical work is the *Relación de las cosas, idolatrías, ritos y ceremonias de la Nueva España* (Account of the Things, Idolatries, Rites, and Ceremonies of New Spain), now lost.[5] It was used by Alfonso de Zorita in his *Relación de Nueva España* (Account of New Spain). The *Memoriales* comprised drafts and notes (Bardot 1985, 53). There is much disorder in the work, which consists of an *Epístola proemial* (Prologue Letter) addressed to the Count of Benavente, divided into two parts. After the first and second chapters, the text skips to chapter 13; chapter 16 contains an Indian calendar. Internal textual evidence points to 1536-43 as the period of composition. Much of the material in Motolinía's History of the Indians can also be found in the *Memoriales,* but there is a larger section on antiquities in the *Memoriales* and Motolinía's classical erudition is more noticeable in the *Memoriales'* citations.

The *Historia de los indios* is generally known today as *Historia de los indios de la Nueva España*. Motolinía was officially charged in 1536 with writing the chronicle. He perceived an urgent need in 1541 to safeguard his project of working among the Indians, which was coming under attack from authorities in Spain and Rome with the threat of the Nuevas Leyes (New Laws) of 1542 and the tightening of papal rules for baptism. He dedicated this chronicle to the Count of Benavente, Don Antonio Pimentel, counselor to Charles V and *padrino natural* (godfather) of Motolinía's native town. He asks two things of the count: to keep his name secret and to have his work reviewed and corrected because he was conscious of his mistakes and poor writing.[6]

The *History* consists of a prologue-letter and three "tratados," or treatises, divided into a number of chapters. Motolinía dated the prologue-letter 24 February 1541 at the Convent of Santa María de la Concepción de Tehuacán. Although Motolinía wanted to remain anonymous, he signed the dedication with the names Motolinía and Fray Toribio de Paredes. The prologue-letter helps understand Motolinía's purpose; the history will trace the origins of the Indians, the origin of the principal Mexican tribes, and the history of some cities and states in Mexico. The prologue-letter outlines the origin of the principal Mexican tribes; treatise 1 covers pre-Columbian civilization and religion; treatise 2 traces the process of evangelization and the administration of the sacraments; and treatise 3 surveys nature, natives, and products, offers praise for the missionaries, and adds a biography of Fray Martín de Valencia.

Fray Gerónimo de Mendieta, a Basque, was born in Vitoria in 1525, one of many children.[7] After spending four months at sea with fellow Franciscans on the outbound voyage, Mendieta reached Veracruz in 1554. He studied arts and theology in New Spain, where he acquired a phenomenally rapid grasp of the Mexican language. Despite having a stutter, he preached eloquently in the Indian language. He employed interpreters and paintings in his missionary work, wrote in defense of the Franciscans and the viceroy against the practices of the audiencia, and returned to Spain in 1570 with health problems and depression. In 1573, he left for New Spain once more.

Mendieta wrote his chronicle, the *Historia eclesiástica indiana* (Ecclesiastical History of the Indies), out of obedience to his superiors, taking 25 years to finish it.[8] He began his history in 1573; the writing was interrupted in 1575, and he finished it in 1597 when he was 72 years old. Mendieta died in 1604. His principal sources were books and documents and the holdings of the Franciscan archives in the Convento de San Francisco de Méjico.

The *Historia eclesiástica* is divided into five books. Book 1 has Las Casas as its source; book 2, concerning Indian religion and customs, relies on Motolinía and the lost chronicle of the friar Olmos; book 3 records the conversion of the Indians and the missionaries' attempts to learn the language, for which Mendieta used Motolinía's *History of the Indians* and Fray Toribio's oral reports; book 4 documents the foundation of the Franciscan provinces of Michoacán, Yucatán, and Guatemala and the activities of other religious orders; and book 5 contains biographies of friars, as well as Mendieta's own experiences. For books 4 and 5 Mendieta consulted several sources: Fray Andrés de Olmos, *Antigüedades de las Indias* (Antiquities of the Indies), which is lost; Fray Toribio de Motolinía, *Venida de los doce primeros padres y lo que llegados acá hicieron* (Arrival of the First Twelve Fathers and What They Did Afterward); a little from Sahagún; a life of Fray Martín de Valencia written by Fray Francisco Jiménez; and for the lives of the other friars, Fray Rodrigo de Bienvenidos, and a Memorial of 1585 largely written by Mendieta.[9] A seventeenth-century chronicler, Fray Juan de Torquemada, may be mentioned here because he was accused of plagiarizing Mendieta's history in his *Monarquía indiana* (Indian Monarchy), published in Seville in 1615.[10]

Fray Bernardino de Sahagún changed his surname, Ribeira, to the name of his place of origin at the time of his profession as a Franciscan.[11] He was born in Sahagún, León province, in 1499 or 1500, studied at the University of Salamanca, and came to New Spain when he was 29 or 30 years old. He was assiduous in learning Nahuatl and taught Latin to Indian students at the Imperial Colegio de Santa Cruz de Tlatelolco. Franciscan provincial Fray Francisco de Toral ordered Sahagún to write in the Indians' language whatever would be useful for doctrine, culture, and the maintenance of the Christian faith among the natives of New Spain. His works include Sunday epistles and gospels and sermons for Sundays and saints days in the Mexican language. He also wrote a life of Saint Bernardine, *Vida de San Bernardino*, at the request of some Indians.

The *Historia general de las cosas de Nueva España* (General History of Things of New Spain) underwent several stages in its elaboration. After receiving the order to write from his superior, Sahagún drafted the *minuta*, or outline, of the work. The first scheme of the history contained the *Primeros Memoriales* (First Reports): (1) gods, (2) heaven and hell, (3) lords, and (4) human matters. His working method resembled that used earlier by Andrés Olmos. His research procedures included the use of Indian paintings interpreted by native informants.[12] Sahagún drafted a questionnaire of points he wanted to investigate, and then between 1558 and 1560 in Tepepulco, he gathered materials. He devoted two years to consulting with a select group of 12 to 16 Indians on points he wanted to cover. A period of revision, writing, and more information gathering took a year and a half in Santiago de Tlatelolco, followed by three more years of reviewing and revising.

After the text was scrutinized by his Provincial Superior Fray Alonso de Escalona, Sahagún prepared a summary and sent it to Spain with a "Breve Compendio de los ritos idolátricos de Nueva España" (Brief Compendium of Rites of Idolatry in New Spain), which he sent to Pope Pius V. A Spanish translation was made from the original Nahuatl text at the order of Franciscan Commissary General Fray Rodrigo de Sequera. In his dedicatory letter to Sequera, Sahagún stated he wanted to compose a work of language, just as Ambrosius Calepinus did for Latin. After 1575, all of Sahagún's work was seized and sent to Spain. Mendieta believed the documents were sent to Spain at the instigation of a viceroy who was trying to help another chronicler doing research on the Indies (Esteve Barba, 184).

The original text was in Nahuatl. The Spanish text is, according to Sahagún, a "commented version," that is, the Nahuatl text is adjusted to the needs of Spanish readers. The history contains a general prologue and 12 books, most of which have their own prologues and some of which have appendices.[13] Two major divisions of the books are evident, the supernatural and the natural; book 6 serves as the nexus between the divine and the human orders.[14] Book 12 presents the conquest of New Spain.[15] Sahagún used Pliny and Bartolomé Anglico as models to structure the history.

Sahagún's purpose in writing the chronicle was principally religious. In the general prologue he cites a medical model as molding his manuscript. Just as the physician must know the cause of an illness before beginning the cure, so the missionary must know the idolatries and superstitions of the Indians to help convert them and eradicate their vices. To further the missionary activity, Sahagún also had a linguistic purpose, namely, to record all the words of the Nahuatl language. The text was planned for a three-column format, one column in Castilian, a second in Nahuatl, and a third consisting of notes.[16]

Franciscan Chroniclers Elsewhere

The Franciscans were very active also in Guatemala and Yucatan. Fray Diego de Landa was born in 1524 in Cifuentes.[17] He became a Franciscan at the age of 17 at the Convent of San Juan de los Reyes in Toledo and was one of the first Franciscans to begin evangelization in Yucatan. He ran into trouble with church authorities because he held an auto-da-fé (burning of heretics at the stake) to counteract the Indians' return to their former religion. Pardoned by the Council of the Indies, he returned to Yucatan as bishop of Mérida in 1573. Again, he demonstrated great insensitivity to Indian culture when he ordered the burning of a great number of books that he judged to contain superstition and falsehoods of the devil. Landa's chronicle *Relación de las cosas de Yucatán (Account of the Affairs in Yucatan)* is valuable for its information on Mayan antiquities.[18] The original was lost; the available text is a seventeenth-century reworking. Landa describes the geography of the Yucatan, and reports the history of the Spanish discovery and conquest of the region. The most valuable part deals with the customs of the Mayas, their history, hieroglyphic writing, and calendar. Landa had native informants, chiefly Nachi Cocom and Gaspar Antonio Chi. (Another Franciscan in Yucatan and Guatemala, Fray Alonso Ponce, was discussed in chapter 4 of this volume for his voyage chronicle.)

Fray Pedro de Aguado was among the Franciscans who worked in Nueva Granada (Colombia) and Venezuela, arriving there in 1561 and proceeding to engage in mass conversions of the Indians. He became guardian in the convent of Santa Fe and eventually provincial of the Franciscan order. Aguado's history, the *Recopilación historial* (Historical Compendium), is a continuation of a chronicle begun by Fray Antonio Medrano, who died on Jiménez Quesada's expedition to El Dorado. Fray Pedro used as a source Francisco Vázquez's manuscript *Jornada de Omagra y Dorado* (The Journey to Omagra and Dorado). The *Recopilación* consists of two long parts, the first being the *Historia de Santa Marta y nuevo reino de Granada* (History of Santa Marta and the New Kingdom of Granada) and the second, the *Historia de Venezuela* (History of Venezuela). The volumes give the history of each region, its geography, and the customs and religious practices of the inhabitants. Aguado favors the use of force in subjugating the Indians. Considerable space is devoted to the military and exploratory expeditions of Jiménez de Quesada, Federman, Ursúa, Lope de Aguirre, and others.[19]

Fray Esteban Asensio came to Nueva Granada in the same expedition that brought Pedro de Aguado to the Indies. His superiors ordered him to write a brief history of his order in Nueva Granada.[20] The *Historia memorial de la fundación de la Provincia de Santa Fe del Nuevo Reino* (Memorial History of the Founding of the Province of Santa Fe of the New Kingdom), covering the period from 1550 to 1585, was not completed. The history mainly treats the accomplishments of his order in the region. Like many friar-chroniclers, Asensio covers ethnographic information – the diversity of peoples and their languages and religions.

Las Casas and the Dominican Chroniclers

The Dominicans arrived in New Spain in 1526, two years after the Franciscans. Bartolomé de las Casas (1474-1566) is the outstanding chronicler of the Dominican order.[21] Las Casas's historical works are essentially three: the *Historia de las Indias* (*History of the Indies*), the *Brevísima relación de la destrucción de las Indias* (*The Devastation of the Indies: A Brief Account*), and the *Apologética historia* (Apologetical History). (The *History of the Indies* was discussed in chapter 5.) *The Devastation of the Indies* is frequently called a polemical rather than a historical work, but it will be treated here because it offers a chronicle of the destruction of the Indies and follows the events in both geographical and chronological order.[22]

Las Casas had already touched on the *Devastation*'s topic while preparing the *History of the Indies*. André Saint-Lu places the *Devastation* in the context of the Dominican's writings during the 1540s intended to call attention to abuses committed against the Indians and to suggest remedies (26). Las Casas had prepared a primitive text of the work in 1542, added some paragraphs in 1546 to denounce noncompliance with the New Laws of 1542 in Peru, and, as the bishop of Chiapas in Mexico, published the text in 1552. Las Casas signs himself Casas or Casaus in the work. Saint-Lu speculates that he added the name Casaus to differentiate himself from the Casas family of Andalusian merchants and *conversos*, or Jewish converts, yet Las Casas is also supposed to be of *converso* descent(40).

The title and other elements in the text indicate the discourse type of the *Devastation*. In the heading and body of the argument, the account is called an epitome, hence the "brevísima," or very brief of the title, and it is also a "relación," or report. Las Casas's polemic contains details derived from various sources of information, including the author as an eyewitness of atrocities, oral testimonies, and written statements by such personages as Columbus reporting on Hispaniola, Fray Francisco de San Román on the mainland, and Fray Marcos de Niza on Peru, as well as documents from the Archives of the Indies in Seville. Fray Marcos de Niza's account of atrocities committed in Peru, reading like a legal deposition, appears to be incorporated wholesale into Las Casas's narrative. To further strengthen the authority of Fray Marcos's report, Las Casas claims it was undersigned by the Bishop of Mexico, Fray Juan de Zumárraga.

The *Devastation*'s structure consists of several parts: the argument, a prologue addressed to Prince Philip, 21 relatively short, unnumbered chapters or divisions, and a final section, added later, titled "A Piece of a Letter." In the argument, Las Casas points out that events in the Indies have evoked wonder in both observers and readers. Las Casas now adds to the category of wonder the negative, that is, the destruction of the Indies. Here wonder is fright, a kind of ecstasy in its own right. Las Casas, having first reported these events at Court, now commits them to writing. He attributes the destruction of the territory to the greed and ambition of the Spanish, causing their degeneration from men to beasts. The conquistadors and settlers are asking the king for a license to continue to commit their barbarous acts against the native peoples. The *Devastation*, Las Casas says, is a summary of what he wrote to Prince Philip in an attempt to get the prince to deny the request of the exploiters.

In the prologue addressed to Prince Philip, Las Casas portrays the king, according to Homeric metaphors, as father and shepherd, whose knowledge of evil is sufficient for its remedy. Las Casas will return to that idea at the end of the work, where in a reference to the New Laws of 1542, promulgated as a result of the emperor's knowledge, he laments the lack of compliance with them. In the prologue and throughout the body of the text, Las Casas calls the perpetrators tyrants, although he does not give the name of any tyrant. Yet, the Indian rulers are named. Las Casas does not name the Spanish perpetrators but says he knows their names and in some cases their relatives in Spain. Las Casas subverts the usual discourse recording services to a record of abuses. It is a way to avoid giving glory to those men, by not mentioning them. They would be mentioned in others' chronicles perhaps in glorious terms. Las Casas writes from a concern for the salvation of the Indians and to prevent the destruction of Spain, which he believes will follow as a divine punishment. If Las Casas were to remain silent, he reasons, he would be guilty of the loss of souls and bodies. To facilitate the king's reading, Las Casas will write about only a few out of the innumerable cases of atrocities.

The plot running through the 21 divisions is the account of the expeditions, invasions, and conquests by the Spaniards in the Indies in a half-century, starting in 1492 with the discovery followed immediately in 1493 by the beginning of settlements. Las Casas finds that the constant increase of atrocities and cruelties by Spaniards, repeated in all the lands of the Indies, is a rule or principle running through the events. He refers to the rule every so often and, essentially, it structures his narrative. The first chapter, or division, presents an overview of the situation in the Indies by way of introduction. The 21 divisions are arranged geographically and chronologically according to the order of the Spanish conquest of territories in the Indies, progressing from the Caribbean to Central America, to New Spain and Guatemala, to South America, Santa Marta, Cartagena, and Venezuela, back north to Florida, then once again to South America to Río de la Plata, Peru, and the Nuevo Reino de Granada. Occasionally, there exists a discrepancy in the amount of space allotted to individual territories.

Las Casas describes the Indians from several perspectives. Politically, they are simple, guileless, obedient, and faithful to their own lords and then to the Christians; morally, they are humble, peaceful, and patient; physically, they are not too strong, but they are sensitive, which Las Casas relates to their good moral qualities. Regarding the natives' customs, Las Casas compares their life to the desert fathers' asceticism, holding no possessions and having simple food, clothing, and bedding. The Indians are intelligent, capable of conversion to the Christian religion, and anxious to learn more once they hear of the faith. Essentially, the Indians are compared with tame sheep, while the Spaniards, on the other hand, are likened to cruel wolves, tigers, and lions. Saint-Lu indicates that the sheep-wolf image is a reversal of the gospel commission for disciples to go as lambs among wolves (33). Later in the chronicle, Las Casas transforms the image of the Indians into dogs and beasts when it comes to the Spaniards' being interested in propagating Christianity among them.

The word "destrucción" in the title refers solely to the destruction of the people of the Indies and, by implication, their cultures, but not to the fauna and flora. Destruction is the opposite of the theme of pacification, usually propagated in other chronicles. The theme of destruction, according to Saint-Lu, enjoys an ancestry going back to medieval Spanish historiography, which viewed the Muslim invasion as a destruction of Spain (39). The threat of divine punishment for Spain is a common theme in the narrative. Occasionally, Las Casas records cases of divine justice punishing the Spaniards, for example, a ship with Indians bound as slaves sinks with the Spaniards aboard and internecine fighting breaks out among Spaniards, particularly in Peru. The Spanish degenerate from men to beasts. Their actions are captured in strong verbs: "despoblar," "matando," "robar," "destruyéndolas y despedazándolas" (depopulate, kill, rob, destroy, tear to pieces). Atrocities are committed against individuals, groups, and whole populations of towns, as in the case of Cholula and Tepeaca.[23] Desire for tribute, slavery and forced labor are the motivations for the destruction.

Justification of reprisals by the Indians appears at times as a theme. When the natives gradually realized that the Spaniards did not come from heaven, they began to fight back. Las Casas claims that the Indians have just cause to fight. Some Indians reject Christianity because of the Spaniards' bad examples. One Indian ruler thought the Spanish god was gold. At the end of the half century there is no more knowledge of the faith in the Indies than in 1492, with the possible exception of New Spain.

The tendency toward hyperbole is characteristic of the *Devastation*'s style. At the end of the narrative, Las Casas adamantly denies he has exaggerated. The speeches of the Indians are vehicles for their reproaches to Spaniards. Ironic formulas, such as the sarcastic "este piadoso capitán" ("this pious captain") occur with frequency. Las Casas leaves the narrative open ended; he can continue it when he hears news of further evils. The author will continue his defense of the Indians in his next work, the *Apologética historia* (Apologetical History), which is more theoretical than the polemical *Devastation*.

The *Apologética historia* is, according to Anthony Pagden, Las Casas's "massive essay in Amerindian ethnology."[24] The work is both natural and moral history, but overwhelmingly ethnographical. Even the natural history serves ethnographic ends, which Las Casas uses in his argument for the Indians' rationality. The argumentative purpose explains the meaning of the word apologetical in the title. The apologetical history can be traced to two early works of Las Casas: the *Del bien y favor de los indios* (Concerning the Good and the Fa-

vor of the Indians), in turn, derived from Las Casas's first book, the
De Unico Vocationis Modo (The Only Way).[25] The *Apologia* was related to the disputation at Valladolid on behalf of the Indians' humanity and reasonableness. Originally intended as part of the
History of the Indies, it proved too extensive, so it was separated.
Las Casas stated in book 1, chapter 67, of the *History* that he originally intended to include in it a natural history and ethnography section. But because the material was so extensive, Las Casas decided to
separate the natural and moral portions from the *History*.

Indications are that the *Apologética historia* was completed
after 1551. Anthony Pagden and Edmundo O'Gorman believe that it
did not have a direct role in the sessions at Valladolid. From its tone,
method, and length, Pagden concludes the history was intended for
a larger audience than the authorities at Valladolid (122). Las Casas's
sources include his knowledge of Indian languages. There are questions about that knowledge, however. His 40 years of experience in
the Indies involved traveling extensively in the Caribbean, Mexico,
and Central America, but not to Peru. Reports from missionaries who
knew Indian languages and had investigated their cultures supplied
Las Casas with valuable information. Las Casas intended to prove in
the apologetical history that the Indians were rational beings capable
of civilized government. His reliance on Aristotle as authority is con-
sonant with the approach of scholastic philosophy and his opponents, who also used Aristotle in their arguments. Las Casas
employed the scriptures and Church Fathers to argue his case.

The *Apologética historia* is structured into an argument, or
preamble, 267 chapters, and an epilogue. Las Casas writes the argument in the third person. He states that the Indians have been slan-
dered to the effect that they lack reason and therefore cannot govern
themselves in an ordered republic. The proponents of the calumny
mistook the Indians' good qualities as signs of lack of reason. Las
Casas wants to demolish that calumny by demonstrating that the
Indians are capable of governing themselves according to the norms
of civilized society. To demonstrate the Indian's rational capacity,
Las Casas considers three elements: a description of the physical
environment, organic considerations, and the historical aspect.

In the section on the physical environment, natural history is
examined. Essentially, it is an examination of one island, Hispaniola,
from which Las Casas extrapolates, claiming for most of the Indies

the characteristics of Hispaniola. He proceeds by making four turns around the island, examining its various provinces. Natural resources are considered. Las Casas's comparative method is evident early on in the work. In a comparison of Hispaniola with islands in the Old World, namely, England, Sicily, and Crete, Hispaniola is judged to have a natural superiority.

In his consideration of the organic aspect, he studies the essential natural causes disposing human beings for intelligence. The six essential causes are (1) the influence of the heavens; (2) the disposition and quality of the regions; (3) the composition of the members and organs of sense; (4) the clement and tranquil nature of the weather; (5) the age of the parents (younger parents being thought more suitable to conceiving and raising children); and (6) the healthfulness of the food supply. The six causes fall into a few categories: the physical environment with the influence of the heavens, the geography of the region, the weather, and the food supply. The remaining category bears on the physical and genetic makeup of the Indians: the composition of the body and the senses and the age of their parents. Las Casas devotes individual chapters to a discussion of each of the six essential causes, concluding that the six essentials are present in the environment and body of the Indian, so the Indian possesses intelligence and is disposed to receive a noble soul.

To demonstrate the Indians' rational capacity from the historical aspect, that is, through an examination of their cultures, Las Casas demonstrates that they are prudent; if they are prudent, they must have rationality, because prudence requires reason. Las Casas employs Aristotle's tripartite division of prudence: monastic, or rational government of oneself; domestic, or of the family; and political, or of the society. Under political prudence, Las Casas reviews the Indians' social life and compares it with that of the nations of the Old World. According to Aristotle, a temporally perfect society must have six categories of citizens: (1) farmers, (2) artisans, (3) warriors, 4) tradespeople, (5) priests, and (6) judges and governors. If the Indians show evidence of possessing these six categories, then it will prove that they are rational. He then examines Indian societies in terms of each of the six classes to conclude that all people, no matter how primitive their society, can be introduced to a political life by peaceful means. Las Casas defends the equality of the human race.

Cases of people lacking in reason, the so-called monsters, are the exception and are mistakes of nature.

Of particular interest are his ideas on the categories of priest and judge, that is, religion and government. Under the category of priests, Las Casas presents a wide-ranging examination of religion in general and then discusses the Indians' religions in terms of gods, temples, ministers, and cult. Throughout this section, Las Casas does a comparative study comparing the religions of the Indians with those of ancient Greece and Rome. Knowledge of the true God is natural to people, but idolatry results when God's grace is not present. Idolatry itself is a natural but misdirected expression of human religiosity. When the devils intervene, idolatry, false portents, and deceitful prodigies occur.

The ancients of the Old World, in Las Casas's opinion, were more idolatrous than the American Indians. The Indians committed fewer errors, were more reasonable in their choice of gods, and were easier to convert to the Christian faith than other peoples have been. It is natural to make offerings and sacrifices to God. People should offer what they most esteem. Human sacrifice, therefore, is a very ancient and almost universal practice, in accord with which the inhabitants of New Spain are the most religious. With what seems to modern people a strange kind of logic, Las Casas concludes that societies that offered human sacrifices presented the best they had to their gods. This shows that they acted according to natural reason and with more prudence than peoples who did not offer such sacrifices. Las Casas views the Indians of New Spain as superior to the Greeks and Romans in the matter of sacrifice.

The fact that Indian societies exist is proof that they had judges and governors with legitimate governments to maintain and perpetuate their societies. The Indians' governments were directed to the common good. The governments were not tyrannical but beneficial. Las Casas views them in a highly optimistic manner: they treated their subjects as a father does his son. This chronicler condemns cannibalism but exculpates the Indians somewhat by claiming that the practice arose accidentally and that many ancient peoples of the Old World indulged in cannibalism.

Fray Diego Durán was a native of Seville, born around 1537. Unlike most missionaries, Durán came to New Spain when he was seven or eight years of age. When he was older and had been ordained a priest, he served in several towns. He wrote his history between 1570 and 1581.[26] Durán's history, *Historia de las Indias de la Nueva España* (History of the Indies of New Spain), consisting of 101 chapters, has an ancient calendar and pen drawings. It presents the social and political history of the Aztecs including their dances, feasts, and songs.

Esteve Barba considers Durán's work the most original in that he did not use Spanish sources (198). He used native sources – codices and the Indians' oral testimony. His own observation of indigenous practices plays an important role in his writing. Durán was looking in the native culture for carry-overs of paganism into the Christian practices of the newly baptized. He had the advantage of observing native culture within a few years after the conquest. He saw two powers in opposition – God and the devil – in the history of the Indians. With a providentialist view of history, Durán links Indian customs to Hebrew practices. He accepts the belief, circulating in those days, that Saint Thomas preached the gospel in the Indies and equates St. Thomas with Quetzalcóatl.

Religious chronicles were written by men officially associated with the church, usually in the role of missionary. They were participants in the so-called spiritual conquest of America. Like the secular chroniclers, they often wrote out of obedience to their superiors, to record the conversion of the Indians, to explain to Europeans the native civilizations they encountered, and, above all, to advance the work of evangelization by presenting valuable information on the Indians' history, languages, and customs. Sometimes the missionaries' interest in Indian culture was to eradicate what they considered idolatry. Their sources varied from their own experience and study of native culture to information from native informants, other religious observers, and conquistadors. The friars used a variety of discourse types – history, the record of services in the form of the *relación*, and the memorial.

Among the corps of works by missionary chroniclers, Motolinía's *History* is a valuable source of information on the Indians' pre-Columbian history and culture. It relies directly on Indian sources, a practice not followed by Mendieta, who is typical of chroniclers who borrowed from other historians. In comparison with other chronicles, secular or religious, Sahagún's multivolume work is commendable for its conscientious elaboration of history based on an early anthropological approach and for its dual-language format in Nahuatl and Castilian, although the Castilian is not a direct translation of the Nahuatl text. The works of Bartolomé de las Casas illustrate the significant use of the chronicle in the defense of the Indian against abuses. *The Devastation of the Indies* is particularly readable for its brevity, narrative style, and the shocking details it provides. His *Apologética historia,* on the other hand, despite its wealth of ethnographic information, makes at times for heavy reading. Several minor ecclesiastical chronicles offer varying glimpses of Indian life, highlighting the Spaniards' ever-widening search for the unattainable, symbolized in El Dorado.

Chapter Seven

Summary and Conclusions

The Spanish chronicles of the Indies of the sixteenth century constitute both literature and history and belong jointly to Spain and to Spanish America. The chronicles are not a separate and distinct genre so much as a discourse type that embraces several subtypes. The chronicle's medieval origins appear among the clergy, with Eusebius of Caesarea (ca. 260-340) being the first model. Medieval chronicles treated the creation of world, historical events through various ages, astronomy, and natural phenomena. Chronicles in Spain date from the eighth century, being cultivated by both Christians and Moors writing in Latin and Arabic. The official chronicler came on the scene in the fourteenth century, or perhaps a little earlier, with the most famous being associated with King Alfonso X "el Sabio" (the Wise). At this stage there was a mutual dependence between king and chronicler.

The cultivation of the chronicle in sixteenth-century Spain was intense. Some authors adhered to the rhetorical rules of humanists, such as Juan Luis Vives, and others incorporated the techniques of other discourses. The typical chronicler of the Indies began as an individual involved in the great adventures and tragedies of the discovery and conquest. Soon the old codependency of chronicler and king reappeared in the appointment of official chroniclers of the Indies. Development of the chronicle of the Indies parallels and is marked by the historical events the chronicles record. The same discourse types appear under the different groups, but they may change and evolve according to the nature of the enterprise they chronicle.

The beginnings of the chronicles of the Indies coincide with the so-called discovery at the end of the fifteenth century and the beginning of the sixteenth. Essentially, they concern voyages that result in discoveries and further voyages, including mention of voyages around the world. The early chronicles of exploration were directed to monarchs and influential figures in government and business to

135

report on monies spent and to seek further financial backing. These early chronicles painted the first images of America with idyllic landscapes and described its flora, fauna, and natives. Columbus is the major chronicler of the first moment of the encounter. His son Ferdinand's biography of him rounds out the picture we have of Columbus, Admiral of the Ocean Sea. Minor chroniclers included men who accompanied Columbus on several of his voyages. Although Columbus wrote ship's diaries and Ferdinand a biography, the minor chroniclers and Columbus himself wrote lengthy official letters. The voyager Amerigo Vespucci used such letters to chronicle his exploits.

Chronicles on the conquest are grouped according to geographical regions; the two major areas are New Spain (Mexico) and Peru. Chronicles also record the conquest in other regions: Central America, Nueva Granada (Colombia), and Venezuela, Amazon Region, Chile, and Río de la Plata (Argentina and Uruguay). The predominant discourse types are letters, service records (*relaciones de servicios*), and history. The nature of the individual conquests and the intended audience for these writings – rulers, statesmen, churchmen, and private individuals – contributed to shaping the structure, style, and themes. Accounts of battles, descriptions of the individual conquistadors, and plans for developing the newly acquired lands also formed part of the repertoire of subjects. A significant phenomenon in this period was writing intended to correct someone else's "mistaken" version of events, as is the case of Bernal Díaz's history versus Gómara's.

A different vision of the New World occurs in the chronicles of exploration, wherein the image of America becomes more realistic and less idyllic. The conqueror now is often conquered, literally and metaphorically. Attempts are made, for example, in the discourse of Cabeza de Vaca, to draw some measure of success out of disaster. Discourse types employed are expanded to include diaries, travel journals, and more personal letters.

General chronicles, an attempt to present encyclopedic information on the Indies, were written by both clergy and laypersons. Chroniclers did not hesitate to correct the scientific views of the ancients, yet they still had to rely on their intellectual predecessors. The two main components of most general chronicles were natural history and moral history. Official chronicles were often encyclopedic in nature. Cosmographic treatises typically began with the biblical moment of creation and continued to the subjects and themes of the general chronicle.

The so-called spiritual conquest of America was recorded in a variety of chronicles classified according to geographical regions; within the regions, one finds subdivisions according to religious orders. The prominent orders are the Franciscans, Dominicans, Augustinians, and Jesuits. The ecclesiastical chroniclers make a greater attempt to understand the Indians as an aid to converting them and to extirpate remaining pagan beliefs and practices. Some such chroniclers produce texts on the culture of the Indians, cataloging their beliefs, rites, and ceremonies as well as their government, their languages, and aspects of their daily life. The image of the Indian varies in the different chronicles from primitive innocence to satanic evil. On occasion, the ecclesiastically authored chronicles are intended to defend the Indians against unscrupulous encomenderos, government officials, and even other missionaries.

The sixteenth-century Spanish chronicles of the Indies retain their value for today's reader. As historical-literary works belonging to both Spain and to Spanish America, they represent the unity of Hispanic culture and trace the origins and early development of Spanish American literature. They offer examples of the evolution of Spanish and Spanish American historiography. The chronicles are noteworthy as a discourse type that includes several subtypes that change and evolve according to the nature of the enterprises they chronicle. The use of traditional literary themes and devices are of special interest to the modern scholarly reader.

Many chronicles have the advantage of being eyewitness accounts of individuals involved in the great adventures and tragedies of discovery, conquest, and colonization. They trace the changing image of America in literature from the first impression of idyllic landscapes and innocent natives to one that is more realistic and even harsh. The chronicles served the valuable task of preserving certain aspects of Indian culture that would otherwise have vanished. They catalog Indian beliefs, rites, ceremonies, government, languages, and daily life.

Today, as humanity stands on the threshold of space exploration, as humankind envisions moving beyond the frontiers of the solar system into the unknown worlds of the galaxy, the chronicles of discovery, exploration, and conquest acquire new meaning. They serve to remind us not only of the human potential for heroism but of the capacity for villainy. They are testament to the incredible destruction wrought in the name of proselytization and colonization, both deliberately and unwittingly, as European bacteria were introduced into virgin ecosystems. The lessons to be learned from these 500-year-old texts transcend history to comprise cautionary exempla that should guide humanity's next great adventure.

Notes

Chapter One

1. Rolena Adorno, "Nuevas perspectivas en los estudios literarios coloniales hispanoamericanos," *Revista de Crítica Literaria Latinoamericana* 14 (1988):16-17; hereafter cited in text.

2. Walter Mignolo, "La lengua, la letra, el territorio o la crisis de los estudios coloniales," *Dispositio* 11, no. 28-29 (1986): 137-60; hereafter cited in text.

3. Enrique Anderson-Imbert, *Spanish American Literature: A History*, 2d ed. revised and updated by Elaine Malley (Detroit: Wayne State University Press, 1969). 1:16-17; hereafter cited in text.

4. José Juan Arrom, *Esquema generacional de las letras hispanoamericanas: Ensayo de un método*, 2d ed. (Bogotá: Instituto Caro y Cuervo, 1977), tackles the problem of ordering five centuries of Spanish American literature and seeks a chronological order based not on periods but generations. He rejects 1492 as the starting date for Spanish American literary generations and posits 1474-1503 as the first generation, calling it the generation of the discoverers. Around 1474 Spain was approaching political unification and Portugal was looking for markets beyond the peninsula.

5. Bellini published this history several years earlier in Italian; the Spanish version is considerably updated.

6. Roberto González Echevarría in his annual review of Spanish American literature in *Handbook of Latin American Studies* 42 (1980): 469 noted the redefinition of literature and its relation to culture taking place in Spanish American literary studies in general, while Daniel Reedy (*Handbook of Latin American Studies* 46 [1984]: 379) reported that studies in colonial Spanish American literature crossed generic and disciplinary boundaries and were rooted in the sociocultural and historical context.

7. In her review, Adorno outlines the formulation of new disciplinary practices (12).

8. Walter Mignolo, "Cartas, crónicas y relaciones del descubrimiento y la conquista," in *Historia de la literatura hispanoamericana, Vol. I: Epoca colonial*, ed. I. Madrigal (Madrid: Ediciones Cátedra, 1982), 59 (hereafter cited in text), and "El metatexto historiográfico y la historiografía indiana," *Modern Language Notes* 96 (1981): 380.

9. Roberto González Echevarría, "Humanismo, retórica y las crónicas de la conquista," *Isla a su vuelo fugitiva: ensayos críticos sobre literatura*

hispanoamericana (Madrid: Ediciones José Porrúa Turranzas, 1983), 16; hereafter cited in text.

10. See in Mignolo, "Cartas,," 103-10, a table of the historiographical treatises and histories of the Indies based on B. Sánchez's *Historia de la historiografía española: ensayo de un examen de conjunto*, 2 vols. (Madrid: Consejo Superior de Investigaciones Científicas, 1941, 1944). The table is a handy reference for the chronological development and relationship of treatises and histories of the Indies.

11. For information on the characteristics of the *relación*, see González Echevarría, "Humanismo, retórica y las crónicas de la conquista," 20-24. González Echevarría studied the model of the *relación* in *Lazarillo de Tormes* and the picaresque novel in "José Arrom, autor de la *Relación acerca de las antigüedades de los indios*: picaresca e historia," in *Relecturas: Estudios de Literatura Cubana* (Caracas: Monte Avila, 1976), 17-35.

12. Alfonso Reyes, *Letras de la Nueva España* (Mexico: Fondo de Cultura Económica, 1948), 46. Anderson-Imbert, following Reyes's lead, wrote of the chronicle and the theater as genres of medieval origin in *Spanish American Literature: A History*, 1: 27.

13. Margarita Zamora, "Historicity and Literariness: Problems in the Literary Criticism of Spanish American Colonial Texts," *Modern Language Notes* 102, no. 26 (1987): 334-46; hereafter cited in text.

14. González Echevarría dealt with this topic earlier in "José Arrom, autor de la 'Relación acerca de las antigüedades de los indios' (picaresca e historia)," *Relecturas* (Caracas: Monte Avila, 1976), 17-35.

15. Enrique Pupo-Walker, *La vocación literaria del pensamiento histórico en América* (Madrid: Gredos, 1982); Pupo-Walker sets forth his theory and approach in the introduction, pp. 9-13, and the first chapter, "Sobre el sesgo creativo de la historiografía americana: esbozos preliminares," pp. 15-95.

16. Stephanie Merrim, "Historia y escritura en las crónicas de Indias: ensayo de un método," *Explicación de textos literarios* 9, no. 2 (1981): 193-200. Merrim bases her investigation in part on the work of historians Hayden White, *Metahistory: The Historical Imagination in 19th Century Europe* (Baltimore and London: Johns Hopkins Press, 1973) and William Nelson, *Fact or Fiction: The Dilemma of the Renaissance Storyteller* (Cambridge, Mass.: Harvard University Press, 1973).

17. Adorno (14n4), singles out studies of discursive stratifications done by Roberto González Echevarría, "Humanism and Rhetoric in *Comentarios reales* and *El Carnero*," in *In Retrospect: Essays on Latin American Literature (In Memory of Willis Knapp Jones)*, ed. Elizabeth S. Rogers and Timothy J. Rogers (York, S.C.: Spanish Literature Publications Co., 1987), 8-23; *Literature among Discourses: The Spanish Golden Age*, ed. Wlad Godzich and Nicholas Spadaccini (Minneapolis: University of Minnesota Press,

1986); and Peter Hulme, *Colonial Encounters: Europe and the Native Caribbean, 1492-1797* (London and New York: Methuen, 1986).

18. Adorno (14-15), believes that Angel Rama's *La ciudad letrada* (Hanover, N.H.: Ediciones del Norte, 1984) is the most important work for colonial literary studies in the last 10 years because of its focus on the existence of different discourses and the variety of positions of the subject and the incorporation of subjects not explicitly mentioned in a text.

19. Beatriz Pastor, *Discursos narrativos de la conquista: mitificación y emergencia*, 2d rev. ed. (Hanover, N.H.: Ediciones del Norte, 1988); hereafter cited in text.

20. Pp. 32-33 of their "Introduction: Allegorizing the New World," in *1492-1992: Re/Discovering Colonial Writing*, eds. René Jara and Nicholas Spadaccini, Hispanic Isssues Vol. 4 (Minneapolis: The Prisma Institute, 1989).

21. Tzvetan Todorov, *The Conquest of America: The Question of the Other*, trans. Richard Howard (New York: Harper and Row, 1984), 3; hereafter cited in text. Todorov presents a typology of the other on pp. 185-201.

22. Rolena Adorno, "Literary Production and Suppression: Reading and Writing about Amerindians in Colonial Spanish America," *Dispositio* 11, no. 28-29(1986): 1-25; hereafter cited in text.

23. Rolena Adorno, *Guamán Poma: Writing and Resistance in Colonial Peru* (Austin: University of Texas Press, 1986), 3.

24. Rachel Phillips, "Marina, Malinche: Masks and Shadows," in *Women in Hispanic Literature: Icons and Fallen Idols*, ed. Beth Miller (Berkeley: University of California Press, 1983), 97-114.

25. Julie Greer Johnson, *Women in Colonial Spanish American Literature: Literary Images* (Westport, Conn.: Greenwood Press, 1983), 14.

26. James Lockhart and Enrique Otte, *Letters and People of the Spanish Indies: Sixteenth Century* (Cambridge, Cambridge University Press: 1976), 14-17.

27. Nati González Freire, "La mujer en la literatura de América Latina," *Cuadernos hispanoamericanos* 138, no. 414 (1984): 84-92; the article is a review of Latin American women writers.

28.Hernán Vidal, *Socio-historia de la literatura colonial hispanoamericana: tres lecturas orgánicas* (Minneapolis: Institute for the Study of Ideologies and Literature, 1985), 2-3.

29. Jean Franco, "La cultura hispanoamericana en la época colonial," in Madrigal, 35-53. In the same volume, Manuel Lucena Salmoral, "Hispanoamérica en la época colonial," 11-33, offers valuable background information on social, political, and economic issues. For a Spanish perspective on the issue, Carlos Blanco Aguinaga, Julio Rodríguez Puértolas, and Iris M. Zavala, *Historia social de la literatura española (en lengua castellana)* (Madrid: Editorial Castalia, 1979), 1:214-18, include mention of

the major historians of the Indies; more important is the chapter "El Impe-
rio y sus contradicciones," 197-247, for the peninsular background of the
events occurring in the New World. Antonio Antelo, "Literatura y sociedad
en la América Española del siglo XVI: notas para su estudio," *Thesaurus* 28
(1973): 279-330, places the New World's literary production of the sixteenth century in its social and essentially ideological context to demonstrate the presence of medieval and Renaissance elements.

30. Much of the information in this section on the sociohistorical context is taken from articles or chapters in *Cambridge History of Latin America* 1, 2 (1984), and Mark A. Burkholder and Lyman L. Johnson, *Colonial
Latin America* (New York: Oxford University Press, 1990). Specialized
studies corresponding to topics discussed in the text are cited where
appropriate in these notes.

31. Edmundo O'Gorman, *The Invention of America: An Inquiry into the
Historical Nature of the New World and the Meaning of Its History* (1961;
Westport, Conn.: Greenwood Press, 1972), 9. O'Gorman's thesis provoked
considerable debate, especially with Marcel Bataillon; see Marcel Bataillon,
"L'idée de la découverte de l'Amérique chez les espagnols du XVIe siècle
d'après un livre récent," *Bulletin Hispanique* 55 (1955): 23-55. See also
Wilcomb E. Washburn, " 'The Meaning of Discovery' in the Fifteenth and
Sixteenth Centuries," *Hispanic American Historical Review* 68 (1962): 1-
21. An interesting collection of papers on first impressions of the New
World is in Fredi Chiappelli, ed., *First Images of America: The Impact of the
New World on the Old*, 2 vols. (Berkeley: University of California Press,
1976). For the perspective of French Royal Cosmographer, André Thevet,
on Canada, Florida, and Mexico, see Roger Schlesinger and Arthur P. Sta-
bler, eds. and trans., *André Thevet's North America: A Sixteenth-Century
View*. (Kingston and Montreal: McGill-Queen's University Press, 1986).

32. Information on the pre-conquest state of the Indians comes from
Burkholder and Johnson, 3-15.

33. For indigenous religious texts of the Mexican region, see Miguel
León-Portilla, ed., *Native Mesoamerican Spirituality* (New York: Paulist
Press, 1980). Miguel León-Portilla, *Pre-Columbian Literatures of Mexico*,
trans. Grace Lobanov and the author (Norman: University of Oklahoma
Press, 1969), presents samples of myths, sacred hymns, lyric poetry, religious festivals, chronicles and history; especially of interest is the last chapter, "Native Chronicles of the Conquest."

34. For much of the information on Spanish conquest I have relied on
J. H. Elliott, "The Spanish Conquest and settlement of America," *Cambridge History of Latin America* 1 (1984): 149-206.For the intellectual
underpinnings of the conquest, see Silvio Zavala, *La filosofía en la
conquista de América*, 2d corr. ed. (Mexico: Fondo de Cultura Económica,
1972).

35. Richard Konetzke, *Descubridores y conquistadores de América: de Cristóbal Colón a Hernán Cortés*, trans. Celedonio Sevillano (Madrid: Editorial Gredos, 1968), is a general and somewhat limited study of the conquistadors. Lockhart and Otte's *Letters and People of the Spanish Indies: The Sixteenth Century* is valuable for English translations of passages from a variety of types of conquistador.

36. Information on the organization and administration of the New World is taken from Burkholder and Johnson, 70-80. C. H. Haring's *The Spanish Empire in America* (New York: Oxford University Press, 1947) is the classic treatment of Spain's political and commercial system in the New World. D. Ramos et al., *El Consejo de las Indias en el siglo XVI* (Valladolid: Universidad de Valladolid, 1970), is a collection of articles on the Council of the Indies, covering its foundation, policies under several presidents, policy on the organization of the church and missionaries in the Indies in the sixteenth century, and the spread of the Castilian language. J. H. Parry, *The Spanish Theory of Empire in the Sixteenth Century* (New York: Octagon Books, 1974), deals with the right of conquest, the *encomienda*, and aspects of imperial government in the colonies. An important collection of manuscripts documenting the government of New Spain, taxation, the Inquisition, and the New Laws of 1542 and their reception by the colonists is found in J. Benedict Warren, *Hans P. Krause Collection of Hispanic American Manuscripts: A Guide* (Washington: Library of Congress, 1974).

37. For information on the organization and workings of a typical *audiencia*, that of New Galicia (Venezuela), see J. H. Parry, *The Audiencia of New Galicia in the Sixteenth Century: A Study in Spanish Colonial Government* (Cambridge: Cambridge University Press, 1948).

38. For a discussion of the trauma of the conquest experienced by the Aztecs, the Incas, and to a lesser extent the Mayas, see Nathan Wachtel, "The Indian and the Spanish Conquest," *Cambridge History of Latin America* 1 (1984): 207-48; hereafter cited in text. For the conquest experience as well as many other aspects of Indian life in Peru, see by the same author *The Vision of the Vanquished: the Spanish Conquest of Peru through Indian Eyes, 1530-1570*, trans. Ben and Sian Reynolds (New York: Barnes and Noble, 1977). Indigenous texts that recount the Indians' reaction to the conquest are presented by Miguel León-Portilla in *Visión de los vencidos: relaciones de la conquista*, 6th ed. (Mexico: Universidad Nacional Autonoma de México, 1972); there is a more recent edition published by Historia 16 of Madrid as well as an English translation. See also León-Portilla's *El reverso de la conquista: relaciones aztecas, mayas e incas* (Mexico: Editorial J. Moritz, 1990). Gordon Brotherston, *Image of the New World: The American Continent Portrayed in Native Texts* (London: Thames and Hudson, 1979), is valuable for the native texts from the Aztecs and other Indians of Mexico, the Mayas, and the Incas; Brotherston also includes Eskimo and North American Indian documents. The author lets the

Indians speak for themselves through their own documents on topics such as invasion from the Old World, defense of traditional values and forms, ritual, calendars, cosmogony and the birth of man, hunting and planting, conquest, healer, singer, and scribe. The cross-cultural approach destroys the myth of a monolithic Indian culture. The book concentrates on texts in native script but also includes texts written in the Roman alphabet.

39. Nathan Wachtel, "The Indians and the Spanish Conquest," *Cambridge History of Latin America* 1 (1984): 207-8.

40. For information on population see Wachtel, 212, and Leslie Bethel's succinct presentation, "A Note on the Native American Population on the Eve of the European Invasions," *Cambridge History of Latin America* 1 (1984): 145-46. Some important studies on the native population are those by Sherburne F. Cook and Woodrow Borah, *The Aboriginal Population of Central Mexico on the Eve of the Spanish Conquest* (Berkeley: University of California Press, 1963), and *Essays in Population History: Mexico and the Caribbean*, 2 vols. (Berkeley: University of California Press, 1971-74); Nicolás Sánchez-Albornoz, "The Population of Colonial Spanish America," *Cambridge History of Latin America* 2 (1984): 3-35; and a book-length study by Sánchez-Albornoz, *The Population of Latin America: A History* (Berkeley: University of California Press, 1974). The classic works of Angel Rosenblat are outdated but still useful: *La población indígena y el mestizaje en América, I: La población indígena, 1492-1950* (vol. 1) and *El mestizaje y las castas coloniales* (vol. 2) (Buenos Aires, 1954).

41. For information on the controversy, see Burkholder and Johnson, 61-62, and J. H. Parry, "The Rights of Conquerors and Conquered," in his *The Age of Reconnaissance* (Cleveland: World Publishing Co., 1963), 303-19.

42. For a classic study of the controversy over the treatment of the Indians, see Lewis Hanke, *The Spanish Struggle for Justice in the Conquest of America* (Philadelphia: University of Pennsylvania Press, 1949). Julio Peñate, "De la naturaleza del salvaje a la naturaleza de la conquista: La figura del indio entre los españoles del siglo XVI," *Cahiers du monde hispanique et luso-brésilien* 43 (1984): 23-34, examines three aspects of the ideological debate on the Spanish presence in the New World: the legitimacy of the domination, the legality of violence against the natives, and – the area in which he is most interested – the nature of the Indians. Mercedes López-Baralt, "La iconografía política de América: el mito fundacional en las imágenes católica, protestante y nativa," *Nueva Revista de Filología Hispánica* 32, no. 2 (1983): 448-61, considers how sixteenth-century ingravings affected the European attitude toward the natives as innocents, vicious and victims; Guamán Poma de Ayala finally turns European iconography against the Spanish.

43. An older but important work on the encomienda system and its evolution is Lesley Byrd Simpson's *The Encomienda in New Spain: The Begin-

ning of Spanish Mexico (Berkeley and Los Angeles: University of California Press, 1950). Valuable for its study of slavery, including pre-Hispanic practices is William L. Sherman, *Forced Native Labor in Sixteenth-Century Central America* (Lincoln and London: University of Nebraska Press, 1979).

44. Wachtel cites his own study, "Pensée sauvage et acculturation: L'Éspace et le temps chez Felipe Guamán Poma de Ayala et l'Inca Garcilaso de la Vega," *Annales, Economies, Sociétés, Civilizations* (May-August 1971): 793-840.

45. Robert Ricard, *The Spiritual Conquest of Mexico: An Essay on the Apostolate and the Evangelizing Methods of the Mendicant Orders in New Spain: 1523-1572*, trans. Lesley Byrd Simpson (Berkeley and Los Angeles: University of California Press, 1966), is an earlier but still valuable study (the French original appeared in 1933) that focuses on the role of the mendicant orders in establishing the church in Mexico. John Leddy Phelan, *The Millenial Kingdom of the Franciscans in the New World*, 2d rev. ed. (Berkeley: University of California Press, 1970) is informative on the Franciscans' millenarian goals.

46. See Wachtel (228-29) on evangelization and attendant problems. A seventeenth-century source on the missionaries' struggle to destroy idolatry among the Indians is Pablo José de Arriaga, *The Extirpation of Idolatry in Peru*, trans. and ed. L. Clark Keating (Lexington: University of Kentucky Press, 1968). Pierre Duviols, *La lutte contre les religions autochtones dans le Pérou colonial: "l'extirpation de l'idolâtrie" entre 1532 et 1660* (Lima: Institut Français d'Études Andines; diffusion: Éditions Orphrys, Paris, 1971), documents the effort made by the church and the crown to suppress the native religions in Peru.

47. A work on religious syncretism and acculturation among the Mexican Indians is Jacques Lafaye's *Quetzalcoatl and Guadalupe: The Formation of Mexican National Consciousness*, foreward, Octavio Paz; trans. Benjamin Keen (Chicago: University of Chicago Press, 1976).

48. On alcoholism and its ravages in Mexico, see Serge Gruzinski, "La mère dévorante: alcoolisme, sexualité, et déculturation chez les Mexicas (1500-1550)," *Cahiers des Amériques Latines* (1979): 22-26.

49. See the article by Frederick P. Bowser, "Africans in Spanish American Colonial Society," *Cambridge History of Latin America* 2 (1984): 357-79. For a survey of scholarship on the topic of Africans in Spanish American colonial society, see Bowser's bibliographical review in the same volume, pp. 848-853. The source on the importation of slaves from Africa is Philip D. Curtin, *The Atlantic Slave Trade: A Census* (Madison, 1969).

50. On the moral problems associated with the slave trade see David Brion Davis, *The Problem of Slavery in Western Culture* (Ithaca, N.Y.: Cornell University Press, 1966).

51. Information on women in the colonies is taken from Asunción Lavrin, "Women in Spanish American Colonial Society," *Cambridge History of Latin America* 2 (1984): 321-55; hereafter cited in text.

52. Source of emigration figures is Peter Boyd-Bowman, "Patterns of Spanish Emigration to the Indies until 1600," *Hispanic American Historical Review* 56, no. 4 (1976): 580-604. On Indian women, see Elinor C. Burkett, "Indian Women and White Society: The Case of Sixteenth-Century Peru," in *Latin American Women: Historical Perspectives*, ed. Asunción Lavrin (Westport, Conn.: Greenwood Press, 1978), 101-28, and William L. Sherman, "Indian Women and the Spaniards," *Forced Native Labor in Sixteenth-Century Central America*, 304-26.

53. Information on cultural life is from Jacques Lafaye, "Literature and Intellectual Life in Colonial Spanish America," *Cambridge History of Latin America* 2 (1984): 663-704 (hereafter cited in text) and Burkholder and Johnson, 221-26; also consult Franco, "La cultura hispanoamericana en la época colonial," in Madrigal.

54. On the topic of utopias in the New World, or in Spanish America, see Stelio Cro, *Realidad y utopía en el descubrimiento y conquista de la América hispana (1492-1682)* (Troy, Mich.: International Book Publishers, 1983).

55. For a discussion of books and printing in colonial Latin America, see Lafaye, "Literature and Intellectual Life," 676-78. Julie Greer Johnson, *The Book in the Americas: The Role of Books and Printing in the Development of Culture and Society in Colonial Latin America*, with bibliographical supplement by Susan L. Newbury (Providence, R.I.: John Carter Brown Library, 1988), is the catalog of an exhibition on the history of the book as an artifact in colonial Latin America. It includes helpful introductory essays on books and printing in Spanish and Portuguese America. Irving A. Leonard's *Books of the Brave* (Cambridge, Mass.: Harvard University Press, 1949) is a classic, essentially about books of fiction in Spanish America in the sixteenth century; it explores the influence of books of chivalry on the conquistadors, the book trade in the New World, and the diffusion of Spanish literature in America.

Chapter Two

1. Among the lives of Columbus, a classic and highly regarded study is Samuel Eliot Morison, *Admiral of the Ocean Sea: A Life of Christopher Columbus*, 2 vols. (Boston: Little, Brown, 1942), and a one-volume abridgement of the work, *Christopher Columbus, Mariner* (Boston: Little, Brown, 1955). Salvador de Madariaga, *Christopher Columbus*, new ed. (London: Hollis and Carter, 1949) is a controversial account; more recently, Gianni Granzotto, *Christopher Columbus*, trans. Stephen Sartarelli (Garden City, N.Y.: Doubleday, 1985). The most recent and complete bibliography on Columbus, his life and writings arranged historically, is Foster

Provost, *Columbus: An Annotated Guide to Scholarship on his Life and Writings* (Providence and Detroit: Published by Omnigraphics for John Carter Brown Library, 1991). Updates on Columbiana issues appear periodically in *1992: A Columbus Newsletter* (Providence, R.I.), ed. Foster Provost. *The Christopher Columbus Encyclopedia*, ed. Silvio A. Bedini, 2 vols. (New York: Simon and Schuster, 1992).

2. On Columbus's language, see Ramón Menéndez Pidal, *La lengua de Cristóbal Colón* (Madrid: Austral, 1942); see pp. 28-32 for a summary of Menéndez Pidal's position. See the more recent study by Joaquín Arce, "Sobre la lengua y el origen de Colón: A vueltas con la tesis de Madariaga," *Arbor 96*, no. 375 (1977): 121-25.

3. Madariaga (54) held that Columbus was a Genoese of Spanish-Jewish origin. Simon Wiesenthal, *Sails of Hope*, trans. R. Winston and C. Winston (New York: Macmillan, 1973), deals with Columbus's Jewish ancestry.

4. On the development of Columbus's plan, see Juan Manzano Manzano, *Cristóbal Colón: siete años decisivos de su vida, 1485-1492* (Madrid: Cultura Hispánica, 1974); Paolo Emilio Taviani, *Cristóbal Colón: génesis del gran descubrimiento*, 2 vols. (Barcelona: Novara, 1977); and Juan Pérez de Tudela y Bueso, *Mirabilis in Altis: Estudio crítico sobre el origen y significado del proyecto descubridor de Cristóbal Colón* (Madrid: Instituto Gonzalo Fernández de Oviedo, C.S.I.C., 1983).

5. Varela gives several of the annotations that contain some autobiographical detail in Cristóbal Colón, *Textos y documentos completos: Relaciones de viajes, cartas y memoriales*, ed. Consuelo Varela (Madrid: Alianza, 1982), lvii.

6. Toscanelli's first letter to Columbus contains within it the Latin letter sent to the Canon Ferdinand Martins of Lisbon, who was interested in the westward route. The letter with a Spanish translation is given in J. Gil and C. Varela, *Cartas de particulares a Colón y relaciones coetáneas* (Madrid: Alianza, 1984), 130-40; the second letter, in Spanish, appears on pp. 140-41. See an English translation of the two Toscanelli letters in Samuel Eliot Morison, trans. and ed., *Journals and Other Documents* (New York: Heritage Press, 1963), 11-15; hereafter cited in text.

7. The Spanish edition of the *Diary* is in Varela, *Textos y documentos completos*. A Spanish edition with an English translation is available in *The "Diario" of Christopher Columbus's First Voyage to America 1492-1493*, transcribed, translated, notes, and concordance, Oliver Dunn and James E. Kelley, Jr. (Norman and London: University of Oklahoma Press, 1989). The complete works of Columbus were published for the four hundredth centenary in 1892 in *Raccolta colombiana*, 14 vols., 1892-96, ed. Cesare de Lollis.

There is a new edition, the *Nuova Raccolta*, 12 volumes of which were scheduled to begin appearing in English translation in 1992 as a joint endeavor of the Instituto Poligrafico e Zecca dello Stato, Rome, and the

Center for Medieval and Renaissance Studies at Ohio State University, under the direction of Fausto Fontecedro and Christian Zacher (according to *1992: A Columbus Newsletter*, no. 13 [Spring 1991]: 5). A serviceable English translation of a large number of Columbus's texts is Morison's *Journals and Other Documents*.

8. Bartolomé de las Casas, *Historia de las Indias*, 2d. ed. ed. Agustín Millares Caro, 3 vols (Mexico: Fonda de Cultura Economica, 1965). Aspects of the abstract are discussed in Margarita Zamora, " 'Todas son palabras formales del almirante': Las Casas y el *Diario* de Colón," *Hispanic Review* 57, no. 1 (1989): 25-41; Diane M. Bono, "The Gospel According to Bartolomé," *Hispanic Journal* 11, no. 1 (1990): 55-59; and Antonio Rumeu de Armas, "El 'Diario de a bordo' de Cristóbal Colón: el problema de la paternidad del extracto," *Revista de Indias* 36, no. 143-44 (1976): 7-17.

9. Rumeu questions attribution of the extract to Las Casas and concludes that Las Casas's role was that of copyist, corrector, and interpolator (14).

10. Peter Hulme finds two discourses functioning in the *Diary*: the discourse of Oriental civilization derived from Marco Polo and the discourse of savagery traced to Herodotus with gold as the element common in both discourses (21-22). For Gilberto Triviños Araneda, the material of the first voyage is the encounter with a military, economic and political paradise ("Los relatos Colombinos," *Ideologies and Literature: Journal of Hispanic and Lusophone Discourse Analysis* 3, no. 1 [Spring 1986-87]: 86-87).

11. On the contributions of the Pinzón family in the discoveries and explorations, see Juan Manzano Manzano and Ana María Manzano Fernández-Heredia, *Los Pinzones y el descubrimiento de América*, 3 vols. (Madrid: Instituto de Cooperación Iberoamericana, 1988).

12. In a note to the *Diary* entry for 18 February, where Columbus records the joy of the Portuguese at news of his discovery of the Indies, Las Casas says the news "[a]ppears fictitious." See Morison, 168n3. The topic of Columbus's vision has been treated in various ways. See Leonardo Olschki's "What Columbus Saw on Landing in the West Indies," *Proceedings of the American Philosophical Society* 84 no. 5 (1941): 633-59; Erwin Walter Palm's "España ante la realidad americana," *Cuadernos americanos* 38 no. 2 (1948): 135-67 (hereafter cited in text); Beatriz Pastor's *Discursos narrativos de la conquista: mitificación y emergencia*; and Mignolo's "Cartas," 61-62.

13. Beatriz Pastor, "Silence and Writing: The History of the Conquest," in *1492-1992: Re/Discovering Colonial Writing*, ed. René Jara and Nicholas Spadaccini (Minneapolis: Prisma Institute, 1989), 128, vol. 4 of *Hispanic Issues*.

14. For Columbus's "Letter to the Sovereigns on the First Voyage" the Spanish edition I use is Varela's *Textos y documentos completos*; the En-

glish translation is Morison's in *Journals*. Morison's is from the original Spanish, not the Latin, as is the case with most English translations.

15. In "The Form of Discovery: The Columbus Letter Announcing the Finding of America," *Revista canadiense de estudios hispánicos* 2, no. 2 (1978), S. R. Wilson points out that "Columbus 'finds' land; only later, in the third voyage, will he begin to use the term 'discover.' To find is a modest, unassuming, almost accidental, occurrence" (157).

16. English translation by Dr. Milton Anastos in Morison, *Journals*, 199-202.

17. Morison's *Journals* contains an English translation by Luisa Nordio from the Italian text published in De Lollis.

18. Gil in J. Gil and C. Varela, eds, *Cartas de particulares a Colón y relaciones coetáneas*, (Madrid: Alianza, 1984), 177.

19. Syllacio's letter, Latin text by DeLollis, in *Raccolta*. English translation by Milton Anastos in Morison, *Journals*, 229-45.

20. Dr. Diego Alvarez Chanca's letter to the Town Council of Seville, Spanish text in Gil and Varela, *Cartas particulares*, 155-76; intro. Varela, 152-55. English translation by Cecil Jane and Spanish text in *The Four Voyages of Columbus*, trans. and ed. Cecil Jane, 2 vols. bound as one (1930, 1933; New York: Dover Publications, 1988).

21. The manuscript of the Las Casas abstract is printed in De Lollis. A reduced version of the abstract is in Las Casas' *Historia de las Indias*, chapters 127-46 (1951, ed. 1, 482-500, ed. 2, 7-73). An English translation is in Morison, *Journals*, 259-83.

22. The letter is an extract made by Las Casas from the lost original. Text in De Lollis; also in Consuelo Varela, *Textos y documentos completos*, 204-23. An English translation along with Spanish text on opposite page is printed in Cecil Jane, trans. and ed., *The Four Voyages of Columbus*, 2 vols. bound as one (1930, 1933; New York: Dover Publications, 1988).

23. Letter to Doña Juana Torres. The Spanish text is in De Lollis and in Varela, *Textos y documentos completos*, 243-51. An English translation is in Morison, *Journals*, 289-98.

24. See Morison, *Journals*, 307.

25. The Italian title is *Copia de la lettera per Columbo mandata a li Serenissimi Re e Regina di Spagna: de le insule et luoghi per lui trovate* (in Morison's translation, *Journals*, 371: "Copy of the letter by Columbus sent to the Most Serene King and Queen of Spain, concerning the Islands and Places by him Discovered"). A Spanish version, corrected by consultation with the Italian translation, is in De Lollis, 175-205; also in Varela, *Textos y documentos completos*, 291-305.

26. Morison, *Journals*, 379, cites as a source for the passage about the keys Seneca in the *Medea*. Columbus believed Seneca was speaking of him.

27. The Italian edition was published in *Le Historie della vita e dei fatti di Cristoforo Colombo per D. Fernando Colombo suo figlio* in 2 vols., ed. Rinaldo Caddeo (Milan, 1930); a Spanish edition of the text is by Ramón Iglesia, *Vida del Almirante Don Cristóbal Colón*, ed. Ramón Iglesia (Mexico: Fondo de Cultura Económica, 1947); a useful English translation is Benjamin Keen's *The Life of the Admiral Christopher Columbus by His Son Ferdinand*, trans. Benjamin Keen (New Brunswick, N.J.: Rutgers University Press, 1959), which is hereafter cited in text as *Life of Columbus by His Son*. Today the authorship of Ferdinand is generally accepted; in the nineteenth century and in the first half of the twentieth, however, some scholars doubted the attribution. The French Americanist Henry Harrisse and the Argentine historian Rómulo D. Carbia suggested that the *Life of the Admiral* was written by or based on a lost work of Hernán Pérez de Oliva. But once Pérez's book was found and a comparison of the two texts made, Leo Olschki, "Hernán Pérez de Oliva's 'Ystoria de Colón'," *Hispanic American Historical Review* 23, no. 2 (1943): 165-96, demonstrated that the two are totally different works. Carbia also claimed that Las Casas had faked the *Life of the Admiral*. See Carbia's studies, *El problema del descubrimiento de América desde el punto de vista de la valoración de sus fuentes*, 26 Congreso Internacional de Americanistas, Sevilla, octubre de 1935, and *La nueva historia del descubrimiento de América* (Buenos Aires: CONI, 1936).

28. A Spanish version of Vespucci's letters is found in the handy volume A. Vespuccio, *Viajes y documentos completos* (Madrid: Akal, 1985).

Chapter Three

1. The classic work on the conquest of Mexico is William H. Prescott's *History of the Conquest of Mexico*, intro. Thomas Secombe, 2 vols. (1886; London: Dent, 1965).

2. Hernán Cortés, *Letters from Mexico*, trans. and ed. Anthony Pagden, intro. J. H. Elliott (New Haven and London: Yale University Press, 1986), xlv; hereafter cited in text.

3. *Cortés: The Life of the Conqueror by His Secretary Francisco López de Gómara*, trans. and ed. Lesley Byrd Simpson (Berkeley: University of California Press, 1964). Modern biographies of Cortés are Salvador Madariaga, *Hernán Cortés: Conqueror of Mexico*, 2d ed. (Chicago: Henry Regnery Co., 1955), and Maurice Collis, *Cortés and Moctezuma* (New York: Harcourt, Brace and Co., 1955).

4. An accessible Spanish edition of the letters is Hernán Cortés, *Cartas de relación*, ed. Manuel Alcalá, 14th ed. (Mexico: Editorial Porrúa, 1985); an excellent English edition is Hernán Cortés, *Letters from Mexico*, trans. and ed. Anthony Pagden. On writing as an obligation, see Mignolo, "Cartas," 59.

5. On Cortés's use of writing techniques to persuade, see Adrián Blázquez Garbajosa, "Las 'Cartas de Relación de la conquista de México':

política, psicología y literatura," *Bulletin Hispanique* 87, no. 1-2 (1985): 5-46.

6. Mignolo, "Cartas," 67, comments on the letters as *cartas* and *relación*. María del Rocío Oviedo y Pérez de Tudela calls the letters a diary because they follow a chronology; see her study, "Las Cartas de relación y el 'renacer' literario," *Revista de Indias* 44, no. 174 (1984): 533-39.

7. Cortés was conscious of rhetorical rules governing letter writing; see Mignolo, "Cartas," 67. Beatriz Pastor discusses Cortés's discourse in his letters in "Hernán Cortés: La ficcionalización de la conquista y la creación del modelo de conquistador," in her *Discursos narrativos*, 75-167.

8. On the lost first letter, see H. R. Wagner, "The Lost First Letter of Cortés," *Hispanic American Historical Review* 21 (1941): 669-72; on the substitute letter, see Julio Caillet-Bois, "La primera carta de relación de Hernán Cortés," *Revista de filología hispánica* 3 (1941): 50-54.

9. For details of testimonials to its existence, see Francisco Esteve Barba, *Historiografía indiana* (Madrid: Gredos, 1964) 137-39; hereafter cited in text. An idea of the content of the lost letter can be had from Gómara's summary of the lost letter printed in Wagner; Gómara had a copy and incorporated it in whole or in part in his *Historia de la conquista de México*.

10. "Cortés, Velázquez and Charles V," in Pagden, xx.

11. See Stephanie Merrim for a study of the discourse of the second letter, "Ariadne's Thread: Auto-Bio-Graphy, History, and Cortés's *Segunda Carta-relación*," *Dispositio* 11, no. 28-29 (1986): 57-83.

12. On Malinche-Marina, see Carlos Seco, "Doña Marina a través de los cronistas," in *Estudios cortesianos*, Instituto Gonzalo Fernández de Oviedo (Madrid: Consejo Superior de Investigaciones Científicas, 1948), 497-504.

13. A constant intention of Cortés was the settling of the conquered territories. See the origin and development of Cortés's policy in Richard Konetzke, "Hernán Cortés como poblador de la Nueva España," *Estudios cortesianos*, 341-81.

14. *Historia de la conquista de México*, ed. J. Gurriá Lacroix (Caracas: Biblioteca Ayacucho, 1979); for an English version see *Cortés: The Life of the Conqueror by His Secretary Francisco López de Gómara*, trans. and ed. Lesley Byrd Simpson (Berkeley: University of California Press, 1964).

15. Biographies of Bernal include Herbert Cerwin, *Bernal Díaz, Historian of the Conquest* (Norman, University of Oklahoma Press, 1963); Alberto María Carreño, *Bernal Díaz del Castillo, descubridor, conquistador y cronista de la Nueva España* (Mexico City: Ediciones Xochitl, 1946); Lesley B. Simpson, "Bernal Díaz del Castillo, encomendero," *Hispanic American Historical Review* 17 (1937): 100-106; and Henry R. Wagner, "Three Studies on the Same Subject," *Hispanic American Historical Review* 25 (1945): 153-211 – "Bernal Díaz del Castillo," 153-90, "The Family of Bernal Díaz

del Castillo," 191-98, and "Notes on Writings by and about Bernal Díaz del Castillo," 199-211.

16. Carmelo Sáenz de Santa María, ed., *Historia verdadera de la conquista de la Nueva España* (Madrid: Quinto Centenario, 1989), iii, found Bernal's oldest extant signature dated 1556 bearing the addition of del Castillo.

17. See Leonard's *The Books of the Brave* and Sáenz's *Historia de una historia: la Crónica de Bernal Díaz del Castillo* (Madrid: Consejo Superior de Investigaciones Científicas, 1984), the section on Bernal's library.

18. See José de Barbón, *Bernal Díaz del Castillo* (Buenos Aires: Centro Editor de América Latina, 1968), 18, for his brief discussion of first chapters of Bernal's history as a "memorial." See also Roberto González Echevarría, "Humanismo, retórica y las crónicas de la conquista," in his *Isla a su vuelo fugitiva: ensayos críticos sobre literatura hispanoamericana* (Madrid: José Porrúa Turanzas, 1983), 9-25, and Mignolo, "Cartas,," 82-83.

19. See Sáenz, *Historia de una historia*, 71.

20. Esteve Barba, *Historiografía indiana*, 160-66, discusses Cervantes de Salazar.

21. Francisco Cervantes de Salazar, *Life in the Imperial and Loyal City of Mexico in New Spain, and the Royal and Pontifical University of Mexico: As Described in the Dialogues for the Study of the Latin Language*, ed. Minnie Lee Barrett Shepard and Carlos Eduardo Castañeda (Austin: University of Texas Press, 1954).

22. Francisco Cervantes de Salazar, *Crónica de la Nueva España*, ed. Manuel Magallón, preliminary study and indices, Agustín Millares Carlo, Biblioteca de Autores Españoles, vols. 244-45 (Madrid: Ediciones Atlas, 1971).

23. Opinions as to its authorship seem divided between Calvete and Gómara. Ramón Iglesia, in *Cronistas e historiadores de la conquista de México: El ciclo de Hernán Cortés* (Mexico: El Colegio de Mexico, 1942), tries to prove that it belongs to Gómara.

24. Fray Francisco de Aguilar, *Relación breve de la conquista de la Nueva España*, ed. Jorge Gurría Lacroix, Serie de historiadores y cronistas de Indias 7 (Mexico: Universidad Nacional Autónoma de Mexico, 1980), 7; hereafter cited in text.

25. For information on Alonso de Aguilar, see Esteve Barba, *Historiografía indiana*, 149-52.

26. On de Tapia, see Esteve Barba, *Historiografía indiana*, 152.

27. Bernardino Vázquez de Tapia, *Relación de méritos y servicios del conquistador Bernardino Vázquez de Tapia: vecino y regidor de esta gran ciudad de Tenustitlán, México*, ed. Jorge Gurría Lacroix, Nueva Biblioteca Mexicana 34, 3d ed. (Mexico: Universidad Nacional Autónoma de México,

Dirección General de Publicaciones, 1973). Esteve Barba discusses Vázquez de Tapia on pp. 153-54.

28. See Gurría, p. 14, on Vázquez's use of legal language. He had experience as a public official.

29. An English translation is available in Anonymous Conqueror, *Narrative of Some Things of New Spain and of the Great City of Temistitan Mexico*, trans. Marshall H. Saville (Boston: Milford House, 1972). See Esteve Barba, 154-156, on the Anonymous Conquistador. Juan Bautista Ramussio published the Anonymous Conquistador's *Relatione di alcune cose della nuova Spagna e della gran città di Tenustitán, Messico, fatta per uno gentil'bomo del signor Fernando Cortese* (Account of Some Things of New Spain and the Great City of Tenochtitlán, Mexico, Done by a Gentleman of Sir Hernán Cortés).

30. Esteve Barba, 269. *Historiadores primitivos de Indias*, Biblioteca de Autores Españoles, vol. 22 (1946). For a study of Alvarado's life, see John Eoghan Kelly, *Pedro de Alvarado, Conquistador* (Princeton: Princeton University Press, 1932).

31. *Relación becha por Pedro de Alvarado a Hernán Cortés, en que se refieren las guerras y batallas para pacificar las provincias del antiguo Reino de Guathemala* (Mexico: Porrúa, 1954). Pedro de Alvarado, *An Account of the Conquest of Guatemala in 1524*, ed. Sedley J. Mackie, with facsimile of the Spanish original, 1525 (New York: Cortés Society, 1924; reprint, New York: Kraus Reprint, 1969).

32. On the search for El Dorado, see J. G. Cobo Borda, *Leyendo El Dorado: la otra imagen de Colombia*, Biblioteca del Nuevo Mundo 4 (Barcelona: Tusquets, 1986).

33. For further information on Jiménez de Quesada, consult Germán Arciniegas, *El caballero de El Dorado, vida del conquistador Jiménez de Quesada*, 2d ed. (Buenos Aires: Editorial Losada, 1950); an earlier English translation is available as *The Knight of El Dorado: The Tale of Don Gonzalo Jiménez de Quesada, and His Conquest of New Granada, Now Called Colombia*, trans. Mildred Adams (New York: Viking Press, 1942). Robert B. Cunningham Graham, *The Conquest of New Granada: Being the Life of Gonzalo Jiménez de Quesada* (New York: Cooper Square Publishers, 1967).

34. On the chronicles of Peru, see R. Porras Barrenechea, *Los cronistas del Perú (1528-1650)*, ed. F. Pease (Lima: Banco de Crédito, 1986). J. M. Oviedo, *La edad de oro: crónicas y testimonios de la conquista del Perú*. Biblioteca del Nuevo Mundo 3 (Barcelona: Tusquets, 1986) is a handsome volume anthologizing the Peruvian chronicles.

35. Raúl Porras Barrenechea, *Las relaciones primitivas de la conquista del Perú* in *Cuadernos de Historia del Perú*, no. 2 (Paris, 1937); cited in Esteve Barba, 646n509.

36. Pascual de Andagoya, *Narrative of the Proceedings of Pedrarias Dávila in the Provinces of Tierra Firme or Castilla del Oro, and of the Discovery of the South Sea and the Coasts of Peru and Nicaragua*, trans. and ed. Clements R. Markham (New York: Burt Franklin [1964]).

37. The letter is in Gonzalo Fernández de Oviedo's *Historia general y natural de las Indias*, part 3, book 46, chapter 15. The letter is also in Biblioteca de Autores Españoles, vol. 19, 494-99, as an appendix to the life of Francisco Pizarro. See also Clements R. Markham, *Reports on the Discovery of Peru*, trans. and ed. Clements R. Markham (New York: B. Franklin, 1964). An earlier life of the Pizarros is Hoffman Birney's *Brothers of Doom: The Story of the Pizarros of Peru* (New York: G. P. Putnmam's Sons, 1942).

38. Raúl Porras Barrenechea, *Las relaciones primitivas de la conquista del Perú*, 45-46; cited in Esteve Barba, 647n517. Porras Barrenechea's opinion is reported by Esteve Barba on his p. 393. See also, Alexander Pogo, ed. *The Anonymous "La Conquista del Perú,"* in *Proceedings of the American Academy of Art and Sciences*, vol. 64 (Boston, 1930). Also, Horacio H. Urteaga, *Los cronistas de la conquista*, Biblioteca de Cultura Peruana, primera serie, no. 2 (Paris: Desclée de Brouwer, 1938), 307-28. Joseph H. Sinclair, a facsimile edition of the chronicle with English translation, New York Public Library, 1929.

39. Francisco de Xerex, *Verdadera relación de la conquista del Perú*, ed. Concepción Bravo (Madrid: Historia 16, 1985). Facsimile of the 1534 Seville edition, *La conquista del Perú* (Madrid: El Crotalón, 1983). Clements R. Markham, *Reports on the Discovery of Peru*, trans. and ed. Clements R. Markham (New York: Burt Franklin [1970]), contains English versions of Francisco de Xeres, Miguel de Astete, Hernando Pizarro, and Pedro Sancho.

40. Pedro Sancho de Hoz, *An Account of the Conquest of Peru*, trans. Philip Ainsworth Means (New York: Cortes Society, 1917; reprint, New York: Kraus Reprint Co., 1969).

41. Pizarro's *relación* is in Fernández de Navarrete's collection, *Colección de documentos inéditos para la historia de España*, vol. 5. There is an English translation by Philip A. Means.

42. Trujillo's *relación* was published by Raúl Porras Barrenechea in 1948.

43. Cieza de León is discussed by Esteve Barba, 413-20, under heading "Los historiadores de las guerras civiles"; for a complete discussion of Cieza and with an emphasis on the literary aspects of the *Crónica*, see Pedro León, *Algunas observaciones sobre Pedro Cieza de León y la Crónica del Perú* (Madrid: Gredos, 1973).

44. Pedro Cieza de León, *La Crónica del Perú*. ed. Carmelo Sanz de Santa María, 3 vols. (Madrid: Consejo Superior de Investigaciones Científicas, 1984).

45. The Third Part, The Discovery and Conquest of Peru, is in Sanz, vol. 1, pp. 225-368. For the English version, see *The Incas of Pedro Cieza de León*, trans. Harriet de Onís. Ed. Victor Wolfgang von Hagen (Norman, Okla.: University of Oklahoma Press, 1959).

46. Esteve Barba, 648n535: *Relación de los servicios en Indias de don Juan Ruiz de Arce, conquistador del Perú* in *Boletín de la Academia de la Historia*, vol. 102 (Madrid, 1933), 327-84.

47. *Libro de la vida y costumbres de D. Alonso Henríquez de Guzmán*, ed. Hayward Keniston, Biblioteca de Autores Españoles, vol. 126 (Madrid: Atlas, 1960). An English version is titled *The Life and Acts of Don Alonzo Enríquez de Guzmán*, trans. Clements R. Markham (1862; New York: Burt Franklin, 1970). On the picaresque qualities of the chronicle, see F. A. Kirkpatrick, "The First Picaresque Novel," *Bulletin of Spanish Studies* 5 (1928): 376-78, and Lesley B. Simpson, "A Precursor of the Picaresque Novel in Spain," *Hispania* 27 (1934): 53-63.

48. Spanish text in Biblioteca de Autores Españoles, vol. 26, 459-547. Studies on Zárate's chronicle include Dorothy MacMahon, "Variations in the Text of Zárate's 'Historia del descubrimiento y conquista del Perú,' " *Hispanic American Historical Review* 33 (1953): 572-86, and Dorothy MacMahon, *Some Observations on the Spanish and Foreign Editions of Zárate's 'Historia del descubrimiento y conquista del Perú'* (Publicaciones de la Sociedad Bibliográfica de América, 1955).

49. P. 5 of her biography of Valdivia, *Pedro de Valdivia: fundador de Chile* (Madrid: Ediciones Anaya, 1988).

50. For the text of the *Cartas*, or letters, see *Crónicas del Reino de Chile*, ed. Francisco Esteve Barba, Biblioteca de Autores Españoles, vol. 131 (Madrid: Ediciones Atlas, 1960), 1-74. See also Robert B. Cunninghan Graham, *Pedro de Valdivia, conquistador de Chile. Su biografía y espistolario* (Buenos Aires: Inter-Americana, 1943), and Rodolfo Oroz, "Sobre el estilo de las cartas de Pedro de Valdivia, conquistador de Chile," in *Studia Philologica: homenaje ofrecido a Dámaso Alonso* (Madrid: Editorial Gredos, 1961) 2:537-40; Oroz hereafter cited in text.

51. In Esteve Barba, *Crónicas del Reino de Chile*.

52. Text in Esteve Barba, *Crónicas del Reino de Chile*.

53. An edition of the German original is Ulrich Schmidel, *Warhaftige Historien einer wunderbaren Schiffart* (Graz, Austria: Akademische Druck-u. Verlagsanstalt, 1962). The English translation is *The Conquest of the River Plate (1535-1555)*, trans. for Hakluyt Society, notes by Luis L. Domínguez (1891; New York: B. Franklin, 1964); hereafter cited in text. The Spanish edition is Ulrico Schmidl, *Derrotero y viaje al Río de la Plata y Paraguay*, ed. Roberto Oviedo (Asunción: Biblioteca Paraguaya, Ediciones NAPA, 1983).

54. See Dominguez's introduction for information on Schmidel, whom he calls Schmidt.

Chapter Four

1. Esteve Barba discusses this *relación* on pp. 237-238 of his *Historiografía indiana*. Text is in Joaquín García Icazbalceta, *Colección de Documentos para la Historia de México*, vol. 1, facsimile ed. (1858; Mexico: Editorial Poviña, 1980).

2. Morris Bishop, *The Odyssey of Cabeza de Vaca* (New York: Century Co., 1933), is an older biography and contains factual errors, but it is serviceable.

3. Alvar Núñez Cabeza de Vaca, *Naufragios*, ed. Trinidad Barrera (Madrid: Alianza Editorial, 1985), 24; hereafter cited in text. Barrera gives this bibliographical reference: *Documentos inéditos del Archivo de Indias*, vol. 14 (Madrid, 1870), 265-79.

4. Cyclone Covey, *Cabeza de Vaca's Adventures in the Unknown Interior of America* (Albuquerque: University of New Mexico Press, 1983); hereafter cited in text.

5. Pedro Lastra, "Espacios de Alvar Núñez: las transformaciones de una escritura," *Cuadernos americanos* 254, no. 3 (1984): 155; hereafter cited in text.

6. Luisa Pranzetti, "Il naufragio come metafora," *Letteratura d'America* 1, no. 1 (Winter 1980): 5-28.

7. See Pastor, *Discursos narrativos*, 212-44.

8. The title of the two volumes of Cabeza de Vaca's works is *Relación de los Naufragios y Comentarios de Alvar Núñez Cabeza de Vaca*, ed. M. Serrano y Sanz, vols. 5 and 6, Colección de Libros y Documentos referentes a la Historia de América (Madrid: Librería General de Victoriano Suárez, 1906). An English translation, *The Commentaries of Alvar Núñez Cabeza de Vaca by Pero Hernández*, was published in *The Conquest of the River Plate (1535-1555)*, notes and intro. Luis L. Dominguez (New York: Burt Franklin, n.d.).

9. See Pastor, *Discursos narrativos*, 201-3, on De Soto's search for the fountain of youth.

10. Esteve Barba, *Historiografía indiana*, 628n327. There is an English translation "The Narrative of the Expedition of Hernando de Soto by the Gentleman of Elvas," ed. Theodore H. Lewis, published in *Spanish Explorers in the Southern United States 1528-1543* (New York: Charles Scribner's Sons, 1907), 133-272; intro. T. Hayes Lewis, 129-32.

11. English translation, *Relation of the Conquest of Florida*, trans. Buckingham Smith in *Narratives of the Career of Hernando de Soto*, ed. Edward Gaylord Bourne, vol. 2 (New York: Allerton Book Co., 1922) 3-40.

12. Ranjel's text is on pp. 46-149 of vol. 2 of *Narratives of the Career of Hernando de Soto in the Conquest of Florida, as Told by a Knight of Elvas and in a Relation by Luys Hernandez de Biedma, Factor of the Expedition*, trans. Buckingham Smith, ed. and intro. Edward Gaylord Bourne, 2 vols. (New York: Allerton Book Co., 1904).

13. The letters of Pedro Menéndez de Avilés are in Bibliotheca indiana, Colección de textos anotados, directed by Manuel Ballesteros Gaibrois, *Viajes por Norteamérica* (Madrid 1958), 907-43; cited in Esteve Barba, *Historiografía indiana*, 618n331 and 619n337.

14. Germán Vázquez, *Las siete ciudades de Cíbola: los españoles en el sur de los Estados Unidos* (Madrid: Ediciones SM, 1990), 37.

15. An English version titled "Report of Fray Marcos de Niza," appears in George P. Hammond and Agapito Rey, eds., *Narratives of the Coronado Expedition 1540-1542* (1940; New York: AMS Press, 1977), 63-82.

16. See Esteve Barba, *Historiografía indiana*, 241-242, for details of Castañeda's life and chronicle.

17. Frederick W. Hodge, *Spanish Explorers in the Southern United States 1528-1543*. Esteve Barba refers to *Narratives of the Coronado Expedition*, ed. George P. Hammond and Agapito Rey (Albuquerque: University of New Mexico Press, 1940).

18. In Bolton, *Spanish Exploration in the Southwest, 1542-1706* (New York: Barnes and Noble, 1908), 1-39.

19. See Esteve Barba, *Historiografía indiana*, 288-89.

20. *Jornada del río Marañón*, prelim. study, Mario Hernández Sánchez Barba, Biblioteca de Autores Españoles 216 (Madrid: Atlas, 1968), 216-358.

21. See Pastor, *Discursos narrativos*, 318-33.

22. In Nueva Biblioteca de Autores españoles 15.

Chapter Five

1. The English translation of Pedro Mártir's *De Orbe Novo* is *De Orbe Novo: The Eight Decades of Peter Martyr D'Anghera*, trans., notes and intro. Francis Augustus MacNutt, 2 vols. (1912; New York: Burt Franklin, 1970); hereafter cited in text.

2. For a discussion of Pedro Mártir consult Alberto Salas, *Tres cronistas de Indias*. 2d ed. (Mexico: Fondo de Cultura Económica, 1986). On Pedro Mártir as a humanist, see Richard G. Cole, "Renaissance Humanists Discover America," in *A Humanist's Legacy: Essays in Honor of John Christian Bale*, ed. Dennis H. Jones (Decorah, Iowa: Luther College, 1990), 11-15, and Paul R. Ziegler, "The New World and Christian Humanism: Three Views," *Proceedings of the PMR Conference: Annual Publication of the International Patristic, Mediaeval and Renaissance Conference* 8 (1983): 89-95.

3. For biographical information, see Esteve Barba, *Historiografía Indiana*, 61-66.

4. See Stephanie Merrim's study of this novel in her article "The Castle of Discourse: Fernández de Oviedo's *Don Claribalte* (1519) or 'Los correos andan más que los caballeros' " *MLN* 97, no. 2 (1982): 329-46, where she points out that some of Oviedo's traits as a historian are noticeable in the novel.

5. Gonzalo Fernández de Oviedo, *Sumario de la natural historia de las Indias*, ed. José Miranda. (Mexico and Buenos Aires: Fondo de Cultura Económica, 1950). An English translation is *Natural History of the West Indies*, trans. and ed. Sterling A. Stoudemire, University of North Carolina Studies in the Romance Languages and Literatures 32 (Chapel Hill: University of North Carolina Press, 1959).

6. Gonzalo Fernández de Oviedo, *Historia general y natural de las Indias*, ed. Juan Pérez de Tudela Bueso, 5 vols. (Madrid: Atlas, 1959).

7. Rómulo D. Carbia, "La superchería en la historia del descubrimiento de América," *Humanidades* 20 (La Plata, 1930): 169-84.

8. The *History* revolves around two main personages, as scholars have pointed out; Saint-Lu, for example, does so in his introduction to Bartolomé de Las Casas, *Historia de las Indias*, ed. André Saint-Lu (Caracas: Biblioteca Ayacucho, 1986), xviii.

9. See Andree Collard's introduction to the English version of the *History of the Indies*, p. xxiii, for a discussion of Las Casas's fashioning of himself as a respectable historical figure (English version edited and translated by Collard [New York: Harper, 1971]).

10. For information on Gómara's life, see R. E. Lewis, "El testamento de Francisco López de Gómara y otros documentos tocantes a su vida y obra," *Revista de Indias* 44, no. 173 (1984): 61-79. Juan Ginés de Sepúlveda is like Gómara in some ways. He was a humanist who never set foot in the Indies, and he also chronicled both the New World and Mexico in his history written in Latin, the *De Rebus Hispanorum Gestis ad Novum Orbem Mexicumque* (About the Deeds of the Spaniards in the New World). The history is not too representative, since it covers only the period from the Discovery to the year 1521. See Esteve Barba, 92-94, for information on Sepúlveda.

11. *La Historia de las Indias y conquista de México*, ed. H. Barcia, Biblioteca de Autores Españoles 22 (Madrid: Atlas, 1877). A modernized Spanish text is available in *Historia General de las Indias "Hispania Vitrix,"* ed. Pilar Guibelalde, intro. Emiliano M. Aguilera, 2 vols. (Barcelona: Obras Maestras, Editorial Iberia, 1954).

12. On Acosta's life and works, see Francisco Mateos, "Personalidad y escritos del P. José de Acosta," in *Obras del P. José de Acosta, de la Compañía de Jesús* (Madrid: Ediciones Atlas, 1954), vii-xlix, and Esteve Barba, *Historiografía indiana*, 102-11.

13. See Luciano Pereña's study of Acosta as a missionary in *De procuranda indorum salute. Pacificación y colonización*, Bilingual ed. (Madrid: Consejo Superior de Investigaciones Científicas, 1984), 3-46. The collected works are in *Obras del P. José de Acosta, de la Compañía de Jesús*.

14. Joseph de Acosta, *Historia natural y moral de las Indias*, ed. Edmundo O'Gorman, 2d rev. ed. (Mexico, Buenos Aires: Fondo de Cultura Económica, 1952). An English translation is Joseph de Acosta, *The Natural and Moral History of the Indies*, reprinted from the English translated edition of Edward Grimston, 1604, ed. Clements R. Markham. 2 vols. (1880; New York: Burt Franklin, 1970).

15. Mignolo, "Cartas," 86.

16. On evolution in Acosta's writing, see E. Aguirre, "Una hipótesis evolucionista en el siglo XVI: El P. José de Acosta, S.I., y el origen de las especies americanas," *Arbor* 36, no. 134 (1957): 176-87.

17. On the official chronicle, see the classic study by Rómulo de Carbia, *La crónica oficial de las Indias Occidentales* (La Plata, Argentina: Biblioteca Humanidades, 1934).

18. Juan López de Velasco, *Geografía y descripción universal de las Indias*, ed. Marcos Jiménez de la Espada, prelim. study, María del Carmen González Muñoz, Biblioteca de Autores Españoles, vol. 248 (Madrid: Atlas, 1971). The preliminary study by González Muñoz is very informative.

19. Alonso de Zurita's chronicle on Indian ethnography in Mexico, the *Relación de los señores de la Nueva España* (Account of the Lords in New Spain), ed. Germán Vázquez (Madrid: Historia 16, 1992), is also an example of a text written in response to an official census questionnaire. A royal order in 1553 had the "audiencias" in the Indies take a census of the Indian lords in the region, the tribute they received from their subjects before and after the Spanish arrived, the tribute system, and other customs. Zurita twice missed out on the opportunity to report such a census because he was changed from one post to another in the Americas, but he was so interested in the project that on his own back in Spain he compiled his summary using notes he had accumulated over the years. Zurita structured his chronicle according to the chapters and information required in the royal order of 1553, although he rearranged the order of the chapters to suit his purpose. For a discussion of Zurita's work, see Esteve Barba, *Historiografía indiana*, 157-59. An English translation is available, *Life and Labor in Ancient Mexico: The Brief and Summary Relation of the Lords of New Spain*, trans. Benjamin Keene (New Brunswick, N.J.: Rutgers University Press, 1963).

20. Antonio de Herrera y Tordesillas, *The General History of the Vast Continent and Islands of America*, trans. John Stevens (1740; New York: AMS Press, 1973). It is an abridged translation of the first three decades of Herrera's *Historia general de los hechos de los castellanos*.

Chapter Six

1. For a handy review of the religious chroniclers with a useful bibliography, see Ernest J. Burrus, S.J., "Religious Chroniclers and Historians: A Summary with Annotated Bibliography," in *Guide to Ethnohistorical Sources, Part Two*, ed. Howard F. Cline and John B. Glass, vol. 13 of *Handbook of Middle American Indians* (Austin: University of Texas Press, 1973), 138-85.

2. For information on Motolinía's life and works, see Esteve Barba, *Historiografía indiana*, 168-72.

3. For a hypothetical list of Motolinía's works, see Fray Toribio de Motolinía, *Historia de los indios de la Nueva España*, ed., intro., and notes G. Baudot (Madrid: Clásicos Castalia, 1985), 41; hereafter cited in text.

4. For the Spanish editions of the *Memoriales* and the *Historia*, see Fray Toribio Motolinía, O.F.M., *Memoriales e Historia de los indios de la Nueva España*, prelim. study Fidel Lejarza, O.F.M., Biblioteca de Autores Españoles 240 (Madrid: Atlas, 1970), For English versions of the history, see *Motolinía's History of the Indians of New Spain*, trans. and ed. Elizabeth Andros Foster (Berkeley: Cortés Society, 1950), and *Motolinía's History of the Indians of New Spain*, trans. and ann. with biobibliographical study, Francis Borgia Steck, O.F.M. (Washington: Academy of American Franciscan History, 1951).

5. Baudot attempts to reconstruct the contents of the lost *Relación* in his 1985 Clásicos Castalia edition of Motolinía's *Historia*, 53-70.

6. Edmundo O'Gorman does not believe the *History* is Motolinía's work. See his *La incógnita de la llamada Historia de los indios de la Nueva España atribuida a Fray Toribio Motolinía* (Mexico: Fondo de Cultura Económica, 1982). O'Gorman came to that conclusion when he noted errors in Nahuatl words and erroneous news of events in early Franciscan history in Mexico (7). O'Gorman maintains that the author is a compiler (28).

7. Biographical information on Mendieta is in Esteve Barba, *Historiografía indiana*, 172-77.

8. Fray Gerónimo de Mendieta, *Historia eclesiástica indiana*, 2 vols., ed. Francisco Solano y Pérez-Lila (Madrid: Ediciones Atlas, 1973).

9. See Phelan, *The Millennial Kingdom of the Franciscans in the New World*, on Mendieta's apocalyptic ideas derived from Joachim of Fiore and others and applied to the Indies.

10. For information on Torquemada, see Esteve Barba, *Historiografía indiana*, 177-81.

11. Information on Sahagún is in Esteve Barba, *Historiografía indiana*, 181-84. A biography is in Mendieta's *Historia eclesiástica indiana*.

12. On consultation with the Indians, see Katherine R. Goodwin, "The Methodology of Fray Bernardino de Sahagún: Oral History in the Sixteenth Century." *E. C. Barksdale Student Lectures* 9 (1985-86): 51-65.

13. A study of the prologues is Howard F. Cline, "Missing and Variant Prologues and Dedications in Sahagún's *Historia general:* Texts and English Translations," *Estudios de Cultura Nabuatl* 9 (1971): 237-51.

14. Leonidas Emilfork, *La conquista de México: ensayo de poética americana* (Santiago de Chile: Editorial Universitaria, 1987.)

15. An English version of book 12 is Bernardino de Sahagún *Conquest of New Spain,* ed. S. L. Cline (Salt Lake City: University of Utah Press, 1989).

16. Anderson and Dibble translated the Aztec text into English: Bernardino de Sahagún, *General History of the Things of New Spain: Florentine Codex,* trans. from the Aztec by J. O. Anderson and Charles E. Dibble (Sante Fe, N.M.: School of American Research, 1950-). An important Spanish edition is Bernardino Sahagún, *Historia general de las cosas de la Nueva España,* ed. Angel María Garibay K[intana], 4 vols. (Mexico: Porrúa, 1977).

17. See Esteve Barba, *Historiografía indiana,* 271-72, for information on Landa.

18. *Diego de Landa's Account of the Affairs of Yucatan: The Maya,* ed. and trans. A. R. Pagden (Chicago: J. Philips O'Hara, 1975).

19. For information on Aguado, see Esteve Barba, *Historiografía indiana,* 292-95. See also studies by Orlando Fals Borda, "Odyssey of a Sixteenth-Century Document: Fray Pedro de Aguado's 'Recopilación historial,'" *Hispanic American Historical Review* 35 (1955): 203-20; "Fray Pedro de Aguado, the Forgotten Chronicler of Colombia and Venezuela," *Americas,* 11 no. 4 (1955): 539-73; and *Fr. Pedro de Aguado. El cronista olvidado de Colombia y Venezuela* (Cali, 1956).

20. Information on Asensio is in Esteve Barba, *Historiografía indiana,* 295-97.

21. For biographies of Las Casas see Manuel Giménez Fernández, *Breve biografía de fray Bartolomé de las Casas* (Seville: Facultad de Filosofía, 1966), and Arthur Helps, *The Life of Las Casas: "The Apostle of the Indies,"* new ed. with an introduction by Lewis Hanke (1868; London, 1970) – a reprint appears in Bartolomé de las Casas, Tears of the Indians and the Life of Las Casas, intro. Lewis Hanke (Williamstown, Mass.: J. Lilburne, 1970). Helen Rand Parish's definitive biography, *Las Casas: The Untold Story,* was scheduled for publication by the University of California Press in 1992. Bibliographies on Las Casas are Lewis Hanke and Manuel Giménez Fernández, *Bartolomé de las Casas: Bibliografía crítica* (Santiago, Chile: Fondo Histórico y Bibliograpáfico José Toribio Medina, 1954), and Almudena Hernández Ruizgómez and Carlos González, "Materiales para una bibli-

ografía sobre fray Bartolomé de las Casas," in *El V centenario de Bartolomé de las Casas* (Madrid: Cultura Hispánica, 1986): 183-231.

22. Bartolomé de las Casas, *Brevísima relación de la destrucción de las Indias*, ed. André Saint-Lu, 3d ed. (Madrid: Cátedra, Letras Hispánicas, 1987); hereafter cited in text. An available English translation is *The Devastation of the Indies: A Brief Account*, trans. Herma Briffault (New York: Seabury Press, 1974); it does not contain the argument, prologue, and final section, titled "A Piece of a Letter."

23. See Raymond Marcus, "La conquete de Cholula: conflits d'intérpretations," *Ibero-Amerikanisches Archiv* 3, no. 2 (1977): 193-213, where Marcus compares versions of the Cholula massacre written by Cortés, Las Casas, Díaz del Castillo, Sahagún, and Muñoz Camargo.

24. Anthony Pagden, *The Fall of Natural Man: The American Indian and the Origins of Comparative Ethnology* (Cambridge: Cambridge University Press, 1986), 120. An edition of the apologetical history is Bartolomé de las Casas, *Apologética historia*, vols. 3-4 in *Obras escogidas*, ed. Juan Pérez de Tudela Bueso, 5 vols. (Madrid: Ediciones Atlas, 1958).

25. Saint-Lu, xxiv. An English translation exists for the work on evangelization; *The Only Way*, ed. Helen Rand Parish, trans. Francis Patrick Sullivan, S.J. (New York and Mahwah, N.J.: Paulist Press, 1991).

26. For biographical and bibliographical information, see Esteve Barba, *Historiografía indiana*, 196-200.

Selected Bibliography

PRIMARY WORKS

Texts in the Original Language

Acosta, José de. *Historia natural y moral de las Indias*. 2d ed. 1940. México: Fondo de Cultura Económica, 1962.

Benavente, Toribio de. *Historia de los indios de la Nueva España*. Edited by G. Baudot. Madrid: Castalia, 1986.

Carvajal, Gaspar de, Pedrarias, P. and P. Teixeira. *La aventura del Amazonas*. Edited by R. Díaz Maderuelo. Crónicas de América 19. Madrid: Historia 16, 1985.

Casas, Bartolomé de las. *Apologética historia*. Vols. 3 and 4 of *Obras escogidas*. Edited by Juan Pérez de Tudela Bueso. 5 vols. Madrid: Ediciones Atlas, 1958.

_____. *Brevísima relación de la destrucción de las Indias*. Edited by André Saint-Lu. 3d ed. Madrid: Cátedra, Letras Hispánicas, 1987.

_____. *Historia de las Indias*. Edited by Agustín Millares Caro. 2d ed. 3 vols. Mexico: Fondo de Cultura Económica, 1965.

Colón, Hernando. *Vida del Almirante: Don Cristóbal Colón*. Edited by Ramón Iglesia. Mexico City and Buenos Aires: Fondo de Cultura Económica, 1947.

Columbus, Christopher. *The Libro de las profecías of Christopher Columbus*. An *en face* edition. Translation and commentary by Delno C. West and August Kling. Gainesville, Fla.: University of Florida Press, 1991.

_____. *Textos y documentos completos: relaciones de viajes, cartas y memoriales*. Edited by Consuelo Varela. Madrid: Alianza, 1982.

Cortés, Hernán. *Cartas y relaciones*. Buenos Aires: Emecé, 1946.

Díaz del Castillo, Bernal. *Historia verdadera de la conquista de la Nueva España*. Edited by Joaquín Ramírez Cabañas. 5th ed. Mexico: Porrúa, 1967.

Esteve Barba, Francisco, ed. *Crónicas del Reino de Chile*. Biblioteca de Autores Españoles, vol. 131. Madrid: Ediciones Atlas, 1960.

Fernández de Oviedo y Valdés, Gonzalo. *Historia general y natural de las Indias*. Edited by Juan Pérez de Tudela Bueso. 5 vols. Madrid: Ediciones Atlas, 1959.

_____. *Las memorias de Gonzalo Fernández de Oviedo*. Edited by Juan Bautista Avalle-Arce. 2 vols. Chapel Hill: University of North Carolina Department of Romance Languages, 1974.

_____. *Sumario de la natural historia de las Indias*. Edited by José Miranda. Mexico: Fondo de Cultura Económica, 1950.

Landa, Diego de. *Relación de las cosas de Yucatán*. Introduction by Angel María Garibay K. Mexico City: Editorial Porrúa, 1959.

López de Gómara, Francisco. *Historia general de las Indias*. Edited by Pilar Guibilalde and M. Aguilera. 2 vols. Barcelona: Iberia, 1954.

Núñez Cabeza de Vaca, Alvar. *Naufragios y comentarios*. Edited by R. Ferrando. Crónicas de América 3. Madrid: Historia 16, 1984.

Sahagún, Bernardino de. *Historia general de las cosas de la Nueva España*. Edited by Angel María Garibay K[intana]. 4 vols. Mexico: Porrúa, 1977.

Zorita, Alonso de. *Relación de los señores de la Nueva España*. Edited by Germán Vázquez. Madrid: Historia 16, 1992.

English Translations

Acosta, José de. *The Natural and Moral History of the Indies*. Edited by Clements R. Markham. 2 vols. New York: B. Franklin, 1970-73.

Carvajal, Gaspar de. *The Discovery of the Amazon According to the Account of Friar Gaspar de Carvajal and Other Documents*. Edited by H. C. Heaton. New York: American Geographical Society, 1934.

Casas, Bartolomé de las. *The Devastation of the Indies: A Brief Account*. Translated by Herma Briffault. New York: Seabury, 1974.

_____. *History of the Indies*. Edited and translated by Andree Collard. New York: Harper, 1971.

Columbus, Christopher. *Across the Ocean Sea: A Journal of Columbus's Voyage*. Edited by George William Sanderlin and Laszlo Kubinyi. New York: Harper, 1966.

_____. *The Authentic Letters of Columbus*. Edited by William Eleroy Curtis. Chicago: May, 1895.

_____. *The Diario of Christopher Columbus's First Voyage to America, 1492-1493*. Edited by Oliver Dunn and James E. Kelley, Jr. Norman: University of Oklahoma Press, 1988.

_____. *Select Documents Illustrating the Four Voyages of Columbus*. Edited and translated by Cecil Jane. 2 vols. London: University Press of Oxford, 1930-33.

Columbus, Ferdinand. *The Life of the Admiral Christopher Columbus by His Son Ferdinand*, trans. Benjamin Keen (New Brunswick, N.J.: Rutgers University Press, 1959).

Cortés, Hernán. *Letters from Mexico.* Edited and translated by Anthony Pagden. New Haven and London: Yale University Press, 1986.

Díaz del Castillo, Bernal. *The Conquest of New Spain.* Translated by J. M. Cohen. 1963. Harmondsworth: Penguin, 1985.

Fernández de Oviedo y Valdés, Gonzalo. *Natural History of the West Indies.* Edited and translated by Sterling H. Stoudemire. Chapel Hill: University of North Carolina Press, 1959.

Landa, Diego de. *Diego de Landa's Account of the Affairs of Yucatán: The Maya.* Edited and translated by A. R. Pagden. Chicago: J. Philip O'Hara, 1975.

López de Gómara, Francisco. *Cortés: The Life of the Conqueror by His Secretary.* Translated by Lesley Byrd Simpson. Berkeley: University of California Press, 1964.

Núñez Cabeza de Vaca, Alvar. *Cabeza de Vaca's Adventures in the Unknown Interior of America.* Translated by Cyclone Covey. 1961. Albuquerque: University of New Mexico Press, 1983.

_____. "The *Commentaries* of Alvar Núñez Cabeza de Vaca." In *The Conquest of the River Plate (1535-1555)*, edited by Luis L. Domínguez, translated for the Hakluyt Society. [1891.] New York: Burt Franklin, 1964.

Sahagún, Bernardino de. *General History of the Things of New Spain: Florentine Codex.* Translated from the Aztec by J. O. Anderson and Charles E. Dibble. Sante Fe, N.M.: School of American Research, 1950-.

Zurita, Alonso de. *Life and Labor in Ancient Mexico: The Brief and Summary Relation of the Lords of New Spain.* Translated by Benjamin Keene (New Brunswick, N.J.: Rutgers University Press, 1963.

SECONDARY WORKS

General Works on the Chronicles

Adorno, Rolena. "Nuevas perspectivas en los estudios literarios coloniales hispanoamericanos." *Revista de Crítica literaria latinoamericana* 14 (1988): 11-28. Examines the methodological assumptions in recent criticsm of Spanish American colonial literature.

Ballesteros Gaibrois, Manuel. *La novedad indiana: noticias, informaciones y testimonios del Nuevo Mundo.* Vol. 1. Madrid: Editorial Alhambra, 1987. 2 vols. A consideration of the chronicles as reportage of news about the New World; contains an analytical study, sections of exemplary texts, and an extensive bibliography.

Cro, Stelio. *Realidad y utopía en el descubrimiento y conquista de la América hispánica.* Troy: International Book, 1983. Addresses the development of the concept of utopia in the New World in the sixteenth and seventeenth centuries.

Bravo-Villasante, Carmen. *La maravilla de América: los cronistas de Indias.* Madrid: Ediciones Cultura Hispánica, Instituto de Cooperación Iberoamericana, 1985.

Chang-Rodríguez, Raquel. *Violencia y subversión en la prosa colonial hispanoamericana, siglos XVI y XVII.* Potomac, Md.: Studia Humanitatis, 1982.

_____, and Malva E. Filer, eds. *Voces de Hispanoamérica: antología literaria.* Boston: Heinle and Heinle, 1988.

Esteve Barba, Francisco. *Historiografía indiana.* Madrid: Gredos, 1964. The standard biobibliographical study in Spanish of the chronicles covering several centuries.

Fernández de Navarrete, Martín. *Colección de viajes y descubrimientos que hicieron por mar los españoles desde fines del siglo XV,* in *Obras de D. Martín Fernández de Navarrete,* edited by Carlos Seco Serrano. Madrid: Ediciones Atlas, 1954-55. 3 vols. Vols. 75, 76, 77 in Biblioteca de Autores Españoles.

Foster, David W. *Handbook of Latin American Literature.* New York and London: Garland Publishing, 1987.

Godoy, Roberto, and Angel Olmo. *Textos de cronistas de Indias y poemas precolombinos.* Madrid: Editora Nacional, 1979.

Goic, Cedomil, and Walter D. Mignolo, eds. "Literature and Historiography in the New World." *Dispositio* 11, no. 28-29 (1986). The articles and notes of the entire edition are devoted to the chronicles.

González de Barcia, Andrés, ed. *Historiadores primitivos de las Indias Occidentales.* Madrid, 1749. 3 vols.

González Echeverría, Roberto. "Humanismo, retórica y las crónicas de la conquista." In *Isla a su vuelo fugitiva: ensayos críticos sobre literatura hispanoamericana,* ed. Roberto Gonzalez Echeveria, 9-25. Madrid: Ediciones José Porrúa Turranzas, 1983. Examines the role of humanist and notarial rhetoric in the production of the chronicles.

Greenblat, Stephen. *Marvelous Possessions: The Wonder of the New World.* Chicago: University of Chicago Press, 1991. Studies European representational practices describing the New World to residents of the Old, with wonder as central to this practice.

Higgins, James. *A History of Peruvian Literature.* London and Wolfeboro, N.H.: F. Cairns, 1987.

Hulme, Peter. *Colonial Encounters: Europe and the Native Caribbean, 1492-1797.* London and New York: Methuen, 1986. Among other topics, presents an insightful study of Columbus's relations with the Indians.

Ideas '92 6 (Spring 1990). Entire issue devoted to the chronicles of America, under the editorship of Julie Greer Johnson.

Jara, René and Nicholas Spadaccini, eds. *1492-1992: Re/Discovering Colonial Writing.* Hispanic Issues 4. Minneapolis: Prisma Institute, 1989. A collection of articles by leading specialists in chronicle literature, containing an introduction on allegorizing the New World, 10 studies emphasizing a rereading of the chronicles, and a bilingual appendix of documents relative to the conquest.

Leonard, Irving. *Books of the Brave.* Cambridge, Mass.: Harvard University Press, 1949. A classic study exploring the influence of books of chivalry on the conquistadors, the book trade in the New World, and the diffusion of Spanish literature in America.

_____. *Portraits and Essays: Historical and Literary Sketches of Early Spanish America.* Edited by William C. Bryant. Newark, Del.: Juan de la Cuesta, 1986. Introductory essays on the major chroniclers.

Madrigal, Luis Iñigo, ed. *Historia de la literatura hispanoamericana. I: Epoca colonial.* Madrid: Editorial Castalia, 1982.

Means, Philip A. *Biblioteca Andina.* New Haven: Connecticut Academy of Arts and Sciences, 1928; reprint, Detroit: Blaine Etheridge Books, 1973.

Merrim, Stephanie. "Historia y escritura en las crónicas de Indias: ensayo de un método." *Explicación de textos literarios* 9, no. 2 (1981): 193-200. Explores the Renaissance concept of history as a literary subgenre at work in the elaboration of the chronicles.

Mignolo, Walter. "Cartas, crónicas y relaciones del descubrimiento y la conquista." In *Historia de la literatura hispanoamericana: Epoca colonial,* coordinated by Luis Iñigo Madrigal, 2:56-125. Madrid: Cátedra, 1982. Excellent survey of the types of chronicle and the characteristics of their discourse.

_____. "El metatexto historiográfico y la historiografía indiana." *Modern Language Notes* 96 (1981): 358-402. Explores the chronicles as adhering to historiographical discourse and, in the process, modifying that discourse.

Pagden, Anthony. *The Fall of Natural Man: The American Indian and the Origins of Comparative Ethnology.* London: Cambridge University Press, 1984. Considers the ethnology of Sepúlveda, Las Casas and Acosta.

Pastor, Beatriz. *Discursos narrativos de la conquista: mitificación y emergencia.* Hanover, N.H.: Ediciones del Norte, 1988. A study of mythification and demythification in the chronicles of the New World.

_____. *The Armature of Conquest: Spanish Accounts of the Discovery of America, 1492-1589.* Translated by Lydia Longstreth Hunt. Stanford, Calif.: Stanford University Press, 1992. An English version of Pastor's *Discursos narrativos.*

Pupo-Walker, Enrique. *La vocación literaria del pensamiento histórico en América*. Madrid: Gredos, 1982. A study of the literary implications of Spanish American historiography.

_____. *Historia de la historiografía española*. Vols. 1 and 2. Madrid: Consejo Superior de Investigaciones Científicas, 1941. 3 vols. An older survey of Spanish historiography that includes the histories of the Indies arranged according to type and chronology.

Rodríguez-Monegal, Emir. *Noticias secretas y públicas de América*. Barcelona: Tusquets, 1984.

Sánchez Alonso, Benito. *Fuentes de la historiografía española e hispanoamericana*. 3d rev. ed. Madrid: Consejo Superior de Investigaciones Científicas, 1952. 3 vols.

_____. *Historia de la historiografía española: ensayo de un examen de conjunto*. Madrid: Consejo Superior de Investigaciones Científicas, 1941, 1944. 2 vols.

Solé, Carlos A., and Maria Isabel Abreu, eds. *Latin American Writers*. Vol. 1. New York: Charles Scribner's Sons, 1989. 3 vols. Contains biobibliographical essays on several chroniclers of the sixteenth century, with essential bibliography.

Todorov, Tzvetan. *The Conquest of America. The Question of the Other*. Translated by Richard Howard. New York: Harper, 1984. A consideration of Columbus, Cortés, Durán, Sahagún, and Las Casas in relation to the concept of the other.

Vidal, Hernán. *Socio-historia de la literatura colonial hispanoamericana: tres lecturas orgánicas*. Minneapolis: Institute for the Study of Ideologies and Literature, 1985. Devotes one of three sections to the literature of the conquest in its social context.

Xirau, Ramón de. *Idea y querella de la Nueva España*. Madrid: El libro del bolsillo, Alianza Editorial, 1973.

Zamora, Margarita. "Historicity and Literariness: Problems in the Literary Criticism of Spanish American Colonial Texts." *Modern Language Notes* 102, no. 26 (1987): 334-46. Addresses the issue of incorporating the chronicle as nonliterary text into the category of colonial literature.

Essays on Specific Writers

Adorno, Rolena. "Discourses on Colonialism: Bernal Díaz, Las Casas, and the Twentieth-Century Reader." *Modern Language Notes* 103, no. 2 (1988):239-58. A consideration of Bernal Díaz and Las Casas as embodying the relationship of the European conquistador and land holder to the Indians.

_____. *Guamán Poma: Writing and Resistance in Colonial Peru*. Austin: University of Texas Press, 1986.

Arrom, José Juan. "Gonzalo Fernández de Oviedo, relator de episodios y narrador de naufragios." *Casa de las Américas* 24, no. 141 (1983): 114-23. Studies some of Oviedo's works to show how he purposely wrote to make a place for himself in Spanish literature.

Barbón, José de. *Bernal Díaz del Castillo*. Buenos Aires: Centro Editor de América Latina, 1968. Comprehensive introduction to Bernal Díaz's life and chronicle.

Barrenechea, Raúl Porras. *Los cronistas de Perú (1528-1650)*. Edited by F. Pease. Lima: Banco de Crédito, 1986. A survey of the chronicles of Peru.

Baudot, Georges. *Utopie et histoire au Mexique. Les premiers chroniqueurs de la civilisation mexicaine (1520-1569)*. Toulouse: Privat, 1976. A study of chronicles produced by missionaries.

Benítez-Rojo, Antonio. "Bartolomé de Las Casas: entre el infierno y la ficción." *Modern Language Notes* 103, no. 2 (1988):259-88. Studies an interpolated episode of Las Casas's history of the Indies to argue for the relevance of other "digressions."

Blázquez Garbajosa, Adrián. "Las 'Cartas de Relación de la conquista de México': política, psicología y literatura." *Bulletin Hispanique* 87, no. 1-2 (1985): 5-46. Examines Cortés's use of writing techniques to persuade.

Boxer. C. R. *Women in Iberian Expansion Overseas, 1415-1815*. New York: Oxford University Press, 1975.

Brody, Robert. "Bernal's Strategies." *Hispanic Review* 55 (1987): 323-36. Uses Hayden White's theory of the historical work to delineate the narrative shape of the chronicle.

Buxó, José Pascual. *La imaginación del Nuevo Mundo*. Mexico: Fondo de Cultura Económica, 1988. A semiotic approach to Columbus's texts.

The Cambridge History of Latin America. Vols. 1 and 2. Cambridge: Cambridge University Press, 1984.

Carreño, Antonio. "*Naufragios* de Alvar Núñez Cabeza de Vaca: una retórica de la corónica colonial." *Revista Iberoamericana* 53, no. 140 (1987): 499-516. Contrasts the picaresque and the chronicle.

Carrillo, Francisco. *Cartas y cronistas del descubrimiento y la conquista*. Lima: Editorial Horizonte, 1987. An anthology of chronicles pertaining to Peru, with general introduction and basic bibliography of authors cited.

Cascardi, Anthony J. "Chronicle toward Novel: Bernal Díaz's *History of the Conquest of Mexico*." *Novel* 15, no. 3 (1982): 197-212. Considers the predominance of the novelistic over the historical in the chronicle.

Cline, Howard F. "The *Relaciones geográficas* of the Spanish Indies, 1577-1588." *Handbook of Middle American Indians* 12 (1972): 183-242. A survey of chronicles concentrating on geographical details, with a useful bibliography.

Cobo Borda, J. G. *Leyendo El Dorado: la otra imagen de Colombia.* Biblioteca del Nuevo Mundo 4. Barcelona: Tusquets, 1986. Details the search for El Dorado.

———. El *Sumario* de Gonzalo Fernández de Oviedo." *Cuadernos Hispanoamericanos* 429 (1986): 63-77. Provides biographical and bibliographical background of Oviedo's writings, although with very little on the *Sumario*.

Dowling, Lee H. "Story vs. Discourse in the Chronicle of the Indies: Alvar Núñez Cabeza de Vaca's *Relación." Hispanic Journal* 5, no. 2 (1984): 89-99. Analyzes the tension between fictional and historiographical devices.

Emilfork, Leonidas. "La doble escritura americana de Oviedo." *Revista chilena de literatura* 19 (1982): 21-38. Argues that Oviedo's work represents the writing of deeds and the writing of recognition.

Estudios cortesianos. Instituto Gonzalo Fernández de Oviedo. Madrid: Consejo Superior de Investigaciones Científicas, 1948. A varied collection of articles, originally published in *Revista de Indias*, on aspects of Cortés's life and letters.

Forster, Merlin H., and Julio Ortega, eds. *De la crónica a la nueva narrativa mexicana: coloquio sobre literatura mexicana.* Mexico: Editorial Oasis, 1986. Articles by well-known Hispanists on the practice of chronicle writing, on Bernal Díaz del Castillo, and on López de Gómara.

Friede, Juan, and Benjamin Keen, eds. *Bartolomé de las Casas in History: Toward an Understanding of the Man and His Work.* DeKalb: Northern Illinois University Press, 1971. A collection of essays by various scholars that considers Las Casas's life, ideology, and literary and historical legacy.

García Calvo, Mercedes. "Lectura de *Historia verdadera* de Bernal Díaz del Castillo desde un 'espacio teórico del referente.' " *Revista chilena de literatura* 27-28 (1986): 17-28. Analyzes the impact of the narrator's continual calling attention to himself in the text.

Gerbi, Antonello. *Nature in the New World: From Christopher Columbus to González Fernández de Oviedo.* Translated by Jeremy Moyle. Pittsburgh: University of Pittsburgh Press, 1985. Explores the representation of nature in the texts of several chroniclers, with an emphasis on Oviedo.

Hanke, Lewis. *All Mankind Is One: A Study of the Disputation between Bartolomé de Las Casas and Juan Ginés de Sepúlveda in 1550 on the Intellectual and Religious Capacity of the American Indians.* DeKalb:

Northern Illinois University Press, 1974. A study of the conflict between the two opponents, its origin, development, and aftermath.

_____. *The Spanish Struggle for Justice in the Conquest of America.* Philadelphia: University of Pennsylvania Press, 1949. A classic study of Las Casas as an advocate of Indian rights.

Iglesia, Ramón. *Columbus, Cortés, and Other Essays.* Edited and translated by Lesley Byrd Simpson. Berkeley: University of California Press, 1969. A collection of essays on the chronicles.

Invernizzi Santa Cruz, Lucía. "*Naufragios e Infortunios*: discurso que transforma fracasos en triunfos." *Revista chilena de literatura* 29 (1987): 7-22. Examines the use of rhetorical procedures in the text.

Jitrik, Noé. *Los dos ejes de la cruz. La escritura de apropiación en el Diario, el Memorial, las Cartas y el Testamento del enviado real Cristóbal Colón.* Puebla: Universidad Autónoma de Puebla, 1983. A semiotic examination of the specific mechanisms employed in Columbus's texts to convey the New World reality.

Johnson, Julie Greer. "Bernal Díaz and the Women of the Conquest." *Hispanófila* 28, no. 1 (1984): 67-77. The use of literary techniques to portray prominent women of the conquest.

_____. *Women in Colonial Spanish American Literature: Literary Images.* Westport, Conn.: Greenwood Press, 1983.

Lagmanovich, David. "Los *Naufragios* de Alvar Núñez como construcción narrativa." *Kentucky Romance Quarterly* 25, no. 1 (1978): 27-37. Discusses the literary nature of the chronicle's narrative.

Lastra, Pedro. "Espacios de Alvar Núñez: las transformaciones de una escritura." *Revista chilena de literatura* 23 (1984): 89-102. Examines the relationship between the *Naufragios* and the *Comentarios* to conclude that they constitute a literary unit.

León, Pedro. *Algunas observaciones sobre Pedro Cieza de León y la Crónica del Perú.* Madrid: Gredos, 1973. Discussion of Cieza with an emphasis on literary aspects of the *Crónica*.

Marchetti, Magda. "Hacia la edición crítica de la *Historia* de Sahagún." *Cuadernos Hispanoamericanos* 396 (1983): 505-40. Traces the elaboration of Sahagún's chronicle and argues for a team effort to edit the definitive edition.

Menéndez Pidal, Ramón. *La lengua de Cristóbal Colón.* Madrid: Austral, 1942. The classic study of Columbus's language.

Merrim, Stephanie. " 'Un mare magno e oculto': Anatomy of Fernández de Oviedo's *Historia general y natural de las Indias*." *Revista de estudios hispánicos* (1984): 101-20. Sees in Oviedo's chaotic chronicle a purposeful correspondence to the disorder and incoherence in the reality he described.

Miller, Beth. *Women in Hispanic Literature: Icons and Fallen Idols*. Berkeley: University of California Press, 1983.

Morison, Samuel E. *Admiral of the Ocean Sea: A Life of Christopher Columbus*. 2 vols. Boston: Little, Brown, 1942. The classic biography containing analyses of Columbus's texts.

1992: A Columbus Newsletter. Edited by Foster Provost. Providence, R.I.: John Carter Brown Library. A semiannual newsletter devoted to scholarly and general matters related to the quincentenary observance of the Encounter.

Orijuela, Héctor H. "Orígenes de la literatura colombiana: Gonzalo Fernández de Oviedo." *Thesaurus* 40, no. 2 (1985): 241-92. A life and works monograph.

Oviedo y Pérez de Tudela, M. del Rocío. "Las Cartas de relación y el 'renacer' literario." *Revista de Indias* 44, no. 174 (1984): 533-39. A consideration of Cortés's choice of the letter as an intermediate form between the literary and the informative in the Renaissance.

Paolucci, Anne and Henry Paolucci, eds. *Columbus*. Council on National Literatures. Whitestone, N.Y.: Griffon House, 1989. A collection of studies reassessing Columbus and his time.

Phelan, John Leddy. *The Millennial Kingdom of the Franciscans in the New World*. 2d ed. Berkeley: University of California Press, 1970. Singles out the missionary labor and chronicle of Gerónimo de Mendieta.

Provost, Foster. *Columbus: An Annotated Guide to Scholarship on his Life and Writings*. Providence and Detroit: Published by Omnigraphics for the John Carter Brown Library, 1991. A recent and complete bibliography, arranged historically.

Pupo-Walker, Enrique. "Los *Naufragios* de Alvar Núñez Cabeza de Vaca y la narrativa de viajes: ecos de la codificación literaria." In *Los hallazgos de la lectura: Estudio dedicado a Miguel Enguídanos*, edited by John Crispin, Enrique Pupo-Walker, and Luis Lorenzo-Rivero, 63-83. Madrid: Ediciones José Porrúa Turanzas, 1989. Places the *Naufragios* within the medieval and Renaissance tradition of voyage narrative.

_____. "Pesquisas para una nueva lectura de los *Naufragios* de Alvar Núñez Cabeza de Vaca." *Revista Iberoamericana* 53, no. 140 (1987): 517-39. Considers the influence of medieval hagiography on the text.

Rabassa, José. "Dialogue as Conquest: Mapping Spaces for Counter-Discourse." *Cultural Critique* 6 (1987): 131-59. A study of Cortés's discourse.

Ricard, Robert. *The Spiritual Conquest of Mexico: An Essay on the Apostolate and the Evangelizing Methods of the Mendicant Orders in New Spain: 1523-1572*. Translated by Lesley Byrd Simpson. Berkeley and Los Angeles: University of California Press, 1966. Supplies helpful background for the chronicles written by Franciscans, Dominicans, and Augustinians.

Sáenz de Santa María, Carmelo. *Historia de una historia: la crónica de Bernal Díaz del Castillo*. Madrid: Consejo Superior de Investigaciones Científicas, Instituto "Gonzalo Fernández de Oviedo," 1984. An extensive study of the different Bernal manuscripts, aspects of the chronicler's life, and the elaboration of the history.

Saint-Lu, André. "Bernal Díaz del Castillo y Bartolomé de las Casas." In *Actas del Sexto Congreso Internacional de Hispanistas celebrado en Toronto del 22 al 26 agosto de 1987*, edited by Alan M. Gordon and Evelyn Rugg, 661-65. Toronto: Department of Spanish and Portuguese, University of Toronto Press, 1980. Argues that despite obvious differences between the two chroniclers, points of agreement exist.

Salas, Alberto M. *Tres cronistas de Indias*. Mexico: Fondo de Cultura Económica, 1959. A biobibliographical study of Pedro Mártir, Oviedo and Las Casas.

Sale, Kirkpatrick. *The Conquest of Paradise: Christopher Columbus and the Columbian Legacy*. New York: Alfred A. Knopf, 1990. A reassessment of the Discovery and the processes resulting from it.

Triviños Araneda, Gilberto. "Los relatos colombinos." *Ideologies and Literature* 3, no. 1 (1988): 81-96. A reading of Columbus's texts as a narrative of the discovery of paradise and the disintegration of the conqueror's ideal of paradise.

Valcárcel Martínez, Simón. "El Padre José de Acosta." *Thesaurus* 44 (1989): 389-428. A life and works study of the chronicler.

Wagner, Henry Raup. *Francisco López de Gómara and His Works*. Worcester, Mass.: American Antiquarian Society, 1949. A pioneering biobibliographical study.

Zamora, Margarita. " 'Todas son palabras formales del Almirante': Las Casas y el *Diario* de Colón." *Hispanic Review* 57, no. 1 (1989): 25-41. An intertextual study arguing that Las Casas subordinated the original Columban mercantile/imperialist discourse to the idealizing/poeticizing discourse.

Index

The Author

James C. Murray, Assistant Professor of Spanish at Georgia State University, has been Director of Graduate Studies in the Department of Modern and Classical Languages at Georgia State and has taught at Duke University. He holds a B.A. from King's College in Wilkes-Barre, Pennsylvania, and a Ph.D. from Cornell University. His field of specialization is early Spanish literature, the Middle Ages, and the sixteenth century. Professor Murray teaches undergraduate and graduate classes in these areas. He has presented papers on medieval and humanist literature at professional meetings and is co-author of *A New Shorter Spanish Review Grammar*.